Bilingual Women

Cross-Cultural Perspectives on Women

General Editors: Shirley Ardener and Jackie Waldren, for The Centre for Cross-Cultural Research on Women, University of Oxford

Bilingual Women

Anthropological Approaches to Second-Language Use

Edited by
Pauline Burton, Ketaki Kushari Dyson and Shirley Ardener

BERG
Oxford/Providence

First published in 1994 by
Berg Publishers

Editorial offices:
221 Waterman Road, Providence, RI 02906, USA
150 Cowley Road, Oxford, OX4 1JJ, UK

Library of Congress Cataloging-in-Publication Data
Bilingual women: anthropological approaches to second language use/
    edited by Pauline Burton, Ketaki Kushari Dyson, and Shirley Ardener.
        p. cm. -- (Cross-cultural perspectives on women: v. 9)
    Includes bibliographical references and index.
    ISBN 0-85496-737-0 (cloth) -- ISBN 0-85496-864-4 (pbk.)
    1. Bilingualism. 2. Women--Language. I. Burton, Pauline.
    II. Dyson, Ketaki Kushari, 1940-. III. Ardener, Shirley.
    IV. Series.
    P115.B5426   1993   93-26394
    404'.2'082--dc20   CIP

British Library Cataloguing in Publication Data
A CIP catalogue record for this book is available from the British Library.

ISBN 0 85496 737 0 (cloth)
        0 85496 864 4 (paper)

Printed in the United Kingdom by Short Run Press, Exeter.

Contents

Preface

Shirley Ardener

This book derives from conversations which arose at the Centre for Cross-Cultural Research on Women in Oxford when Pauline Burton began to describe an experience of teaching English to Chinese men and women. The different responses to language learning and use which she had encountered inspired the proposal that we hold a workshop to explore such issues. Contacts with colleagues with the relevant field experience and interests were made and Pauline Burton returned to Oxford to make the final arrangements, in consultations with Ardener, for the weekend workshop which was held in October 1989. All the papers in this book were delivered first on that occasion. In addition two interesting papers drawing on their experience in Japan, by Roger Goodman and Alison Chapman, one on literature by African women by Adeola James, and another on dialogue involving Arab and Jewish women in Israel by Juliet Pope, which were presented at the workshop could not be included here, but are being incorporated in other writings by these authors.

The editors wish to thank all those, including the contributors here, who participated in our workshop. In particular we are grateful to Helen Callaway, Hiroko Minimikata, Sarah Skar, Julia Leslie and Mai Yamani who chaired various sessions. The discussions were extremely helpful. We would also like to thank those at the Cherwell Centre in Oxford where the workshop took place for the smooth efficiency of their arrangements.

Pauline Burton, together with Shirley Ardener, shaped the present volume and took on the first editorial tasks. Burton being based in Hong Kong, and having other heavy academic obligations, the advantage of drawing in another editor located in Oxford became apparent. Accordingly, despite her own packed schedule, one of our contributors, Ketaki

Kushari Dyson, kindly agreed to become a co-editor; her assistance in communicating with contributors, and with the final editing, certainly added to the quality of the volume and speeded up its production. Meanwhile Pauline Burton proceeded with writing the chapter which provides the very helpful introductory frame for this collection.

The Centre has sponsored other books now in the current Berg Publishers series which have particular relevance for language use, for example *Defining Females* (Croom Helm, 1978; Berg edition, 1993) and *Women and Missions: Past and Present* (Berg 1993); *Perceiving Women* (Dent, 1975) is also relevant to some of the discussions below.

1

Women and Second-Language Use: An Introduction

Pauline Burton

Women's Linguistic Choices

The papers in this book, collectively, present anthropological approaches to women and second-language use in a wide range of cultures. This is an exploration of an apparent gap between studies of gender and single-language use, and 'ungendered' accounts of bilingualism. With a few notable exceptions,[1] the considerable body of work on language and gender [2] deals with monolingual situations, whatever the cultural context. In the literature on bilingualism, on the other hand, gender is hardly mentioned; here, it seems, is an area in which the experience of women is little documented.

This lack of information is reflected in general texts on bilingualism; for example, in Hamers and Blanc (1989), a detailed and comprehensive account of recent work, there are only three citations of papers in which gender is a factor.[3] In Hamers and Blanc and in Baetens Beardsmore (1982) the bilingual individual is referred to generically as 'he' throughout; and in his book on language policy, Tollefsen (1991) analyses inequality in language planning without addressing the issue of women's access to second-language learning.

Such gender-blindness is a cause for concern for practical as well as intellectual reasons. Women, like men, are affected by language and educational planning decisions. In their study of language contact and bilingualism, Appel and Muysken argue that such decisions need to be supported by 'a thorough and dispassionate analysis of bilingual language behaviour' (1987:4). It is hard to see how such an analysis can be achieved without taking into account the language behaviour of women as well as that of men; we cannot assume that they are identical, nor that gender-related differences are subcultural and unimportant.

Some indication of the importance of women's choices appears in Gal's (1979) study of language shift in Oberwart, Austria. Gal shows that the shift from Hungarian to German is facilitated by women's choice of marriage partners, as well as by choice of occupation (by men and women) and change from one generation to the next. Thus, women's decisions can have far-reaching structural consequences. In a recent study of language and ethnic identity, Edwards comments: 'General linguistic evidence ... suggests that women are more likely to be favourably disposed towards prestigious varieties (including dialects within a language) than are men. This can be an important factor, given women's traditionally important role with children, in the decline of languages in contact with powerful, higher-status rivals' (1985:72).

The 'general linguistic evidence' that women automatically prefer high-prestige language varieties has been called into question by a number of sociolinguistic studies (notably, Nichols 1983; Milroy, 1987; Coates and Cameron, 1989). Where such gender-related preference does occur, it seems important to investigate (as in Gal's study) how it is related to social strategies[4] in specific contexts. However, Edwards raises two important points: first, that women's experience of bilingualism is likely to be different from that of men; second, that these differences can be significant for the fate of minority languages, because of women's role as mothers.

Why should women, as second-language users, be different from men? Surely, because women usually have a different life-cycle and life experience from men, though the ways in which these differ vary widely across cultures. As Gal puts it, in her classic paper 'Peasant Men Can't Get Wives', 'sexual differentiation of speech is expected to occur whenever a social division exists between the roles of men and women – that is, universally' (1984:292). Gender, like age and race, is a common basis for social inequality; lack of power may limit women's access to privileged forms of language, and to public forums in which such forms are used. One may recall Dr Johnson's famous comparison of a woman preaching with a dog walking on its hind legs, an attitude which has much in common with the Quechua contempt for women speaking Spanish, recorded by Harvey in this book.

Stereotyping may, of course, be positive as well as negative; our papers also record the perception of women as 'good at languages', or as the 'guardians' of a minority mother-tongue – in itself, a powerfully emotive phrase. How can one reconcile these contradictions? One possible explanation is provided by Steiner's argument that women, like children, 'are maintained in a condition of privileged inferiority. Both suffer obvious modes of exploitation – sexual, legal, economic – while benefiting from a mythology of special regard' (1984:375). Certainly, this comment fits several of the cases described in this book, though it is not necessarily a description the women themselves would recognise or endorse. However, though a persuasive explanation, it is incomplete; it does not take into account women's perceptions of themselves as language users, nor their capacity to construct their own identities (individually or collectively) through their use of the languages available to them. Moreover, though the analogy between women and children is a compelling metaphor for the social and linguistic disadvantage of women in many different cultures, it disregards the point made by Edwards: that women, as mothers, are commonly (if not universally) responsible for children. Therefore, their 'strategic and socially meaningful linguistic choices' (Gal, 1984:293) affect their children's life chances as well as their own.

The papers in this book (with the exception of Tonkin's contribution) were originally presented at the workshop on 'Women and Second-Language Use' held at Oxford in Oxtober 1989 by the Centre for Cross-Cultural Research on Women. The issues of language choice, and of constraints upon that choice, were explored through participants' own experience as anthropologists, writers and second-language users. I have taken the title of the workshop as the title of this introductory essay, in which I shall attempt to draw out some common themes in the papers which follow.

Dominant Languages, Subordinate Women?

The use of the word 'bilingual' in the title does not imply that all the women referred to in these papers have equal competence in two languages. Indeed, some of them – like the 'closed Aymara' (non-Castilian-speaking) Andean peasant women in Spedding's paper – may be regarded as monolingual within their own communities. Moreover, three or even more languages may be involved, as in Joan Burke's description of a Zairean convent, in which French – 'nobody's language, therefore everybody's' – is used as a lingua franca. We have adopted a flexible definition of 'bilingual' as denoting the possibility of using more than one language as part of an individual linguistic repertoire.

Our papers deal with the experience of women in different situations of language contact. Applying Appel and Muysken's historical typology of such situations, the cases fall into two main categories: those in which language contact has occurred through European colonial conquest, and those in which 'individual pockets of speakers of minority languages ... [are] cut off by the surrounding national languages' (Appel and Muysken, 1987:5–6). There is considerable variation between individual cases in the status of the first language, and in its relationship with second and other languages. Bengali (for example) is a majority language within its own geographical boundaries, as Dyson's paper below shows: it can be defined as a 'minority language' only in the context of migrant communities in Britain (and possibly, if unfairly, in the context of international academic writing). Breton, on the other hand, might be popularly described in France as a 'patois' rather than a language. Some of the first languages referred to seem to be stable; others are undergoing shift and are apparently dying, or (as in the case of East Sutherland Gaelic) already dead. Most of the papers here show dyadic relationships between dominant and subordinate languages; in some the relationship is less simple, as historical complexities present the choice of more than one possible second language, new first language or lingua franca. One paper (Liu Hong's) falls outside Appel and Muysken's typology altogether, as it recounts the experience of a bilingual individual within a powerful monolingual society; Liu's personal 'situation of language contact' arises through her work as an interpreter.

Nearly all of the papers here are studies of bilingual women for whom a second or third language is the language of a dominant group, associated with power, prestige and access to economic benefits. The dominant languages to which our papers relate are English, French, Russian and Spanish (and to a lesser extent, Portuguese). For those who are native speakers of one of the powerful world languages, monolingualism is an attribute of dominance and may even (as in the English-speaking West) be regarded as a human norm. There is rarely such a pressing need for the members of dominant groups to learn the languages of minorities as for the reverse to happen. Hence bilingualism may be associated with inequality and social disadvantage, as Haugen points out: 'for many people, "bilingual" is a euphemism for "linguistically handicapped"' (1979:73). This attitude may be reflected in the negative stereotyping of bilingual minority speakers as incompetent users of more than one language, including their own.

Such a negative perception of bilingualism may create a double bind for poor women in minority groups, disadvantaged by gender as well as by race and class. In her analysis of women's speech in the Malinche Volcano area of Central Mexico, Hill (1987) describes how bilingual women are stigmatised (by Mexicano men) as incompetent in their use of Mexicano as well as Spanish. They are regarded as 'lagging' linguistically behind men in their use of Spanish; their Mexicano, on the other hand, is considered to be less pure than that of men, lacking the 'power code' associated with male Mexicano solidarity. Hill comments: 'Rather than think of the speech norms of women as marginal to a core of male norms, we might instead think of women's speech as highly constrained within a narrow range of possibilities, at the same time less Mexicano and less Spanish than men's speech, whereas men are able to use the full range of code variation' (1987:158). Hill adds that the women themselves do not perceive their own speech as in any way deficient; it is appropriate to their own needs and patterns of language use, which are different from those of men. This difference, however, rests on severe economic disadvantage and exclusion from 'male-dominated social arenas' such as paid employment.

Language contact may itself be mythologised in terms of sexual conquest, as Harvey's discussion below of Quechua ritual demonstrates. In their book Appel and Muysken exhort the reader to 'think of Cortes' conquest of Mexico in 1532 not as an outrageous narrative of bravery, cruelty and betrayal, but in terms of the crucial role of his Indian mistress Malinche, interpreter between Aztec and Spanish' (1987:1). It is worth noting, however, that the present-day descendants of this glamorous figure are the disadvantaged women described by Hill.

As Steiner has persuasively argued, there is a strong metaphorical association between the exchange of language and sexual intercourse: 'Eros and language mesh at every point' (1984:375). Hence, bilingual women may be seen as being sexually as well as linguistically promiscuous. This kind of stereotyping is summed up neatly in Elizabeth Tonkin's account in this book of the myth of the 'sleeping dictionary'. The 'sleeping dictionary' may, of course, have a certain basis in historical fact. It is a recognisable pattern, early in colonial conquest, for the women of the colonising power to remain at home, and for the men to seek local partners.

This image of bilingual women mediating between cultures through sex as well as language is not necessarily a negative one. Susan Abeyasekere has described how women acted as 'cultural intermediaries' in nineteenth-century Java. As servants, slaves, nannies, concubines – and, after a change in the law in 1848, sometimes as wives – Indonesian and Eurasian women brought about 'the acculturation of Batavian Europeans and Chinese' (1983:21). For a certain period, Abeyasekere argues, their influence helped to create a 'social idyll' within this relatively small, isolated society; 'a distinctive Batavian culture with ethnic variants' (*op.cit.*, p.28).

It is tempting to see this as a specifically female form of power through bilingualism. However, as Abeyasekere indicates, this influence was exercised at a price; Eurasian women especially (as the products, as well as the agents, of ethnic mixing) were stigmatised by English and Dutch colonisers alike: 'Eurasian women in particular are described by [nineteenth-century Dutch] writers ... as promiscuous, selfish, cunning, lazy and superstitious – and also extremely sexually attractive' (1983 :22). Abeyasekere describes (p.27) how, from the late nineteenth century onwards, ethnic separateness was reinforced, as further immigration of Europeans and Chinese (including women) created distinctive groups. To Europeans, Chinese and Indonesians alike, ethnic mixing was seen as a form of adulteration, and criticisms of it focused on the idea of women as 'guardians of the culture'. This is an idea which recurs in several of the cases described below.

In the early stages of colonial regimes, local girls may be excluded from 'legitimate' means of acquiring the language of the conquerors, if formal education is restricted to preparing local boys for service to the colonial regime. In addition, such exclusion may be defended on the grounds of sexual morality. In nineteenth-century Hong Kong, fear of the corrupting effects of second-language education was used as an excuse to end early attempts to provide English-language schools for local girls: 'the experiment of educating Chinese girls in English proved to be a blunder and had to be dropped, since most of them became mistresses of Europeans' (Endacott, 1964:143).[5]

This colonial motif is echoed here in Joan Burke's paper, referring to the competence in French of Zaïrean nuns. The language of instruction in Belgian Congo schools was the vernacular until the late 1950s. The senior Zaïrean sisters – those who had joined the sisterhood before 1960 – were affected by this policy. Moreover, Burke comments, 'I often heard them say jokingly – but also with a degree of resentment, because of the resultant language limitations – that they were not allowed to study French in their youth because of the missionaries' fear that it would encourage them to converse with expatriate men!' Burke adds, scrupulously, 'None of the older missionaries ever confirmed or denied this statement in my presence.' Nevertheless, within the convent itself – an extreme yet illuminating case of an all-female community – the sisters create their own linguistic universe with the resources at their command.

'Difference and Dominance'

In the last paper in this book, Tonkin relates our subject – bilingual women – to 'ungendered' accounts of bilingualism, and to sociolinguistic studies of gender and language. Our papers share some common concerns with recent community-based studies of women and language, as Tonkin shows. If, as she argues, linguists cannot make a clear-cut distinction between languages and language varieties, some of the questions raised by 'monolingual' studies of language and gender may usefully be pursued in studies of bilingualism.

One of the earliest collections of papers on gender and language (Thorne and Henley, 1975) is subtitled 'difference and dominance'[6]. In her introduction to the second part of a recent collection of papers by British women linguists (Coates and Cameron, 1989) Coates argues that these two themes have emerged as the two main approaches in sociolinguistic studies on women and language (65–71). The 'difference' theme stresses subcultural differences between men and women: 'dominance', the effects of hierarchy. I will consider both of these themes in turn, and their bearing on the papers presented here.

Is women's use of language everywhere different from that of men, and if so, is it different in the same way? The evidence from sociolinguistic and anthropological studies (including our own) suggests a cautious 'yes' to the first question, though to varying degrees; 'no' to the second. Cross-cultural ethnographic studies, by their very nature, undermine generalisations and challenge what Kramarae has described as the 'folk-linguistics of women's speech' (1982:87). For example, politeness in women's speech appears to be widespread, as Brown's work in Mayan communities (1980) and evidence from Japan (Ide et al., 1986; Shibamoto, 1985) attests; but it is by no means universal. Sherzer, examining speech-roles and gender-related genres among the Araucanians and the Kuna, comments that 'women's language, women's speech, and women's verbal activities are not everywhere socially and culturally inferior, domestic and polite' (1987:120).

Since the mid-1970s, work on language and gender has developed beyond simple monocausal explanations of difference. Several studies of language variation and speech styles suggest that apparent gender difference can be explained through intervening variables. Nichols (1983) argues that occupation, rather than gender in itself, creates differences between men's and women's use of standard forms of Creole in South Carolina Black communities. Milroy (1987) argues that variation in men's and women's speech in Belfast is related to the density of their personal networks. Ochs (1987) shows how gender interacts with age and political status in determining speech forms in Samoan society, and argues that it is (in this particular context) the least salient factor of the three. Ide et al., considering politeness in language use by women and men in Japan, present a similar case. They conclude that difference in language use is not 'a direct consequence of speaker of sex per se, but a phenomenon determined by complex factors' (1986:26).

What conclusions may be drawn from such findings? First, that care needs to be taken in recording the patterns of language use in particular societies. In their monograph on politeness, Brown and Levinson comment: 'we need to specify more closely some claim of the sort that 'women are more polite than men' – more polite than whom, to whom, about what and in what circumstances?' (1987:30). Next, that caution is needed in interpreting data: gender interacts variably with other bases of social differentiation, as Ochs suggests. However, it is not surprising that gender may be mediated through other factors – such as occupation, network or seniority – since it is itself culturally constructed. Ide *et al.* argue that, all things being equal, men's and women's use of language would be identical. But are all things ever equal in this sense? An anthropological explanation would suggest that biological sex is the basis for social marking of certain features (such as motherhood); the 'complex factors' noted by Ide *et al.* are the social groupings and expectations through which gender is given meaning in a particular society.

Brown and Levinson (1987) claim that research which assumes the existence of language differences between men and women has been empirically disappointing; that such differences, where they exist, are either minimal or can be attributed to other factors. According to this argument, gender differences such as those described in Brown's own Mayan data (1980) can be explained in terms of rational speaker strategies. They acknowledge the existence of gender stereotyping, such as that in Japanese soap operas recounted by Shibamoto (1985); however, they argue, it should be contrasted with realities (Brown and Levinson, 1987:56).

Our own papers offer ample evidence of rational speaker strategies. However, these still operate within the limitations of collective ideologies (as in the Goan case described by Mascarenhas-Keyes). It is doubtful whether 'ideology' and 'realities' can be so neatly opposed: as Hastrup argues in her study of breastfeeding in seventeenth- and eighteenth-century Iceland, collective values 'cannot be reduced to a sum of individual choices for an explanation' (1992:93).[7]

Moreover, as Brown and Levinson themselves observe, perceiving gender difference in language use is as much a matter of definition as it is of empirical observation (1987:31). One does not have to prove the existence of phonemic variation or distinct genderlects to observe differences in men's and women's use of language. There has been a shift in language and gender research (also observed by Brown and Levinson) towards observing speech styles and the patterning of discourse in actual contexts. This is the approach taken in our papers (with a varying degree of linguistic detail) to second-language use. Our evidence also suggests that there is more scope for observing gender difference in the choice and application of second languages than in the minutiae of sentence-level variation. Appel and Muysken argue that sociolinguistic issues 'reappear in enlarged form' in the context of language contact (1987:5); this may well be true of gender-related differences in the use of language.

Do differences between men and women in second-language use simply reflect male oppression of women? As Harvey argues in her paper below, this is the least helpful of the explanations offered for gender-based differences in language. This is not to deny the existence of inequality but to recognise that this model presents a one-dimensional view of social relations in general and gender relations in particular. It may offer the starting-point for an explanation but cannot, in itself, provide one; nor does it account for the value that women themselves set on their own experience and their own language.

Nevertheless, explanations which stress difference at the expense of dominance omit a vital element (as do arguments which seek to explain class and racial inequality at a purely subcultural level). Power becomes an issue as soon as women's life chances are affected by limitations on their access to a particular language or language variety. Such limitations may be created at least as much by colonial domination and poverty as by male strategies of exclusion; but, as Tonkin points out, women are still educationally disadvantaged worldwide, and therefore lag behind men in access to prestigious languages and language varieties.

Despite its crucial importance as an issue in economic development, equality of access to second languages does not in itself create identity of language use between men and women. In her paper below on the Aymara in Bolivia, Spedding states that both men and women have access to learning Castilian, and that the competence of both sexes is equal. Nevertheless, she argues, women and men use their available languages differently. This might be explained as simply reflecting subcultural differences between male and female spheres of activity; indeed, several of our papers do illustrate such differences of domain. However, gender-based differences in language use go deeper than this. Humphrey, MacDonald, Spedding and Harvey all demonstrate the importance of symbolism in language choice; in a multilingual situation, different languages are associated not only with different domains, but with different sets of values, which may themselves be conceptualised as masculine or feminine. Indeed, as Harvey demonstrates in her analysis of Quechua ritual, the relationship between 'masculine' and 'feminine' may serve as a metaphor for the domination of one ethnic group by another. Thus, gender is not merely a subcultural variable in a complex equation; it may be a vehicle for expressing social oppositions of a general kind.

Language Use: a Feminine Skill?

Though there is ample cross-cultural evidence of formal and informal constraints on women's access to powerful second languages, there is also a widespread belief that women are naturally 'good at languages'. Roger Goodman commented, in a paper given at the workshop (though not published here), on the currency of this belief in Japan and on its importance in women's educational choices and employment patterns. Liu Hong, in this book, observes the same perception in China; and in Hong Kong, the United States and in Britain, proficiency in language learning is widely regarded as a typically female attribute, from early childhood onwards.

Are women, given equal access to learning opportunities, linguistically more competent than men? As with most generalisations about 'women' as a distinct category, it is impossible to give a simple answer to this question. It seems unlikely that an answer could be derived directly from biological sex differences alone.[8] Studies of possible cognitive differences between males and females, and of how such differences might affect their linguistic ability, have so far appeared contradictory and inconclusive (Philips, Steele and Tanz, 1987:263–7).

However, there are more accessible reasons for female language skills. Verbal wit may be developed as a compensation for lesser physical strength, or economic dependence; it may also reflect the need (noted by Steiner) for social inferiors to know the language of their masters. This theme is expressed in the old story of Scheherazade, who wins the king's love and saves her own head through telling him tales of the Thousand-and-One-Nights – cunningly pausing in her narration each morning before the end of the tale. In her paper here, Humphrey refers to the verbal dexterity of Buryat daughters-in-law, who create alternative terms for the names of the male elders of the husband's lineage, which they are forbidden to pronounce (see also Humphrey, 1978). This skill – in which the new wife is tested by her father-in-law – is the appropriate response for a newcomer and an outsider, as well as a demonstration of women's intelligence. So, we return to the idea of linguistic strategies, or, as Tonkin aptly puts it, 'the skilful and intelligent practices of women'.

The use of language to gain face or outwit a more powerful adversary is not an exclusively female manoeuvre; Special skill in using the language of powerful others is a resource of the disadvantaged. Kay McCormick comments on the attitudes to the use of English of 'coloured' adults in District Six, Cape Town. 'The confident use of English is seen as a challenge to whites who are thought to stereotype coloureds as uneducated, unsophisticated, and working class ... It is felt that those whites who "don't like it" take it as a sign that coloureds are leaving their "proper place" in society if they speak English, because English is seen as a marker of upward social mobility' (1986:295; see also Ridd, 1981). Therefore, echoing Steiner's view again, it is possible to draw parallels between the experience of bilingual women and that of other 'muted groups'; in learning more about women, we may learn more about humanity in general.

Ironically enough, the ability to display apparent incompetence in the use of a second language can also be a strategic skill; it may be used to escape censure for inappropriate fluency, or simply as a device to withhold information. Spedding refers below to the way in which Aymara peasant women evade official questions through feigned ignorance of Castilian: 'Peasant women are expected to be "closed Aymara" and exploit this belief.' Bilingual women, therefore, often need communicative competence in their use of second languages, that is, knowing 'who may or should speak, how, when and where, to whom' (Hymes, 1971:72).

Second-language competence is not value-free; its acquisition, its use and the way in which it is perceived are affected by the status of the users. Liu, Mascarenhas-Keyes and Dyson all point out below the connection between second-language education for women and socially acceptable occupations such as teaching, translation, writing, and even (in Mascarenhas-Keyes' study of Goa) 'progressive motherhood'. Such positive images are clearly ideological constructs, no less than the 'sleeping dictionary'. The question is, whose constructs are they, and to whose benefit do they operate? To consider this point further, let us move on to an image of virtuously monolingual womanhood: women as the 'guardians' of a minority language.

Women as 'Guardians of the Language'

In several papers here, it appears that women may be regarded as the 'guardians' of a minority language and, by implication, of ethnic identity. In this scenario, women are held responsible for maintaining the vernacular both by speaking it themselves and by transmitting it to their children. In discussions at the workshop, Tamara Dragadze suggested that women's responses to this role vary from one society to another, spanning a continuum from active support to rejection. In their note on Georgian women in the former USSR, Chinchaladze and Dragadze argue that women were traditionally seen as 'the guardians of literacy' in Georgian villages; this has continued up to the present day, with women's enthusiastic backing for the Georgian language as the medium of education and for the Georgian nationalist cause.

In any beleaguered linguistic minority, women's continued use and transmission of the vernacular may be a demonstration of loyalty to the group, as well as a strategy for survival. This loyalty can be communicated in other ways as well; for example, by maintaining a distinctive mode of dress. Muslim migrant communities in Western Europe are a case in point (Krozjl, 1986). Yet if the way of life associated with the vernacular is not one which women wish to perpetuate and if they have access to a dominant language, they may opt for change. They may migrate, if there are employment opportunities elsewhere; they may marry men outside the group (as recorded by Gal, 1984), or they may decide not to transmit the language to their children (MacDonald, Constantinidou below).

In considering linguistic loyalty, it might be argued that women are not themselves a minority, and that they share the status of the speech community to which they belong. This may often be the case; in her paper here, Dyson reveals a pride in her Bengali literary heritage which is not marked by gender, and which was encouraged by both her mother and her father. However, a 'speech community' is almost impossible to define except through its reality for its members; not only 'in terms of the sharing both of some one primary form of speech, and of rules for its use', as Hymes puts it (1971:64), but as a focus of linguistic loyalty and a source of personal identity. This focus is not necessarily the same for women as it is for men; indeed, in the Breton case described here by MacDonald, the very women who are regarded as the core of a minority speech community simply do not perceive its reality in their own experience.

Do women simply opt for a 'high-prestige' variety in all situations of language choice, as Edwards suggests? Our cases indicate that the issue is far more complex than this; yet again, women cannot be regarded as an undifferentiated category. Women in an ethnic minority may or may not perceive their own interests as being the same as men's; these interests will probably differ between classes, between generations, and even (as Constantinidou points out below) from one community to another within the same region. Also, their perceptions will be different from those of an outside observer, who may judge their choices as short-sighted and even disloyal when they reject a minority language, or self-limiting when they embrace it. The anthropological solution – cogently argued here by MacDonald – is to give full value to the world-view of informants; for women as language users to be the subject, not the object, of enquiry. Let us now take a closer look at the papers, to see the various ways in which the task of 'engendering bilingualism' is approached.

The Papers: Anthropological Approaches

All but two of the papers in this book are by social anthropologists: these two – by Liu Hong and by Ketaki Kushari Dyson – are personal accounts by women whose work and lives have been shaped by their bilingualism. The papers deal with language choice; which languages women speak or write, for what purposes, and how this choice is perceived by themselves and by others. Though these 'anthropological approaches' are by no means uniform, there is a shared emphasis on the diversity and richness of women's language use, on the importance of the local context and the individual voice.

For anthropologists, the use of other languages is an essential aspect both of method and of analysis. Indeed, as Edwin Ardener points out, 'language penetrates the social'; thus, translation and anthropological fieldwork have much in common (1989:172–3). Characteristically, anthropologists see language as a mode of defining individual and group identity, of presenting the self to others, of marking and crossing the boundaries between groups. Such issues are particularly salient in situations of language contact; our papers reflect the relative power of different ethnic groups and the consequent development of dominant and minority languages. We can see how such asymmetries are worked out in the lives and language use of women – and conversely how women's choices can influence linguistic events.

The first two papers (by Spedding and Harvey) deal with indigenous communities in South America and women's use of Castilian (Spanish), the dominant language originally introduced by colonial conquest. The two groups, the Aymara and the Quechua, are geographically close and the history of defeat and domination is basically the same. However, attitudes to Castilian and women's use of it are very different indeed. Among the Quechua, women are largely excluded from use of the high-prestige form of Castilian reserved for speaking in public: an exclusion which may be enforced by ridicule and insult. The Aymara also associate Castilian with the male and the indigenous language with the female; but, Spedding states, 'men and women have equivalent opportunities to learn the national language and levels of bilingualism do not differ much between the sexes, though the choices each sex makes about language use are rather different'. Aymara women improve their Castilian through trade, selling their coffee, fruit and coca in the city. Moreover, middle-class women control the commercial unions set up to organise trading from rural to urban areas. Using Castilian, they can deal with middle-class urban bureaucracy; but this is primarily to their own benefit, not that of peasant women. Spedding comments, 'women, equally with men, are divided and subjected by the external forces of class and race'.

In the case of the Quechua, on the other hand, it appears that such subjection is not equal; that racial and gender inequality reinforce one another, to the detriment of women's presumed competence in Castilian and their native language alike. Harvey develops her interpretation of the use of Quechua and Castilian through considering other modes of communicating meaning in Andean culture: silence and ritual. She gives a detailed and fascinating account of festivals in which 'female' and sexually ambiguous characters are enacted by men and are associated with indigenous identity, defeat, and powerlessness. She argues convincingly that 'gender is used as a metaphor to express other power differences ... the use of this gender metaphor allows men to negotiate the ambiguity of their racial status but at the expense of women'.

Two of our studies (by Humphrey and by Chinchaladze and Dragadze) deal with women in ethnic minority groups in the former Soviet Union. They are very different in approach; Humphrey gives a detailed analysis of an oral text of an informal interview of a Buryat woman, apparently talking freely about her domestic affairs and personal feelings to a Buryat linguist (also a woman). This is set within a historical account of the development of Russian hegemony through the twentieth century, and the varying position of the Buryat – men and women – both in the local economy, and in access to education. However, discourse analysis is the heart of this paper. Humphrey argues the importance of 'casual chat' as a means of self-disclosure, and shows how code-switching is used not only in response to changes in referential domain, but to encode feelings of alienation or solidarity.

Chinchaladze and Dragadze, on the other hand, deal with language use at the level of the group, not the individual. This paper is mainly concerned with Georgian nationalism before the break-up of the old Soviet system, and with the importance of women to the nationalist movement as 'the guardians of literacy and the agents of social control in village life'. Chinchaladze and Dragadze point out the difference between men and women as users of Russian, the dominant language. Men, through wider travel and army service, have had both access to Russian and the need to use it; women have tended to stay within their locality and (until fairly recent times) to be far less competent in Russian than men. This has not been seen as a deficit, because of the positive value placed on Georgian as the national language. Though this pattern has been modified by equal access to education for girls, the reaction against Russian (even as a compulsory school subject) has continued. Women, as 'home educators' in the Georgian language, are key figures in the preservation of national identity.

In these two papers we see how women may be affected by differences in the power balance of language contact. Humphrey describes the geographical separation of Buryat communities and the different forms of the Buryat language, ethnic minority enclaves in a sea of Russian. Georgian, on the other hand, is a national language, by its official recognition as such within the USSR at the time of the study and in the perception of Georgians themselves. Though Chinchaladze and Dragadze doubt the economic viability of a completely autonomous Georgian state, they indicate the ethnic loyalties which underlie the current disintegration of the former Soviet empire and the importance of women's language behaviour in that process.

The potential importance of women's language choice is also apparent in the papers by Maryon MacDonald and Evi Constantinidou. Both these papers deal with language shift and ethnic identity; in Constantinidou's paper, with reference to the death of East Sutherland Gaelic. Both papers show how women are seen as the guardians of the local language and of ethnic identity; in MacDonald's Breton case, quite explicitly so, through the activities of the largely middle-class Breton nationalist movement. Both papers insist on the validity of the world-view of women themselves and of their apparent decision not to transmit the minority language – the 'mother tongue' – to their children. An important difference between the two cases is in timing. Constantinidou, through conversations with the 'fishergirls' of the village of Embo and their families, consciously attempts to 'engender' the process of language death recorded elsewhere by Nancy Dorian; the death of East Sutherland Gaelic has already effectively taken place. Though Breton appears (from the evidence presented by MacDonald in this paper and elsewhere) to be passing through a similar process, its fate is by no means decided.

The imposition of colonial power, or of an educational policy actively imposing the majority national language, is not a theme of these 'language death' papers; indeed MacDonald comments that 'it is not the case that ... adoption of French has been any straightforward imposition from Paris'. Suppression of Celtic languages (and of Celtic ethnic identities) has of course taken place in the past; the Breton case is fully recorded in MacDonald's book (1989), and she comments here on the centralising tendency of the French state over the past two hundred years. However, both writers are concerned with (to use Dorian's terms, quoted by Constantinidou) the association of a subordinate language with a stigmatised group. More accurately perhaps, since none of these women appear to regard themselves as in any way inferior, the subordinate language is associated with a way of life which they do not wish to perpetuate.

MacDonald presents an interesting opposition between national and local attitudes to the Breton language. She shows how, since the Celtic revival of the nineteenth century, Breton has been conceptualised as feminine in opposition to French culture; within the Breton nationalist movement, it is the 'mother tongue' (*yezh mamm*). However, for the women of Kerguz –the village in which MacDonald carried out her fieldwork – Breton is associated with a hard, dirty way of life, with 'cowshit'. French, on the other hand, is the language of femininity, refinement and sophistication. MacDonald's paper makes an explicit connection between language use and domestic detail. One particularly striking vignette is of a New Year party in Kerguz: 'the women sit together at one end of a long table with their sweet cakes and sweet wine and speak predominantly in French, and the men pack together at the other end in a haze of cigarette smoke, eating cheap paté, drinking hard liquor, playing dominoes or cards, and speaking predominantly in Breton'.

Constantinidou's informants have passed beyond this stage of choice. She reconstructs their part in the death of East Sutherland Gaelic through her own interaction as a student of Gaelic with older Gaelic-speaking women and their non-Gaelic-speaking adult children; also, through documentary evidence from newspapers of the 1930s and 1940s.

Constantinidou recounts the women's rejection of older ways of life, extending to their destruction of old furniture – of the kind that was elsewhere being dubbed 'antique' and valued accordingly – and its replacement with new. The tone of her paper, though not judgemental, is gently elegiac; she notes the current revaluation of the fishergirls' way of life, now celebrated in museums and picture postcards, and a source of pride to her older informants.

In Embo, the apparent decision of so many women not to transmit Gaelic to their children was, as Constantinidou puts it, 'retrospectively muted'; never apparently discussed, and not put on record at the time.

Joan Burke's paper deals with women's use of language in a speech community of a rather unusual kind, one which is based not on a shared first language, but on the choice of a shared life and religious beliefs: a community of nuns, the Sisters of Notre Dame in Zaïre. This community came into being in the early twentieth century, within a situation of colonial language contact. Burke shows how colonial language policy in Zaïre reflected attitudes to language in the mother country, bilingual Belgium; this in turn affected the language skills available to the indigenous sisters. The senior Zaïrean sisters, who were educated in the vernacular till the late 1950s, do not have the same command of French as their juniors; and French, though it is the first language of only seven out of a total community of nearly a hundred nuns, is the lingua franca.

However, the older Zaïrean sisters are not at a disadvantage in their total linguistic repertoire; the younger sisters do not have 'the same command of the richness of Kikongo', specifically, the register of persuasive oratory, in which the older sisters are acknowledged to excel.

Burke, like Harvey, Spedding and Chinchaladze and Dragadze, considers the positive values given to the vernacular. In this Zaïrean convent, as in Andean village communities and in Georgia, the vernacular is the language of solidarity, of belonging fully to the community. For the sisters, this takes the form of interpreting their relationships of Catholic sisterhood (and, in some cases, motherhood) through redefinition of Kongo kinship terms; also, through their Kongo-speaking educational work in the wider community. Burke, like Humphrey, shows how the indigenous language is used not only in specific practical domains, but in the articulation and shaping of personal relationships. The sisters' use of French as their lingua franca is historically constrained, but individuals still make choices within the limitations of their own repertoire. This paper shows how important it is, in discussing language use, to be aware of historical change; Burke recounts shifts in patterns of address even within her own fieldwork period and indicates the possibility of vernacular languages other than Kongo becoming prominent in the future.

In her paper on the Goan diaspora, Stella Mascarenhas-Keyes considers another form of language contact: migration. However, rather than analysing Goan migrant groups within host societies, she examines the impact of migration on language use in Goa itself; and specifically the language choices of women, whom she sees as having a positive role in shaping modern Goan identity, through their support for English as the first language of the International Catholic Goan Community. According to her account of colonial language policy, gender equality was a feature of education in Portuguese from a fairly early date, as a result of Catholic ideology. In 1745, Mascarenhas-Keyes notes, a local candidate for the priesthood had to be a Portuguese speaker, and this also applied 'to his close relatives of both sexes'.

Mascarenhas-Keyes examines the language choices of a relatively privileged population. She shows how women have gained access to English through education, and through the availability of 'appropriate' work (nursing, teaching) in the Goan diaspora in mainly English-speaking countries. This paper echoes the 'language death' theme of accounts of ethnic minorities elsewhere. However, there is no suggestion here that women are seen as the 'guardians' of the indigenous language. In their enthusiastic promotion of education in English, women are in line with the mainstream ideology of the International Catholic Goan Community, in which provision for learning Konkani (the vernacular) is 'minimal'.

Liu Hong's autobiographical note brings us a personal and individual voice, though wider implications are apparent. This is an account of her own experience as a second-language user. She learned English as a foreign language within her own culture, not in a situation of language contact. The target language appeared to be value-neutral, at least in the early learning stages, or was used to translate the values of the users (Mao's thoughts, for example). Women and girls are seen, in the society as a whole and by Liu herself as a language teacher, as good at languages. This theme is developed in Liu's account of her first experience of direct language contact, as an interpreter. Here, it becomes apparent that being good at languages is part of a wider feminine role as an intermediary between supposedly equivalent linguistic groups. An interpreter (Liu suggests) needs to be flexible and conciliatory, and also to be a willing scapegoat, bearing the brunt of the wrath of both sides. This, in her own cultural experience, is a role that men are unwilling to play; women can be seen to lose face as they have by definition less face to lose. However, there are compensations for women with language skills: relatively high pay and status (teachers in other subject areas 'eat vinegar' at the good fortune of English graduates), and the less tangible rewards of moving into a wider world through reading, research and travel.

Ketaki Kushari Dyson also speaks from personal experience. She describes a situation of educational privilege in an independent postcolonial country. As an heir to a rich literary tradition, in Sanskrit as well as Bengali, Dyson has no sense of linguistic inferiority; indeed, her experience of language learning as intellectual discovery and personal growth is one which monolinguals may well envy. However, she shows how the imposition of colonial rule on India in the nineteenth century has cast a shadow on the status of Indian languages worldwide, and recounts the repercussions of the supremacy of English on her own career as a bilingual writer. Unlike Konkani, Bengali flourishes as a national language: but as a world language, English is still dominant, and access to its privileged uses is still controlled by gatekeepers, as Dyson demonstrates. However, this muting takes place only in her British life, not in her Bengali life, as a result (she argues) of her refusal to become a monolingual writer; she describes different situations in two different geographical locations. This paper emphasises the imbalance between dominant and subordinate languages, rather than gender-specific muting; yet the situation which led to Dyson's life as a writer in two worlds – her marriage and subsequent residence in Britain – suggests a predominantly female pattern of life choices.[9] This is an account of the personal costs and rewards of bilingualism in the context of such choices, forcefully and elegantly expressed.

Our final paper, by Elizabeth Tonkin, was specially written for this book. In her discussion of 'engendering language difference', Tonkin argues the vital importance for women's life chances of access to prestigious languages and language varieties. She examines some recent studies of gender and language in Britain and draws on her extensive knowledge of sociolinguistic issues worldwide to comment on women's resourceful responses to inequality and disadvantage. In this paper, Tonkin considers both theoretical concerns and the practical consequences of sociolinguistic structures (such as diglossia) for women's lives. She indicates several areas in which our knowledge is incomplete and proposes directions for further research.

Muted Group Theory

Can one conclude, from the varied testimony of these papers, that generalisation is impossible? Certainly, it appears that women's use of language is best understood in the context of specific communities with their own economic constraints and unique history. However, the ideology of language use is central to all these papers; how women are perceived as second-language users, and how they perceive themselves. Liu describes how, in China, being a language teacher or an interpreter is seen as a suitable job for a woman; Mascarenhas-Keyes presents the ideal of 'progressive motherhood' which leads Goan women to intervene actively in the education of their children. Such images can be empowering, and they may even lead women into positions of relative privilege; but they also limit choice, by cutting women off from a wide range of other options which are commonly (if not invariably) open to men. What is the source of these 'mind-forg'd manacles'? I would contend that it is mutedness; that this is the main shared theme of these diverse accounts of bilingual women, and that this is an analytical model which is sufficiently flexible and powerful to illuminate them all.

The idea of mutedness, and of women as a classic case of a muted group, was first mooted in Edwin Ardener's paper 'Belief and the Problem of Women' (1972). In it, Ardener enquires why women, who are half of any normal human population, so rarely speak for themselves in ethnographic studies. When he wrote, if women were perceived or described, it was largely through information given by men; as Ardener puts it, 'mere birdwatching indeed'.

The theory of muted groups which arose from this enquiry has been developed by Edwin and Shirley Ardener in a series of papers

(E.Ardener, 1975, 1986: S.Ardener, 1975, 1978, 1986). Shirley Ardener sums up the central idea of muting thus: 'the gist of this is that there are dominant modes of expression in any society which have been generated by the dominant structures within it' (1978: 20).

Women are commonly (though not inevitably) muted in this sense; they express themselves in public (if at all) through socially sanctioned modes of expression in the generation of which they have often been less prominent than have men. If verbal modes are inadequate to express what they wish to communicate, muted groups may articulate their world-view through other channels, such as song, dress, ritual, or even political protest. Edwin Ardener's original case study was of the Bakweri *liengu* mermaid ritual. At a paper given at the workshop, though not published here, Juliet Pope outlined the importance of symbolic action by women's peace groups in Israel. Harvey's account of Quechua ritual, which I have already discussed, shows both the muting of Quechua men, and their assumption that male/female relations are a fitting symbol of their historical defeat.

The concept of muting has had considerable influence on the work of feminist ethnographers and linguists (see for example Warren and Bourque, 1985; Kramarae, 1981). Nevertheless, as Edwin Ardener argues, it is part of a general theory of dominance, not a statement about gender as a universal condition. He points out that 'dominance when applied to women is ... only patchily related to the economic structure' (1986: 98). Dominance, he states, is a 'problem of humanity' (1986: 99), which can originate in a simple, unmarked difference (for example, left- and right-handedness, or biological differences between men and women). Such a difference leads to an imbalance, thence to imparity, and finally to inequality (1986:100).

The muting of subordinate groups takes place through two processes, which are by no means mutually exclusive. First, through the actual exercise of power by dominant groups, through which the muted are excluded from highly-valued modes of expression or handicapped in their use of them. This is part of the wider mechanisms of social closure: 'mechanisms for devaluing their contribution, squeezing them out from the arenas in which rewards are distributed' (S.Ardener, 1986:4). The papers in this book provide ample illustration of the exercise of power: by one ethnic group against another, by men against women, by middle-class women against peasant women. Tonkin and Burke both record colonial restrictions on women's access to education; Harvey describes the ridicule from men and women alike which greets Quechua women's attempts to speak Castilian; Dyson, after a childhood and early adulthood of educational privilege in India, recounts how so much of this education was discounted in Britain: 'British society … alienated, marginalised and trivialised us.'

Second, muting takes place through the general acceptance of the dominant world-view as the norm: the taken-for-granted version of events. Shirley Ardener, discussing the muting of women in academic discourse, comments: 'more often than not it is done unconsciously, by people who would be the last to wish to discriminate in, say, an inegalitarian way' (1986:5). Thus, muting continues even in the absence of deliberate exclusion and is therefore even harder to challenge or confront without inviting indignant rebuttals or (worse still) ridicule.

And what of the muted themselves? They too may regard the dominant model as the norm, and find it difficult to specify or express any feelings of alienation from it. As Shirley Ardener remarks, achieving a way of expressing oneself depends on interaction and reciprocity. To be visible, one must be seen; to speak, one must be heard: 'words which continually fall on deaf ears may, of course, in the end become unspoken, or even unthought' (1978:20).

This is the aspect of muted group theory which is most controversial, and which has attracted some criticism. Deborah Cameron, in a generally sympathetic account of the theory, finds 'a hint of determinism' in the suggestion that mutedness can cause problems in linguistic self-expression (1985:104), though she agrees that the theory of mutedness is not inherently deterministic. She also argues that 'the question of power is the one the Ardeners appear to shy away from' (op.cit:106). This judgement rests mainly, it appears, on the Ardeners' choice of words: '"structures of dominance" rather than "the oppression of women"'. The question of power is in fact central to muted group theory, but (as in Edwin Ardener's 1986 paper) it is presented in analytical rather than programmatically feminist terms. Unlike the Ardeners, Cameron seems to view muting as a necessarily conscious process: a 'survival tactic' for women, and deliberate coercion by men. She comments on 'the social rules and taboos used in many cultures to silence women', adding 'it is a pity that the dominant/muted model does not go into the implications of these practices more thoroughly' (1985:106). Perhaps what is needed is not further elaboration of the model, but more investigation of specific cases, as in the papers below.

Muted group theory has suffered from being misunderstood, sometimes by writers whose own work appears to exemplify it. I have already discussed Hill's paper on Mexicano women, which reads like a case study of mutedness. Yet Hill dismisses the idea of the muted woman as a 'stereotype', belied by the liveliness of her informants' speech and the positive values they ascribe to it (1987:127). However, muting is not a condition of physical silence, as both Edwin and Shirley Ardener have pointed out; nor are women necessarily 'downtrodden "invisibles"' (E.Ardener, 1986:103). Muted groups can and do generate alternative models of society. Such a model is apparent in Okely's (1975) account of Gipsy women, whose interpretations of their own virtue and sexuality differ both from that of house-dwellers and that of their own men. The theme of alternative models continues in this book: MacDonald's Breton peasant women, Burke's Zaïrean nuns, even Harvey's disadvantaged Quechua women, all construct individual and group identities through interaction with other women.

In this process, the use of a second language may offer women the possibility of encoding meanings which their first language does not permit them to express. Anny Tual comments that Iranian women will speak freely in a second language, even in the presence of men: 'as if this other language does not bind them in the same way in the social structure' (1986:66). On the other hand, continued use of a mother tongue may enable women from minority groups to assert a self and way of seeing the world which cannot be so naturally expressed in the dominant language. This may involve the use of a genre which is specific to a particular culture, as Edwards and Katbamna's account of the wedding songs of British Gujarati women shows (1988). Dyson's account below of her language choices is particularly interesting; her novels are in Bengali, which indicates a choice of audience and of 'universe' as well as medium. The point is that a linguistic repertoire which contains several languages offers more scope for self-expression than does monolingualism.

Can one therefore argue that mutedness is a myth? Should one simply celebrate women's language, created largely within all-female groups, in its own right? I would suggest not, given the facts of power and inequality. Sometimes (as Shirley Ardener has argued) women can dominate a domain of discourse, thereby muting any men present. In a wider context of relevance, that domain may be highly valued, but it may also be disparaged or disregarded. The alternative models of muted groups may simply not be perceived (let alone accepted) in society at large. The positive self-evaluation of Hill's Mexicano and Harvey's Quechua women is not shared by their men; in both cases, they are despised as inadequate speakers both of the vernacular and of Spanish. According to MacDonald, Breton peasant women's attachment to French is dismissed by middle-class Breton activists as 'false consciousness'.

In a sympathetic account of the twentieth-century history of the Canadian Doukhobors,[10] Shirley Ardener describes how the perceived threat of mainstream social values to their group identity led to desperate forms of mass protest: public nudity, arson, and even bombing. These tactics were not supported by most Doukhobors, who 'embraced success' (1983:261) and accepted a measure of social integration as the necessary price of change. As she points out elsewhere, the alternative models of muted groups are commonly generated in response to the dominant model; they may therefore be distorted and restrictive (1978:21). However, such 'templates for thought and action' are not immutable. Change is often possible, as our papers show; and bilingual women, through their use of more than one language, may be the agents of such change.

Directions for Further Research

Each of the papers in this book has its own unique value: each can be read as a self-contained study of some aspect of women and second-language use. There are themes which crop up in more than one paper, some of which I have attempted to bring out in this introduction. In doing so I have not covered all of the arguments presented below: I may well have made generalisations with which not all the contributors would agree. I therefore leave the last word with the papers themselves (and the reader's interpretation of them).

Above all, these papers raise questions and open up new lines of enquiry. Tonkin's paper in particular raises several issues which call for further research. I will add my own comments on possible research directions, and finally discuss how anthropology can help to 'engender language difference'.

First, the question of coverage. In one sense, ethnographic information is never complete; more data can always be collected. However there are still some conspicuous gaps in our knowledge, as Tonkin points out. We need more comparative material on bilingual women from an even wider linguistic, cultural and structural range. This is particularly important where women's life chances may be affected by policy decisions based on research findings. We lack adequate detailed information, for example, on bilingual women who cross boundaries between languages by marriage or migration; on the language problems of women refugees; on monolingual women in bilingual communities; and on women within Third World migrant communities in industrialized societies.

We also need to know more about the part played by women in the transmission of language. I suggested earlier that women's choices are particularly salient because of their responsibility as mothers. However, this responsibility cannot be taken for granted, since motherhood is a social construct open to change as well as a biological state. In addition, the real or symbolic responsibility of mothers for language transmission interacts with a number of external factors (for a list of such factors and discussion of their importance in language maintenance see Romaine, 1989:39–45). Romaine comments that 'in mixed marriages there is usually a shift to the majority language' (1989:41). She cites Williams' (1987) study of language maintenance in Wales, in which data based on the 1981 census show that 'mothers in mixed marriages have a better chance of passing Welsh on to their children than Welsh-speaking fathers, though this pattern is not replicated in all areas of Wales' (Romaine, 1989:41–2). In her paper below, Constantinidou unpacks the particular circumstances through which mothers (and grandmothers) in Embo became key figures in language death. This is the level of information which is needed and which only ethnographic studies can supply; survey data can show gender patterning in language transmission within the family, but cannot in itself explain it.

Further information on bilingual women as linguistic innovators would also be welcome. This is the theme of MacDonald's paper on Brittany; Humphrey's and Burke's papers also show the linguistic creativity of bilingual women. Most of our papers address the question of choice between languages, either as a global preference or within particular domains. These three papers also examine the micro-level of second-language use; borrowing, code-switching and (in Humphrey's paper) the emergence of mixed forms. All this suggests that the effect of gender on cross-linguistic influence merits further investigation. Romaine cites the case of Indoubil, a hybrid language used in urban areas of Zaïre, which 'has its origins in the early 1960s as a language of defiance used mainly by young males' (1989:67). Given the importance of women as traders (see Tonkin's paper below) might one not also find traces of female influence on some pidgins and creoles? Interdisciplinary research could well prove fruitful in areas such as this.

Some convergence between the theoretical concerns of anthropology and those of sociolinguistics has already taken place, as Tonkin argues. This is particularly apparent in recent work on the minority languages of the British Isles, which asserts the value of multiculturalism and multi-lingualism (Alladina and Edwards: 1991). Romaine argues cogently against the traditional view of monolingualism as the norm and biling-ualism as inherently problematic, pointing out that this view is rooted in the ideology of the West and does not reflect the realities of language use throughout the world (1989:6,8). This fits well with the classic anthropological approach of fieldwork in 'other cultures' (which need not always be in geographically remote spots).

Romaine also argues that 'bilingualism cannot be understood except in relation to social context' (1989: Preface). This can surely best be achieved through careful, intellectually-informed ethnography, as in the papers presented here. For the anthropologist, social context is more than explanatory background material; language use needs to be decoded in combination with other modes of communicating meaning, and in relation to informants' own interpretations of experience. Hence, the experience of women should be as central to our understanding of second-language use as that of men. We hope that the papers in this book, through presenting some aspects of this experience, will encourage further study of the needs and perceptions of bilingual women worldwide.

Notes

1. Such exceptions include Hill's (1987) paper and Gal's work on language shift, which are discussed here. There are thirteen entries under bilingualism in the extensive annotated bibliography in Thorne, Kramarae & Henley (1983).

2. I use the term 'gender' in preference to 'sex' to denote a category which is socially rather than biologically constructed. However, linguists tend to prefer the term 'sex' because of the specialised technical meaning of 'gender' in linguistic terminology.

3. Hamers and Blanc, pp.13–139 and 145. The papers cited deal with inter-ethnic (and intra-ethnic) face-to-face encounters, applying the theory of accommodation developed by Giles and his associates at Bristol University. The only paper among these to take gender as a central theme is Valdes-Fallis (1977), which is based on the taped conversations of four Mexican-American women with other bilinguals (women and men).

4. The 'strategy' approach is developed in the work of Brown (1980) and Brown and Levinson (1978/1987). A useful account of this model is given in Kramarae (1981).

5. I am indebted to Dr Gillian Bickley of the Department of English, Baptist College, Hong Kong, for kindly giving me the sources on which this comment by Endacott is based, and for discussing the historical background to this incident with me. Endacott's reference is to the closure of the Diocesan Female Training School. Frederick Stewart, the second Inspector of Schools in Hong Kong, called this school 'one of the most disastrous experiments which the Colony has ever witnessed' (ISs Rep 1873, para 23). According to E.J. Eitel, the third Inspector of Schools, this is what happened:

> the ladies' Committee (under the late Bishop Smith), which started the Diocesan Female Training School in 1862 [sic] found itself compelled in 1865 to close the school on the ground that almost every one of the girls, taught English in that School, became, on leaving school, the kept mistress of foreigners. (E.J. Eitel, 'Girls' School', Hong Kong, Presented to the Leg-

islative Council, by Command of His Excellency the Governor, No. 18 of 1889 [dated 5 July 1889] para 4.)

Dr Bickley, who is currently working on a biography of Frederick Stewart, points out that at that time most Chinese girls were denied education of any kind; limited access to English-language education must therefore be seen in that context. Chinese parents were generally unwilling to let their daughters go to school, and even more unwilling to let them learn English. After the closure of the Diocesan School, Frederick Stewart opposed the teaching of any foreign language to Chinese girls, who were to be 'simply educated for the proper discharge of their duties as wives and mothers in the humble homes from which they come, and to which they return on leaving school' (ISs Rep 1874, para 21). This policy was questioned by Stewart's successor, Eitel, and in 1890 the Belilios Public School was opened, offering an English-language education to girls. This venture had no scandalous consequences, though the continued reluctance of Chinese parents to let their daughters study English was recorded as late as 1915 (Bickley, 1988: also personal communication).

6. In a later collection of papers (1983), Thorne, Kramarae and Henley discuss the changes in approach to gender and language difference since the mid-1970s, notably the shift towards context-specific explanations.

7. Individual choices may indeed bring about a structural change, as in language death; but such choices are shaped by collective values, as well as by economic rationality (see Constantinidou below).

8. I am grateful to Dr Martha Pennington, Reader in English at the City Polytechnic of Hong Kong, for her comments on this issue. Dr Pennington, a linguist trained at the University of Pennsylvania, argues that many linguistic differences between males and females have a basis in natural (biological) differences. She cites the larger size of the vocal tract in adult males; difference in the perceptual bias of males and females for processing acoustic information; and differences in the developmental schedule for language acquisition. Dr Pennington comments on the interaction of the biological and the social, suggesting (for example) that 'children would be more likely to identify with adults who are physiologically similar than those who are physiologically different' (personal communication). Clearly this is a research area worth watching, and one in which anthropologists and sociolinguists should be aware of new developments.

9. I am conscious that this comment appears to endorse gender stereotyping, and that this particular mould can be broken by male exogamy. However, the pattern of the wife's domicile following her husband's, rather than the reverse, is reinforced by the immigration rules of many countries (including the UK).

10. The Doukhobors were a minority religious sect of Russian origin.

References

Abeyasekere, S., 1983, 'Women as Cultural Intermediaries in Nineteenth-Century Batavia' in L. Manderson (ed.), *Women's Work and Women's Roles: Economics and Everyday Life in Indonesia, Malaysia and Singapore*, The Australian National University Development Studies Centre, Monograph 32.

Alladina, S. and Edwards, V. (eds), 1991, *Multilingualism in the British Isles 1: The Older Mother Tongues and Europe*, 2: *Africa, the Middle East and Asia*, London and New York: Longman.

Appel, R. and Muysken, P., 1987, *Language Contact and Bilingualism*, London: Edward Arnold.

Ardener, E.W., 1972, 'Belief and the Problem of Women' in J. LaFontaine (ed.), *The Interpretation of Ritual*, London: Tavistock. Reprinted in S.Ardener (ed.), 1975, *Perceiving Women*, London: Malaby/Dent.

_____, 1975, 'The Problem of Women Revisited' in S.Ardener (ed.), *Perceiving Women*.

_____, 1986 (1981), 'The Problem of Dominance', *Journal of the Anthropological Society of Oxford*, vol.7, no.2. Reprinted in L. Dube, E. Leacock and S. Ardener (eds), 1986, *Visibility and Power*, Delhi: OUP.

_____, 1989 (1977), 'Comprehending Others' in M. Chapman (ed.), *The Voice of Prophecy and Other Essays*, Oxford: Basil Blackwell.

Ardener, S. 1973, 'Sexual Insult and Female Militancy', *Man*, vol.8, no.3. Reprinted in S. Ardener (ed.), 1975, *Perceiving Women*.

_____ (ed.), 1975, *Perceiving Women*, London: Malaby/Dent (reprinted Berg 1992).

_____ (ed.), 1978, *Defining Females: the Nature of Women in Society*, London: Croom Helm (rev. edn, 1993, Oxford and Providence: Berg).

_____, 1983, 'Arson, Nudity and Bombs among the Canadian Doukhobors: A Question of Identity' in G. Breakwell (ed.), *Threatened Identities*, Chichester: John Wiley and Sons Ltd.

_____, 1986, 'The Representation of Women in Academic Models' in L. Dube, E. Leacock and S. Ardener (eds), *Visibility and Power*, Delhi: OUP.

Baetens Beardmore, H., 1982, *Bilingualism: Basic Principles*, Clevedon: Tieto Ltd.

Bickley, G., 1988, 'Should Hong Kong Chinese Girls Learn English? Nineteenth Century Attitudes', paper read at the Hong Kong Association of University Women's Annual Scholarship Presentation Meeting, 24 October.

Brown, P., 1980, 'How and why are Women more Polite: some Evidence from a Mayan Community' in S. McConnell-Ginet, R. Borker and N. Furman (eds), *Woman and Language in Literature and Society*, New York: Praeger.

Brown, P. and Levinson, S.C., 1987, *Politeness: Some Universals in Language Usage*, Cambridge: Cambridge University Press. First published 1978 as part of Esther N. Goody (ed.), *Questions and Politeness*.

Cameron, D., 1985, *Feminism and Linguistic Theory*, Basingstoke and London: Macmillan Press.

Coates, J. and Cameron, D. (eds), 1988, *Women in their Speech Communities: New Perspectives on Language and Sex*, London and New York: Longman.

Edwards, J., 1985, *Language, Society and Identity*, Oxford: Basil Blackwell in association with André Deutsch.

Edwards, V. and Katbamna, S., 1988, 'The Wedding Songs of British Gujarati Women' in J. Coates and D. Cameron (eds), *Women in their Speech Commu-*

nities, London and New York: Longman.

Endacott, G.B., 1964, *A History of Hong Kong,* Hong Kong: OUP. Rev. edn 1973.

Gal, S., 1984, (1978), 'Peasant Men Can't Get Wives: Language Change and Sex Roles in a Bilingual Community', *Language in Society*, vol.7. Reprinted in J. Baugh and J. Sherzer (eds), 1984, *Language in Use: Readings in Sociolinguistics*, Englewood Cliffs, N.J.: Prentice-Hall.

_____, 1979, *Language Shift: Social Determinants of Linguistic Change in Bilingual Austria*, New York: Academic Press.

Hamers, J.F. and Blanc, M.H.A., 1989, *Bilinguality and Bilingualism*, Cambridge: Cambridge University Press.

Hastrup, K., 1992, 'A Question of Reason: Breast-Feeding Patterns in Seventeenth- and Eighteenth-Century Iceland' in V. Maher (ed.), *The Anthropology of Breast-Feeding: Natural Law or Social Construct*, Oxford: Berg.

Haugen, E., 1979, 'The Stigmata of Bilingualism' in J.B. Pride (ed.), *Sociolinguistic Aspects of Language Learning and Teaching*, Oxford: Oxford University Press.

Hill, J., 1987, 'Women's Speech in Modern Mexicano' in S.U. Philips, S. Steele and C. Tanz (eds), *Language, Gender & Sex in Comparative Perspective*, Cambridge: Cambridge University Press.

Humphrey, C., 1978, 'Women, Taboo and the Suppression of Attention' in S. Ardener (ed.), *Defining Females*.

Hymes, D., 1971, 'Sociolinguistics and the Ethnography of Speaking' in E. Ardener (ed.), *Social Anthropology and Language*, Association of Social Anthropologists of the Commonwealth 10, London: Tavistock.

Ide, S., Hori, M., Kawasaki, A., Ikuta, S. and Haga, H., 1986, 'Sex Difference and Politeness in Japan', *International Journal of the Sociology of Language*, no. 58.

Kramarae, C., 1981, *Women and Men Speaking*, Rowley, London, Tokyo: Newbury House.

_____, 1982, 'Gender: How She Speaks' in E.B. Ryan and H. Giles (eds), *Attitudes Towards Language Variation: Social and Applied Contexts*, London: Edward Arnold.

Krozjl, C., 1986, 'Refusing To Be Invisible: Turkish Women in West Berlin' in R. Ridd and H. Callaway (eds), *Caught Up In Conflict: Women's Responses to Political Strife*, Basingstoke and London: Macmillan Education.

MacDonald, M., 1986, 'Brittany: Politics and Women in a Minority World' in R. Ridd and H. Callaway (eds).

_____, 1989, *We Are Not French*, London: Routledge.

McCormick, K., 1986, 'Women's Use of Language in District Six' in S. Burman and P. Reynolds (eds), *Growing Up in a Divided Society: The Contexts of Childhood in South Africa*, Johannesburg: Ravan Press.

Milroy, L., 1987, *Language and Social Networks*, Oxford: Basil Blackwell.

Nichols, P.C., 1983, (1978), 'Linguistic Options and Choices for Black Women in the Rural South' in B. Thorne, C. Kramarae and N. Henley (eds), *Language, Gender and Society*, Rowley, Mass.: Newbury House.

Ochs, E., 1987, 'The Impact of Stratification and Socialization on Men's and Women's Speech in Western Samoa' in S.U. Philips, S. Steele and C. Tanz (eds), *Language, Gender and Sex in Comparative Perspective.*

Okely, J., 1975, 'Gypsy Women: Models in Conflict' in S.Ardener (ed.), *Perceiving Women.*

Philips, S.U., Steele, S. and Tanz, C., 1987, *Language, Gender & Sex in Comparative Perspective*, Cambridge: Cambridge University Press.

Ridd, R., 1981, 'Where Women Must Dominate: Response to Oppression in a South African Urban Community' in S.Ardener (ed.), *Women and Space: Ground Rules and Social Maps*, London: Croom Helm.

Romaine, S., 1989, *Bilingualism*, Oxford: Basil Blackwell.

Sherzer, J., 1987, 'A Diversity of Voices: Men's and Women's Speech in Ethnographic Perspective' in S.U. Philips, S. Steele and C. Tanz (eds).

Shibamoto, J.S., 1985, *Japanese Women's Language*, Orlando: Academic Press.

Spender, D., 1980, *Man Made Language*, second edition, 1990, London: Pandora Press.

Steiner, G., 1984, *George Steiner: a Reader*, Harmondsworth: Penguin.

Thorne, B. and Henley, N. (eds), 1975, *Language and Sex: Difference and Dominance*, Rowley, Mass.: Newbury House.

Thorne, B., Kramarae, C. and Henley, N. (eds), 1983, *Language, Gender and Society*, Rowley, London, Tokyo: Newbury House.

Tollefsen, J.W., 1991, *Planning Language, Planning Inequality: Language Policy in the Community*, London: Longman.

Tual, A., 1986, 'Speech and Silence: Women in Iran' in L. Dube, E. Leacock and S. Ardener (eds), *Visibility and Power.*

Valdes-Fallis, G., 1977, 'Code-switching Among Bilingual Mexican-American Women: Towards an Understanding of Sex-related Language Alternation', *International Journal of the Sociology of Language*, 7.

Warren, K.B. and Bourque, S.C., 1985, 'Gender, Power, and Communication: Women's Responses to Political Muting in the Andes' in S.C. Bourque and D. Robinson Divine, *Women Living Change*, Philadelphia: Temple University Press.

Williams, G., 1987, 'Bilingualism, Class Dialect, and Social Reproduction', *International Journal of the Sociology of Language*, 66.

2

Open Castilian, Closed Aymara? Bilingual Women in the Yungas of La Paz (Bolivia)

Alison Spedding

Introduction: A Sketch of the Region

This paper concerns bilingualism in the Chulumani sector of Sud Yungas province, department of La Paz, in Bolivia. Chulumani is the capital of a very mountainous province, which drops rapidly from peaks of more than 5,000 metres above sea level, through crumpled subtropical valleys to the lowland forests. The town itself stands at about 1,700 metres above sea level. Before the agrarian reform carried out between 1953 and 1964, the region was divided between free peasant communities and haciendas operated by labour tenure; since then it has been dominated by peasant smallholders (Leons 1967, 1979). The community where I worked was a hacienda which had been founded in 1560 and reformed (that is, the land distributed to the tenants) in 1964; I will refer to it as 'Takipata'. The principal activity is agriculture[1], and the principal crop is coca. Coca has a multitude of religious and social uses in the Andean world, and since about 1971 it has provided the raw material for a huge export boom, although it has to be emphasised that cocaine is quite distinct from coca and the vast majority of peasant coca farmers have nothing to do with it. This boom collapsed in 1986, but coca continues to maintain a relatively buoyant local economy, evidenced by the presence of numerous young men and women in the towns and countryside. It is highly labour-intensive, and Sud Yungas is a recipient of labour from higher regions of Bolivia, especially male labour for the less specialised agricultural activities.

While men plant coca, women harvest it. This is a skilled job which only local residents can do properly, and families try to retain their female members while bringing in husbands from outside, often immigrants. As a result, rich families are formed round a power bloc of

30

daughters and uxorilocal husbands, while men migrate into the area rather than out of it[2]. Men and women migrate seasonally to the coca plantations in the lowland sectors of the province, but there is no significant migration to the cities or mines elsewhere in the country; it is typical of many regions of Bolivia that, if there is any labour migration, it is seasonal and agricultural rather than urban-directed. As a result one does not find the situation reported for many parts of the Andes and elsewhere, where women stay home struggling on a diminishing agricultural base and cut off from contact with the national society, while men migrate to the cities and become semi–proletarians with a command of the national language and associated urban customs[3]. In Sud Yungas, men and women have equivalent opportunities to learn the national lang-uage, and levels of bilingualism do not differ much between the sexes, although the choices each sex makes about language use are rather different. I am going to describe women's choices, with comments on the cases where these differ from men's, before going on to consider what each language represents within the social system of the region.

In Chulumani two languages are widely spoken: Aymara and Castilian. Aymara is a native South American language spoken by some three million people in total (Hardman, Vasquez and Yapita, 1988:1). It is the only Andean language to have withstood in number the colonial and postcolonial spread of Quechua. In the Inka period, Quechua was the language of government, but numerous other languages which have now been lost, such as Mochica, Tallan, or Cunsa, were spoken. Aymara was spoken over a wide area of the southern Andes. The majority language in the region I am concerned with, basically the circum-Titicaca region and adjoining valleys to the east and west, was Aymara, but the population included many speakers of Puquina, a language which has only disappeared from the area in this century, together with other lang-uages such as Uruquilla about which nothing is known. Quechua was restricted to the upper classes and by the late sixteenth century those who spoke it were the *ladinos*, that is Indians who could speak Castilian. The Spanish government encouraged the use of Quechua as they did not wish to learn more than one indigenous language, and in most of the former Inka dominions Quechua is now the only indigenous language used. The Aymara–speaking regions are the main exception to this rule. It is important to remember that the contemporary bilingual condition of much of the Andes is in fact the residue of a far richer range of languages, rather than a dual formation which parallels the dualism so common in Andean social organisation[4].

Sud Yungas is a region of embedded Aymara ethnicity, with few connexions with Quechua–speaking regions of Bolivia but links with the adjacent Aymara–speaking regions in Peru. Some immigrants speak Quechua, but it is always lost after the first generation, and I shall not be further concerned with it. It is worth noting, however, that this is a strictly bilingual region, unlike other nearby areas which are trilingual (Aymara, Quechua, Castilian). Quechua is locally associated with the region of Cochabamba, in central Bolivia, which is regarded as ethnically distinct from La Paz, and the refusal to use Quechua is part of the pronounced loyalty people from La Paz have to their local area. Castilian is the name I give to the local dialect of Spanish, which is mutually comprehensible with standard Spanish but somewhat different from it. The rural Castilian dialect is heavily contaminated with Aymara loan-words and syntax[5].

Most adults in Sud Yungas can understand both these languages, although they differ in their competence to express themselves in each. There are a small number of Aymara monolinguals; the local expression for this (in Castilian, since in Aymara there is no need for such a term) is *Aymara cerrada*, closed Aymara. Monolingual Yunguenos are usually old, dating from the time before the reform when landlords dissuaded peasants from speaking Spanish – which in turn forced the landlords to speak Aymara so as to be able to communicate with their tenants. The older generation of the upper class is usually bilingual for this reason, while young upper–class people are monolingual Castilian speakers. If they know a second language, it is more likely to be English. There are some young monolingual Aymara immigrants, but after a few years in Sud Yungas most learn to speak Castilian as well. Castilian monolinguals are also few in number and almost all resident in the towns. A proper adult should be able to speak both languages, and someone who can only understand one is pitied, if they only understand Aymara, or mocked (in Aymara) if they only understand Castilian. In conversations people frequently switch between the two, even in the course of a single utterance:

Esa mandarina ya esta jovencita, panqaraskaniwa.
That mandarin tree's growing up now (Castilian), it'll soon be in bloom (Aymara).
Se van a k'ichirar depacio.
All of you pick the coca slowly (Castilian, but using Aymara verb stem k'ichi- plus the verbal modifier -ra- indicating multiple but non-serial action).

When two people meet, therefore, they usually have the choice of speaking either in Castilian or in Aymara. I will describe a series of contexts and the language preferred in each, before attempting to distil from this the variables which control language choice.

Languages in Context

The context in which most men and women spend most of their time is labouring in the fields. This work is always carried out in Aymara. Family members who speak Castilian at home together will speak Aymara while working, and anyone who works in the fields for a period of time learns some Aymara. The disappearance of Aymara among the upper classes is a symptom of its disengagement from the agrarian sphere, while middle-aged people of the lower-middle classes insist that they grew up speaking Castilian and only learnt Aymara because they had to work on the land. Aymara has a rich verbal vocabulary[6], and each verb has a more precise meaning than is general in Indo-European languages. Much of this vocabulary and nouns denoting things encountered in agriculture are borrowed into Castilian when talking about agricultural production.

Aymara is also preferred in religious contexts. The rites of indigenous religion, such as liberating the earth spirits or divining by looking at a scatter of coca leaves, are always carried out in Aymara. The ritual drinking which is indispensable to every occasion in the Andes is a part of this; Aymara is so embedded in the activity of festive drinking that even people who cannot speak the language are capable of repeating the formal Aymara requests with which one offers and accepts a drink. Aymara is also used in Catholic religious rites. Weekly *rezos*, or Catholic prayer meetings, are carried out in Aymara. These are led by a *catechista*, a local man (often quite young) who has received basic religious instruction. *Catechistas* lead funerals in Aymara, taking the place of priests who do not attend rural burials. Once or twice a year a priest comes to say mass in the chapel; the service is the standard Spanish form, but even here some hymns in Aymara are usually included. In some parts of the Andes many people have converted to evangelical Protestantism, and the evangelical movement produces religious texts in Aymara; however, in Chulumani only marginal members of the community were active evangelicals, and when I attended their service it was in Castilian. It was led by a man from the nearby town of Irupana, who was definitely of 'Hispanic' rather than 'Indian' ethnicity, although the congregation were Indian peasants. The majority prefer Catholic worship in Aymara. Indigenous rituals and curing ceremonies are understood to be part of orthodox Catholic religion – evangelical converts are expected to give them up – which strengthens the association between Catholicism, at least in its Andean folk form, and Aymara.

Local government in rural areas consists of the syndicate, a monthly meeting of household heads. Each household is represented by the senior married man, or if he is dead, absent or incapacitated, by the senior married woman. In practice some wives usually go instead of

their husbands, while poor families cannot spare the time to send anyone at all. All syndicate business is carried out in Aymara. There is a
strong convention that an adult man should speak up in the meetings,
and it provides an opportunity for older men to display their skill as
Aymara orators. In most meetings, about a fifth of the people present are
women. Decisions are reached by consensus after everyone who feels
she or he has something to say has contributed. The leading clique try to
get as many people as possible to speak as this obliges people to accept
the decision made; if people remain silent, it is likely that they will later
try to reject the decision on the ground that they were not given a chance
to influence it. The women may be asked to speak if it is thought that
they have failed to express their views. If they are questioned, it will be
on a topic concerning the whole community and not an issue solely concerning women, which would be dealt with in the meetings of the Mothers' Union which I discuss below. In the large meetings held to organise
communal labour projects, perhaps a third of those present are women,
but in most cases they keep quiet and speak up only if asked to do so.

Women's political activity proper is carried out in the context of the
work process, especially the coca harvest. Coca gives three harvests a
year, and rich women have coca to harvest all year round. They regularly convene large work parties. The nature of the harvest work is such
that women can talk constantly while doing it, and this gives the women
in charge an opportunity to manipulate public opinion in the course of
the working day. The activity of rich women in the harvest thus comple-
ments that of their husbands in the syndicate; in fact it is more influential, if the constant complaints in syndicate meetings about policies
which have been undermined by 'the talk in the harvest' are any guide.
This talk is, of course, in Aymara.

Syndicate meetings in Takipata are held in a small one-roomed hall.
Next to it stands a much larger hall which is the property of the Club de
Madres, or Mothers' Union, giving the impression of a women's organisation parallel to, and indeed more prosperous than, the male-dominated syndicate. In practice, since sexual segregation has no place in
Andean culture, there is always a small silent minority of men in the
women's meetings, but these meetings are not equivalent to those in the
syndicate. The Club de Madres meetings are held in Castilian, which is
not what one would expect, given the association general in the Andes
between women and indigenous languages. Before discussing why this
should be so, I will cite the other occasions where Castilian is preferred.

The most noticeable use of Castilian in the countryside is for speaking to children. Even women whose active knowledge of Castilian is
scant try to use it with their children. The children, in return, usually

speak to parents and each other in Castilian, except when addressing a 'closed Aymara'. To use Aymara in public is an index of emerging adult status. Using Castilian with children is primarily an attempt to improve their educational chances, since all school teaching is done in Castilian, but it also indicates that, until they have married and settled permanently in the community, they are not full members of it even if they were born there.

While Aymara is the speech of rural space, Castilian is the urban language. It is not actually necessary for going to market in Sud Yungas, since virtually all sellers are bilingual, but it would be considered an index of ignorance in Chulumani town to make purchases in Aymara; it is more prestigious to be seen speaking Castilian in the town. Oddly enough, it is more acceptable to speak Aymara in the markets of the capital, which are dominated by women from the Aymara-speaking communities of the Altiplano. Policemen and teachers often come from a rural Aymara background, but they also insist on using Castilian with clients to emphasise their official status, and all high officials speak Castilian. Nowadays the latter are likely to be Castilian monolinguals from the capital. Castilian is also used in the army. Conscription does not exist in Bolivia, but in the countryside the year of military service is viewed in La Paz as a rite of passage to manhood and most peasant youths volunteer for it as a prelude to marriage (which usually follows within a year of returning from the army[7]. Young men improve their Castilian in the army, while young women do the same through travelling to the city to sell their fruit, coffee and coca. On marriage, men are as likely as women to find themselves tied down to a lifetime of Aymara field labour: it is notable that ethnic groups such as the Laymi, whose knowledge of Castilian is very limited, neither do military service nor engage in trade to any significant degree.

Another way for young women to better their Castilian is through domestic service; but in Takipata this was regarded as something which was not only degrading but which exposed girls to the risk of sexual abuse, and most parents preferred their daughters to work in trade or agriculture. Retail trade is dominated by the so-called *cholas*, lower-middle-class women who maintain 'Indian' dress (principally the full skirt called a *pollera* and the rectangular shawl fastened with a pin), and these women are often heard using Aymara in city markets.

I found that women in general displayed a public preference for Aymara, both in the country and in towns. They were happy to converse with me in Aymara in the street and often addressed me in this language while men, even in the countryside, more usually spoke to me in Castilian. This is also true of peasants in contact with officials. Women often reply to official questions in Castilian with a curt comment in Aymara, giving the impression that they barely understand Castilian and are certainly incapable of replying in it. Officials are rarely prepared to engage in a lengthy conversation in Aymara, so they usually give up on women who refuse to speak Castilian; the belief that rural women are ignorant, barefoot drudges who have never been to school and cannot understand the national language reinforces this attitude. Peasant women are expected to be 'closed Aymara' and they exploit this belief, while men are not only expected to know Castilian, but are disgraced if they cannot speak it, so they cannot evade outsiders by pretending not to understand. This association between Castilian and manhood, however, does not carry over into an obligation to use Castilian for the activities which define manhood in the Yungas countryside: acting as a head of household in the syndicate and performing the exclusively male tasks of felling trees and building terraces for coca.

Membership of the syndicate is carefully controlled, and the heads of newly established or immigrant households often have to struggle for admission as full members. The Club de Madres, however, includes women not only from adjacent peasant communities but from Chulumani town, and during my period of residence there it was headed by a lower-middle-class townswoman whose connexion with Takipata had begun when her tractor-driving husband was hired to do some logging on the forested upper slopes. It appears to be true elsewhere in the region of La Paz that Clubes de Madres with rural constituency are organised by urban women. The basic activity of the Mothers' Union is not political but commercial. Apart from a few attempts, rarely successful, to set up consumers' co-operatives or co-operative ventures to produce honey and other saleable goods, they act as agencies for the distribution of foodstuffs donated to Bolivia in aid by the EC and other countries. Members pay a fee, which is described as a transport charge, and each receives a sack of wheat flour, a container of cooking oil and so on – stamped all over with the legend FOR FREE DISTRIBUTION. This charge is much higher than the actual lorry fare from the capital where these goods are received, but it is lower than their free market price. The Clubes de Madres are organised into provincial and national federations parallel to those of the peasant syndicates, and the aid is delivered to the national headquarters in La Paz. Subsequent distribution is definitely in favour of some and not others, and only those local unions who have managed to set up good connections with the national hierarchy – and who pay the prices demanded – obtain any food.

The patterns of authority in the Takipata Mothers' Union have changed over time. In the early days it was headed by local women from rich peasant households, who conformed to the traditional Andean pattern where the holder of an office has to pay out of their own pocket all the costs incurred while acting on behalf of the community. By the time I arrived, it had been taken over by its urban members, who followed the modern, middle-class pattern of demanding *viaticos*, or travelling expenses, to be paid from collections taken up among the membership. It appears that the national hierarchy of the clubs had been taken over by the middle classes, who are notorious in Bolivia for their *empleomania* or desire for bureaucratic jobs. The ethnic division of labour means that this involves a change in the ethnic composition of the leadership from 'Indian' to 'Hispanic'. Even rich peasants, who are almost all 'Indians', find it difficult to deal with middle-class Hispanicised bureaucrats, and I think that the Takipata union had survived in large part because its middle-class members could overcome the barriers set up in the city to exclude peasant women. Other Clubes de Madres which did not have such a leadership had been unable to get their share of the foodstuffs and had collapsed; but the surviving unions did so only because they replicated the forms of commercial and class-based relations which are the established links between urban and rural women in the Andes. As Elinor Burkett (1977) pointed out, the common experiences of motherhood and domestic activity, though they may be shared by most women, do not in fact overcome the divisions of class and race.

Conclusions

Aymara is only one of many indigenous languages used in Bolivia. Multilingualism has a long history in the Andes, and I regard the bilingual society of today as merely the residue of a much greater range of languages.[8] Language is certainly elementary in establishing the ethnic differences that are so important in the Andes, but the dualistic parallel between 'Indian' and Aymara (or, in most regions, Quechua) and 'Hispanic' and Castilian should be seen as a form reduced to the minimum rather than an essential element of the binary ethnic division.[9] Dress codes, iconography and other cultural forms encourage an extension of this dualism to suggest that 'Indian' is to 'Hispanic' as woman is to man; for instance, items of dress like the poncho which are both male and definitive of 'Indian' status in the lower classes are shunned by upper-class or 'Hispanic' men but worn by upper-class women. It is tempting to extend this association between women and indigenous culture to explain women's public preference for Aymara as parallel to women's retention of 'Indian' dress styles when men abandon them, but I do not think that gender *per se* is a determining factor in bilingualism or the lack of it; rather, language choice corresponds to a dynamic of group structure, inclusion and exclusion.

The morality of Andean society, like that of the Han Chinese, regards the individual as subject to the group, defined by it, and bound to obey group demands before furthering individual desires. Aymara and Quechua make a sharp grammatical distinction between the inclusive 'we', binding speaker and hearer, and the exclusive 'we' which cuts out the hearer from the activity referred to. The idea of a united community, one that can act together as a group in defence of its lands and members, is highly valued by all social classes in Sud Yungas. Being part of such a community has definite value, not only in terms of self-defence, but also in the economic benefits obtained through communal labour projects which a united community can motivate its members to perform; psychologically it provides great warmth and support – as long as one is happy to go along with the accepted views and customs of the group. The mass-based, egalitarian mentality developed within such a community gives it the ability to respond very rapidly to disasters, acting as a group without need for charismatic leaders or individual ringleaders who motivate action; I saw an impressive display of this when a lorry overturned in a stream in Takipata, and people immediately rushed out *en masse*, rolled the lorry over again and rescued the passengers. The number of dead and wounded would probably have been higher if people had waited for someone to tell them what to do, and they were able to act as a group without need for an authority figure.

But this unity has disadvantages for the individual; at times being part of such a group can be extremely oppressive, and the same people who value communal unity complain about the insistent gossip which keeps them in line and lack of choice in matters such as consumption which more individualistic societies leave free. In a united community nothing is ever truly private; the dominance of the group over the individual is expressed in the way in which people think that individual moral transgressions, such as incest, are punished by climatic disasters which affect the whole community. This threat of communal victimisation for the sins of a few individuals justifies constant prying and powerful social control.

It is this sort of life which is associated with the use of Aymara. Peasant communities in Yungas are nearer the open than the closed end of the continuum established by Eric Wolf (1966); they have a constant need for labour, and are thus always willing to accept an outsider with initial hospitality – followed up by a series of increasingly severe demands, as the outsider moves closer in, climaxing in the case where the outsider actually joins the community through marriage and becomes a full member receiving all the warmth and all the controls as well. The rewards of joining the community in this way, especially for a poor immigrant who owns nothing in her or his home community, can be great, but they require an unstinting personal commitment which is expressed above all by backbreaking labour in the fields. All who go through this process, if they did not already speak Aymara, would be able to speak it by the end – and indeed could not be so accepted if they did not. They are also invested with the formal political equality which is part of the ideology of the peasant community. Unlike Castilian, Aymara does not distinguish between formal and intimate 'you'. This certainly makes a difference to bilingual speakers; I have seen a pair of them decide, in the course of their first meeting, to call each other '*tu*' in Castilian on the ground that there was no formal '*you*' in Aymara. It has a range of structures for expressing respect and supplication which the Bolivian upper classes regard as 'grovelling' but which Aymara speakers regard as expressing proper humility and respect for others on the part of the speaker; the curt Aymara forms, stripped of the polite suffixes, should only be used to children or animals, and are great insults if used to other adults, such as outsiders who do not understand Aymara well and thus fail to notice the insult they are being dealt. I was warned by my Aymara teacher that I would receive a lot of this sort of mockery when I first tried to speak the language, although halting Aymara is also well received by many, who see it as a sincere attempt to express respect for indigenous customs.

Agricultural labour is one of the things which defines an 'Indian' in the Andes and which imposes Aymara in Sud Yungas. The organisation of work also expresses political equality. In peasant work parties, no distinction (in terms of how much work is expected, whether or not workers are seen receiving food from the convening household, and so forth) is made between household members, people working in *ayni* (mutual aid) and *minga* or wage labourers, although *minga* is in fact an inferior thing to be and *ayni* is prestigious. Instead, everyone must be seen to be equal in the work process. This extends to the rate at which work is done; there is a strong convention that everyone must proceed across the field at the same rate, and anyone who 'shows off' by pressing ahead is insulting the people she or he is working with. The use of Aymara in the work indicates not only inclusion in the labour pool of the community and thus membership in its most essential aspect, but also equality between all participants. To summarise, speaking Aymara is associated with the peasantry, insider status, adulthood, full community membership and with equality of status.

Castilian is associated with the upper classes, with outsiders, with exclusion and hierarchy. This is brought out strongly by the way in which officials use Castilian to peasants, and within the rural community, by the use of Castilian with children, who are like residential out-siders; full membership of the group is only possible for one who can participate fully in production and politics, which children are incapable of. Peasant speakers of Castilian generally use '*tu*' to everyone, except in the context of begging a favour, when the person entreating wants to appear as inferior to the person entreated even if in fact she or he is not, or when the speaker specifically wishes to exclude the person addressed from the speaker's own group. They do not use the formal '*Usted*' as a polite way of addressing someone of equal status, as is the case with city speakers. The use of Castilian in Club de Madres meetings is indicative firstly of their outward orientation, contrasting with the in-group mentality of the syndicate and secondly of their leaders-and-fol-lowers structure. In the syndicate, everyone has a right to speak which most exercise, and authority rotates annually, ideally passing through all households in the community, but in the Club de Madres the masses remain silent, although entitled to speak, and only a few people are con-sidered for positions of authority, for which full competence in urban Castilian is a prerequisite.

So where does this leave women's public preference for Aymara rather than Castilian? If Andean dualism is expressed in a concentric rather than a vertical or horizontal form, then women are the core while men are the periphery. This is expressed in such ritual contexts as death rites where it is important that anyone who comes into contact with the body should be in some way marginal: corpse-washers are all men, whether the corpse is male or female, and corpse-bearers are not only men but usually unmarried men or men who fail in some way to be full community members – either through refusal to participate in other aspects of communal life or because they are lifelong bachelors. Histor-ical evidence, such as Hidalgo's 1985 study of migration in the eigh-teenth century in what is now central Chile, indicates that the home town of a community might be inhabited almost entirely by women, while the men went to work in distant regions, often staying away for years. In this context the maintenance of the local group as such would be entirely the work of women.

In Sud Yungas female centrality is given extra salience by the prac-tice of uxorilocal marriage; a large number of the adult men in Takipata came from elsewhere and are known as 'sons-in-law of Takipata', while most of the adult women were locally born. This implies that as wife-takers, they owe ritual service to the community as a whole, and they can indeed be observed performing this role in the patronal fiestas. The genealogical definition of community membership is established nei-ther patrilineally nor matrilineally, but through endogamy. Someone who is really from Yungas is someone whose parents and grandparents were all born there, that is, the offspring of at least two generations of locally endogamous marriages. Anyone else is not a real Yungueno. Women are central in reproducing Andean cultural practices, both agricultural and domestic: modes of childrearing and cooking are especially important in this. Marriage is strongly controlled for status equality and the few exceptions to this are usually men who marry into a slightly higher social class; women stay put, socially and geographically, while men move around. In Andean terms this means that women are more genuine members of the indigenous community than men are, and they express this by speaking Aymara, the insider's language.

I have claimed that the use of Aymara is associated with political equality. I also associate it with Andean notions of sexual equality which are very different from the ideas about men and women which prevail in 'Hispanic' society. There is no grammatical gender in Aymara, no distinction of gender in pronouns, and no difference between formal and informal pronouns. In formal terms, men and women are said to be equal in Aymara society, but men possess a symbolic dominance expressed, for instance, by their role as political representatives of the household. Men's attempts to convert symbolic dominance into genuine control over their women are actively combated by the women. The women of Sud Yungas are favoured in this by the economic structures which place a high value on female labour and which keep men in the countryside. It seems that there are other areas of the Andes where the collapse of the local economy and its conversion to an existence as a peripheral reserve supported by its remittances from the cities has defeated women, whose labour is not in demand in the urban areas. Women may have spoken to me in Aymara because they felt that I was equal to them whereas men addressed me in Castilian because gender alone, apart from other social differences, made me unequal.

By speaking Aymara one can evade insertion into the hierarchy which governs national society; it is an expression of the insular peasant utopia, the self-governing, self-sufficient, egalitarian community, where the only differences in status are those of age and generation[10]. In practice there are real differences between the poor families whose wage labour supports the rich and the rich peasants who head the factions which struggle for control in the syndicate; but the manners of speech and work within the community conceal the way in which some members of the community exploit others. Speaking Castilian, one cannot avoid national issues of class and hierarchy; and in the Castilian meetings of the Club de Madres it is made plain that women, equally with men, are divided and subjected by the external forces of class and race.

Notes

1. Agriculture is in fact virtually the only activity most people engage in. Unlike most parts of the Andes, where an agropastoral regime prevails, the climate in Yungas makes it impossible to herd small stock, and only the upper class can afford to keep cattle.

2. Coca production and the concomitant social structures are examined in detail in Spedding (1989), especially chapters 2 and 3.

3. An Ecuadorean case of this is found in Weismantel (1988). General surveys of the effect of labour migration are given for Africa in Levine (1966) and worldwide in Rogers (1980, pp. 163–70).

4. The variety of languages in the Lake Titicaca area in the fifteenth and sixteenth centuries is described in Bouysse-Cassagne (1987). Numerous works deal with Andean dualism in one or another aspect; the best short account of it is Platt (1986).

5. As is, to a less pronounced degree, the Castilian dialect of the city of La Paz; the amount of Aymara in the vocabulary is reduced, but the syntax, especially the tense structure, is distinct from that of European Spanish. See Hardman (1981) for examples.

6. See Hardman (1981) for examples of this.

7. Most men in Sud Yungas do military service, and those who have not are mocked by those who have when they are all drunk. The same applies on the Altiplano; Carter (1980) describes how a youth is not considered man enough to marry until he has spent a year in the army.

8. Salomon (1987) cites an Aymara-speaking people from Arequipa in Peru, who, in the eighteenth century, also spoke Quechua, Isapi, Puquina, Coli and the Chinchaysuyo language. Puquina was spoken into this century by the Uru people living round Lake Titicaca, and the Chipaya in the central Altiplano maintain their own language; Bouysse-Cassagne (1987) describes the variety of languages used in the sixteenth century in what is now the Bolivian Altiplano. Jean Jackson (1983), though studying an area a long way from Bolivia, describes the Tukanoan peoples whose rule of linguistic exogamy means that almost everyone grows up speaking at least two or three different languages, and often learns more later in life. I think that this multilingualism is something which typified most of the aboriginal cultures of South America. It is also notable that since a Tukanoan woman must marry a husband who speaks a different language from her and go and live in his community, she will not be confined in a monolingual situation any more that her husband is.

9. I put 'Indian' and 'Hispanic' in quotation marks because these two categories are symbolic constructs rather than components of a genuine ethnic division. Part of the ideology of this construct is that 'Indian' things are descended unchanged from the days of the Inka while 'Hispanic' customs represent pure European style. In practice there is far more in common between the two groups than is usually admitted, and many 'Indian' things – such as most of the traditional costumes used today – are in fact derived from colonial European models, while the 'Hispanic' classes have taken on many Andean ways of life.

10. This ideal of the peasant utopia which liberates its members from outside forces is expressed for Chuschi in Peru in Isbell (1978).

References

Bouysse-Cassagne, T., 1987, *La identitad aymara. Aproximación histórica (siglo XV, siglo XVI)*, La Paz.

Burkett, E., 1977, 'In Dubious Sisterhood: Class and Sex in Spanish Colonial South America', *Latin American Perspectives*, 4.

Carter, W., 1980, 'Matrimonio de Prueba en Los Andes' in Mayer and Bolton (eds), *Parentesco y Matrimonio en Los Andes*, Lima.

Hardman, M. J., 1981, *The Aymara Language in its Social and Cultural Context*, Gainesville, Fla..

Hardman, M. J., Vasquez, J. and Yapita, J. de D., 1988, *Aymara. Compendio de Estructura Fonológica y Gramatical*, La Paz.

Hidalgo Lehuede, J., 1985, 'Ecological Complementarity and Tribute in Atacama: 1683–1792' in Masuda, Shimada and Morris (eds), *Andean Ecology and Civilisation*, Tokyo.

Isbell, B. J., 1978, *To Defend Ourselves. Ecology and Ritual in an Andean Village*, Austin, Texas.

Jackson, J. E., 1983, *The Fish People. Linguistic Exogamy and Tukanoan Identity in Northwest Amazonia*, Cambridge.

Leons, M. B., 1967, 'Land reform in the Bolivian Yungas', *America Indigena*, 27.

_____ , 1979, 'The Political Economy of Agrarian Reform in the Bolivian Yungas' in M.B. Leons and F. Rothstein (eds), *New Directions in Political Economy*, Westport, Conn..

Levine, R. A., 1966, 'Sex Roles and Economic Change in Africa', *Ethnology*, 5.

Platt, T., 1986, 'Mirrors and Maize: the Concept of Vanantin among the Macha of Bolivia in Murra, Wachtel and Revel (eds), *Anthropological History of Andean Polities*, Cambridge.

Rogers, B., 1980, *The Domestication of Women. Discrimination in Developing Societies*, London.

Salomon, F., 1987, 'Ancestor Cults and Resistance to the State in Arequipa, ca. 1748–1754' in S. Stern (ed.), *Resistance, Rebellion and Consciousness in the Andean Peasant World, 18th to 20th Centuries*, Madison and London.

Spedding, A. L., 1989, 'Wachu Wachu: Coca Cultivation and Aymara Identity in the Yunkas of La Pax (Bolivia)', Ph.D. thesis, London School of Economics.

Weismantel, M. J., 1988, *Food, Gender and Poverty in the Ecuadorian Andes*, Philadelphia.

Wolf, E. 1966, *Peasants*, Englewood Cliff, N.J..

3

The Presence and Absence of Speech in the Communication of Gender

Penelope Harvey

Introduction

The events and practices described in this chapter took place in Ocongate, a small Andean town in Southern Peru.[1] It is a relatively busy place, situated on an important though unpaved road which connects the highlands of Southern Peru to the tropical lowlands of Amazonia. Migrant workers, supplies and raw materials travel through daily on the lorries that work the route from Puerto Maldonado to the southern Peruvian cities of Cusco, Puno and Arequipa. The road is important to the livelihood of the villagers. Besides their basic subsistence from agriculture and herding, most people are involved in some way in business. They travel frequently in connection with these business activities, trading products from the local district, from the lowlands and from the cities. Many people also spend at least some time every year working as migrant labour in the cities or in the forest.

As a district capital Ocongate also has important administrative links to Cusco, the departmental capital.[2] Although the population of the village itself is relatively small, 1,300 approximately, it serves a district of some 8,500 people, who come into the village not only to trade but also to visit the town hall, the schools, the health post, the judge's office, the police post and the parish church. Until recently tourism has also played an important part in the local economy. At 3,600 metres the village lies at the foot of the highest snow peak in the area, Mt Ausangate, and climbers and walkers hire local guides and pack-horses in the cold summer months of the dry season.[3]

Ocongate is thus not an isolated town, and in the last three decades the expansion of education and communications has dramatically extended the access to Spanish by people from this area, and the vast majority of young people are fully bilingual in Spanish and Quechua.

Despite the increased use of Spanish by the younger generations, bilingualism in the area appears at present to be stable. Quechua is still the first language of all adults who come from the district. Children continue to be brought up either as Quechua speakers or as bilinguals. Those few families who do not bring their children up as Quechua speakers are those who intend to educate them outside the district. This outside orientation is linked to economic possibility, and thus there is also a degree of correlation with economic status. Nevertheless, those who stay, even those who return, always know Quechua. As a result the only adult monolingual Spanish speakers living in Ocongate are found among the outsiders, the school-teachers, the police, the medical and mission workers.

However, when we look at the monolingual Quechua speakers the striking distinction is not between insiders and outsiders, but between men and women. Indeed, as illustrated in Table 1, gender is a significant variable at all levels of bilingual competence.

Table 1: Bilingual Competence and Gender

Competence	Gender				
	Men	%		Women	%
Category A	87	52		37	24
Category B	41	24		39	25
Category C	13	8		22	14
Category D	4	2		50	32
Unknown	23	14		9	5
Total	168	100		157	100

Note: 168 men and 157 women referred to in this table were drawn from 181 households.
The categories in this table are as follows:
Category A: Those who speak Spanish and Quechua with equal ease and fluency, although not necessarily with equal frequency, and who are recognised by others in the community as fully competent in both languages.
Category B: Those bilinguals who show a marked preference for speaking in Quechua and whose Spanish is strongly marked by Quechua influences in lexicon, phonetics, morphology and syntax.[4]
Category C: Quechua speakers who use Spanish for very limited functions. Such speakers will usually have a basic passive knowledge of Spanish.
Category D: Quechua monolinguals.

Thus it can be seen that the majority of men (76 per cent) are either fully bilingual, or fluent in Spanish despite heavy influences from Quechua. This compares with 49 per cent of the women, of whom less than half are fully bilingual. Conversely 46 per cent of women are either monolingual Quechua speakers or have only extremely limited Spanish, as compared with a mere 10 per cent of men. Furthermore, it should be noted that among all categories of bilinguals, men actually use Spanish more than women. Women generally prefer to use Quechua.

There is one further distinctive difference in the use of Spanish by men and women which concerns a particular Spanish register, used exclusively by men, primarily for making speeches in formal public meetings. This register is characterised by long and complex utterances, with multiple clauses and qualifications. Special vocabulary is used which would rarely be heard in other circumstances, and there is a marked usage of proverbs and clichés. Statements are qualified with the frequent citing of names and dates, and the intonation of the delivery is also distinctive. The formal meetings at which this register is used are concerned with the relationship between the community and the wider social environment, particularly the state and the church.

Women do not have an equivalent register for these public meetings and prefer not to speak at all; some even feel ashamed to attend. This is not to say that women are always silent or absent from political discussion. There are less formal meetings which take place in similar locales and under the direction of the same male authorities. These meetings refer to immediate practical issues, such as setting the prices of goods. Given the division of labour in this community, such meetings are attended primarily either by men or by women. In either case a similar style is employed: people speak when they feel like it, talk over each other, shout and show no inhibitions about dealing with the male village authorities. Women can be extremely vocal and forceful in these meetings but they will tend to speak in Quechua (Harvey, 1989).

The point I want to emphasise here is that women are not intimidated by the presence of men or village authorities. Women's silence in the formal meetings is associated with the nature of the meeting and the fact that a particular style of Spanish, which they do not command, is deemed not only appropriate but also authoritative.

In outlining these differences in the use of Spanish by men and women in Ocongate I do not intend to present a simple division of the population into two homogeneous groups. As I have indicated, there are important variations between men and women, according to age, future orientation and economic possibility. As I will discuss below, people may use more or less Spanish at different times of their lives, depending on the nature of the social relations in which they are engaged. Nevertheless, as Table 1 indicates, there is a marked difference in the use of Spanish by women, emphasised by the fact that women do not use the formal Spanish register described above.

This difference in usage is critically dependent on women's attitudes towards the Spanish and Quechua languages. Spanish competence is generally thought of as an asset. Younger monolingual women go to adult literacy classes in the evenings, and parents will do whatever they can to ensure that their children receive some education, at least enough to learn Spanish. Older women are reluctant to learn, but not because they do not value the language. They say that they are too old, but that their children will learn and as a consequence will not have to suffer as they have had to. One woman said quite explicitly that if she were to try speaking Spanish, people would criticise, stare and make insulting comments. They would think that she was trying to pass herself off as a *mestiza*,[5] a more cultured or educated women than her background would allow. She had heard someone say about a friend of hers, who had put on *mestiza* clothes for a special festive occasion: 'A *mestiza* has come out of the dog shit; she doesn't even know how to talk Spanish.' She added that her friend actually spoke very good Spanish. However, to speak Spanish or to wear *mestiza* clothes is to make an explicit statement about your social identity, a statement which others will not necessarily allow you to make, however good your Spanish, whatever the quality of your clothes. This sense of shame at not speaking well enough is commonly given as a reason for not actively using Spanish. The young women who attend night classes are similarly afraid of ridicule. Consequently many of them have a good passive understanding, but seldom speak in Spanish. Young girls will use Spanish more frequently at those times in their lives when they are attending school, or when they are working as migrant labour, either in the cities or in Amazonia. However, when they return to the village, or when they finish their studies, they increasingly use Quechua, again retaining a passive knowledge of Spanish, but rarely using it in conversation.

Language and Gender

Discussion of speech differences such as those described above has generally taken place within the wider debate on the nature and workings of gender hierarchy.[6] Within this literature several distinctive positions have emerged, some more useful than others. The least useful, although perhaps the most common, explanation of gender difference is that the negative values associated with women's speech reflect women's subordinate position in society. The literature on gender and speech difference has shown that women's pronunciation is generally closer to the prestige standard than men's (see for example Cameron, 1988). Analyses for this gender-marked behaviour quite frequently point to the fact that women strive to speak correctly in order to counteract their low social status (Trudgill, 1972). Where gender hierarchy is salient, men are offered a greater range of ways to fuel their self-esteem and to gain prestige in the eyes of other people and thus do not have the same need to protect themselves with the use of prestige standard forms.

The problem with this type of explanation is that it offers a very passive model of the nature of social relatedness and in fact 'explains' very little. Hierarchy tends to be assumed as a social given, and thus little if any attention is given to looking at the nature of hierarchy, at how hierarchy is constituted and maintained in social relations and at the particular role of language in this social process.

More recently writers such as Milroy (1980) and Nichols (1984) have suggested that language use should be interpreted in terms of social networks. They have argued that people tend to speak most like those with whom they speak most frequently and interact with in a variety of different social roles. These dense, multiplex social networks constitute a supportive linguistic environment which allows speakers to use non-standard features which may be stigmatised by more powerful sectors of the population whose identities are constituted in very different networks of relatedness. Milroy and Nichols thus argue that it is not gender that determines the use of standard forms but rather the nature of the relationships in which men and women are involved. Thus Nichols (1984) argues that in her study of coastal South Carolina it was because the men had denser and more multiplex social networks within the community than women that they used more non-standard features in their speech. Analysis of gender differences in speech must therefore address the whole range of social relations in which men and women are involved.

This focus on the social relations within which gender differences are constituted and expressed is also evident in Brown's work on women's use of politeness in a Mayan community (1980). Expressions of politeness mediate the hierarchy and social distance between speakers by lessening imposition (attending to negative face) or asserting common ground (attending to positive face) (Brown and Levinson, 1978). The greater the insecurity on the part of the speaker, the more drastic the politeness strategy required, to the point where the speaker might not speak at all. Brown's discussion of why women use more politeness expressions than men looks carefully at the nature of social power and social distance in the community, at residence patterns, at networks of social interaction and at values associated with masculinity and femininity. She focuses on the notion of linguistic strategies, on looking at what men and women are doing by speaking in particular ways, at how they are using language to negotiate social relationships. This approach allows her to explore what the linguistic differences mean to speakers and how they are used to both maintain and undermine power differences. Language is thus no longer simply reflecting particular kinds of social relations, but is revealed as an active component in the constitution of those social relations.

This explanation of linguistic strategy links the use of particular linguistic forms to positions of relative powerlessness, but the emphasis on the active nature of this link, on the strategies adopted by speakers, generates a paradox. If politeness forms are generally interpreted as an expression of insecurity, as a relatively weak and indirect method of communication, it would appear that speakers are themselves perpetuating their powerlessness as they seek to protect themselves from the immediate threat raised by the linguistic interaction.

In Ocongate, as I will argue below, the demonstrated ability to use both Spanish and Quechua, together with competence in the formal Spanish register described above, are commonly used to constitute the authority of the speaker. Women have access to these forms: they recognise them as empowering, but are reluctant to use them. Thus by protecting themselves from ridicule and using Quechua instead of Spanish, women are in effect refusing to use the language which could constitute their authority. Why do women adopt the strategy that appears to perpetuate the need for this protection? Before moving on to look more closely at the set of assumptions that renders such practice meaningful, I first address certain standard explanations as to why those in relatively powerless positions do not use those linguistic forms that could confer prestige and authority.

In many cases speakers do not have access to prestige forms. Historically women's lesser bilingual competence in Ocongate was explicable to an extent in terms of their distinctive participation in those spheres of social relations in which Spanish was, and still is, most commonly acquired: education and migrant labour. Thus many poorer women over the age of thirty never went to school. If parents had to choose between their children as to who would receive education, it was deemed that men were more likely to have to deal with local Spanish-speaking authorities and with the Spanish-speaking world outside the village. In Ocongate this criterion is less relevant today. All children over the age of six are now required to attend school, and in the town itself where the school is accessible and absences noticeable, such gender differences are no longer salient.

Similarly, in terms of migration experience women still do not get drafted into the army, but as roads and transport have improved and wage labour has become more available, they frequently work in Spanish-speaking environments outside the village and also travel considerably for business purposes. Once a woman has children she is likely to travel less, but before this time both young men and women supplement family incomes and begin to find their own financial independence by working for periods outside the village. Indeed, many leave school in order to participate more fully in such work. Furthermore, women interact constantly with Spanish speakers in the village itself, even within their own homes. Women's unwillingness to use Spanish cannot therefore be explained in terms of opportunity to learn, and we thus have to consider how their attitudes towards Spanish are acquired and perpetuated.

Socialisation offers the standard explanatory paradigm for the acquisition of attitudes and behaviours. It has been argued by Coates (1986), for example, that young children are treated differently and are thus socialised into gender-specific practices. While I am not arguing against the notion that children learn gender-specific behaviour, I would emphasise here that children are themselves actively engaged in the process of acquisition. They are not socialised into a set of rules and practices that exist independently as a cohesive and commonly-held set of values. Learning is an interactive process, and discussion of the acquisition of norms and values must show how people come to acquire and normalise patterns of behaviour that ostensibly work against their interests. The appeal to ideology, the argument that social actors are mystified, operating on the basis of a false consciousness, still leaves unanswered the question of how the misrecognised values are acquired.[7]

The women of Ocongate quite clearly recognise that their inability to use Spanish has negative implications for their social position. This brings me back to a discussion of value and prestige. The notion of covert prestige in sociolinguistics has been extremely useful in demonstrating that speakers are not simply socialised into a dominant set of values which they adopt and seek to emulate. For example, men as much as women seek prestige and recognition through their language use, but frequently do not appeal to standard forms, but rather rely on the validation offered by an appeal to an alternative 'vernacular culture' (Labov, 1972a, 1972b). Covert prestige refers to the oppositional values that emerge in response to the imposition of hierarchy. These values are sustained in the dense multiplex social networks which Milroy and

Nichols have described. Thus a particular language usage, such as Black English Vernacular, can operate to constitute and perpetuate a powerless position in certain relationships with powerful white speakers, but in such a way as to produce a sense of autonomy and difference from which to resist domination and which thus subverts the values by which powerlessness itself is constituted and experienced. In this case to speak Black English Vernacular is not a direct attack on white power, but a process of disarticulation from the values that constitute the language of the white speakers as powerful. The fact that women more commonly use standard prestige forms than men indicates that they are in some sense excluded from the social relations that generate and sustain the values of covert prestige.

In Ocongate women's speech does not appeal to an alternative covert prestige, nor do women speak more 'correctly' than men. In general terms, women's pronunciation of Spanish demonstrates a higher level of Quechua influence and thus does not approximate the prestige standard of the higher-ranking monolingual Spanish speakers in the village. It is more difficult to estimate whether women's Quechua pronunciation could be said to be more or less standard as there is no accepted outside standard, Quechua itself being a minority, non-prestige language. In more general terms women's lesser Spanish competence is obviously further from the national standard than men's. Although Quechua has the status of an official language in Peru, Spanish is the language of government, law and education, and all official business of the state is conducted in Spanish.

However, women's language use is not more prestigious in terms of an alternative vernacular culture, despite the fact that women are involved in dense, multiplex social networks within the community that should uphold such an alternative. These women have considerable economic autonomy and do not see themselves as subservient to men in the ways that Brown described for the Mayan community. Labov refers to vernacular culture as the source of covert prestige, and claims that 'men are the chief exemplars of the vernacular culture' (Labov *et al*, 1968:41). Despite Labov's unwarranted generalisation,[8] this statement is in fact appropriate to the Ocongate case if the vernacular is understood as a prestigious alternative rather than as simply a non-standard one.

The subsequent sections of this chapter demonstrate how certain discursive practices associated with the constitution of racial or ethnic identities articulate with salient representations of masculinity and femininity. The use of a gendered idiom to articulate racial domination, negatively affects the ways in which women's speech is understood, undermines the possibility of constituting such speech as an instance of covert prestige and makes it difficult for women to become confident bilingual speakers.

Latent Meaning in Talk and Silence

In this section it is argued that the important differences in the speech of men and women lie in the latent meanings that affect the way in which talk is interpreted. Spanish and Quechua are not semantically equivalent, nor are the utterances of men and women. Their meanings are constituted in social interactions that are themselves historically situated and thus relate to previously constituted meanings. The speech of men and women thus reproduces rather than reflects gender difference, constantly articulating anew the ways in which such difference can be understood.

Before looking in detail at Quechua and Spanish usage, it is worth considering the ways in which silence operates as a meaningful aspect of communication. Silence is obviously not a gendered feature of discourse *per se*, as the use of silence is an essential aspect of any communicative repertoire. However, silence can communicate many different meanings. I will here concentrate on four inter-related meanings that commonly attach to silence in Ocongate: power, powerlessness, resistance and respect.

Silence can be understood as an expression of power, a refusal to enter into the intercourse that a social inferior is demanding. In face-to-face interactions such silence communicates its meaning in association with particular body postures, facial expressions, eye movements, gestures and so forth. Silence also holds meaning in non-face-to-face interaction, and in Ocongate this is particularly relevant to the experience of communication with the supernatural world. The Awkis, powerful hill spirits who control the natural fertility essential to the agricultural and herding economy, are believed to communicate verbally among themselves and when represented in ritual, are invariably noisy, somewhat disruptive characters. However, they do not speak to human beings. Their silence is noted with regret as an indication of the difficulties involved in maintaining satisfactory contact with this source of power. The silence with which appeals to secular power are often received is frequently interpreted in a similar fashion.

The classic Andean silence of resistance is related to the idea of silence as power. Silence in the face of authority can signify the absence of agreement, a refusal to participate, an act of defiance.

Silence as lack of power refers to a submissive silence, intrinsically connected to non-linguistic symbols such as body posture. Silence here denotes recognition of another's superiority and a simultaneous sense of shame (*verguenza*) in one's own inferior position. An extreme of this meaning is silence as stupidity, silence as indication that a potential speaker can think of nothing to say.

Finally, there is the silence of respect, a silence which I feel depends to some degree on both power and powerlessness for its meaning. Respectful silence essentially constitutes the silent participant as powerless and thus gives status to other participants, yet respect does not imply a sense of shame in oneself. Such respectful silence can be observed, for example, during Andean wedding celebrations when the bride and groom are expected to show extreme respect to their god-parents who have sponsored the marriage. The couple sit silent and sober amidst the noisy drunken partying of their god-parents, family and friends. Respect in a situation such as this is about not saying everything that you might feel; people emphasise that one of the problems with drinking alcohol is that things that should remain unsaid are voiced and problems arise as a result.

Perhaps the most interesting feature of silence is precisely the lack of material content which heightens the ambiguity of its meaning. Silence can thus be seen as potential antagonism, as submission and recognition of inferiority, as respect, or as distraction and lack of interest. Silence marks the calm, self-contained *tranquilo* as opposed to the crazy *loco*, but also the stupid, slow *sonso* as opposed to the lively, quick-witted *vivo*.

The use of Quechua and Spanish is similarly multivocalic. Quechua is associated with insider status. The indigenous deities that reside in the local landscape, the hill spirits and the earth powers, the Awkis and Pachamama, are the source of regeneration for this local social space. These spirits are always addressed in Quechua and are reported to speak Quechua among themselves. The Quechua-speaking world is organised through networks of kin and spiritual kin relations, networks in which these supernatural powers also have their place as pre-Hispanic ancestors. It is thus through reference to a pre-Hispanic past that people establish their enduring right to the land of the locality and to the benefits that the Pachamama and the Awkis can bring by ensuring its fertility. Here we come close to the source of an alternative prestige, the identification of a conquered people with a glorious past – a past that goes back in time beyond the Inkas to the land itself and the original source of productive social life. Their present status as moral, worthy human beings is sustained through kinship relations which extend to and embrace these supernatural forces. It is in terms of these meanings that Quechua comes to be the most appropriate language for the home, for affection and love-making, and for ritual. However, this past also has a negative image which concerns beliefs in Quechua people's ultimate inferiority in the face of the Spanish-speaking state.

The positive image of Quechua speakers co-exists with a representation of the pre-Hispanic past as a time of ignorance and barbarity. The Inkas could not read and write, and in these terms ignorance of Spanish implies ignorance both of modern technology and of the material comforts that money can buy. It also implies a sense of weakness: for all their power, indigenous deities were defeated by the Spanish God. This feeling is exacerbated by the notion that the Quechua spoken locally is not real Quechua, but a degenerate Hispanised version of some imagined 'pure', 'traditional' form.

To be a monolingual Quechua speaker thus implies insider status, legitimacy and a certain access to the regenerative powers of the animate landscape, but at the same time this identity carries with it a sense of disadvantage and discrimination in the modern world, vulnerability, innocence and ignorance in the face of dominant, powerful outsiders.

Spanish by contrast is the language through which contact can be made with the powers of the state and the material goods produced in the market economy. Spanish is also the language of education and the kinds of knowledge that allow people to function effectively in the modern world. However, a monolingual Spanish identity is problematic to the people of Ocongate because Spanish is ultimately associated with outsider status, and with a world organised around impersonal relations of production which do not respect the moral values inscribed in kinship. Monolingual Spanish speakers thus have a certain knowledge and power, but as outsiders they have no moral basis for the exercise of authority in the locality.

It is in terms of the salient meanings outlined above that bilingualism operates as the language of legitimate authority in the village. In bilingual discourse the positive aspects of both forms of power and/or history can be evoked, while the negative implications are simultaneously denied. To speak Spanish cannot imply the illegitimate abuse of the outsider if the speaker simultaneously invokes insider status through the use of Quechua. Similarly, to use Quechua does not imply ignorance if reference is made to an ability to speak Spanish and to operate effectively outside the village.

Thus, Quechua in this community only operates as a prestigious vernacular in so far as it articulates with, or implies a facility in, the Spanish culture of urban areas and state institutions. The use of Quechua must carry the possibility of choice, implying a decision to distance oneself from the Hispanic. Given that everyone in this community is a first-language Quechua speaker, it is thus understandable that it is Spanish rather than Quechua competence that is emphasised in public, particularly in those formal political meetings that most directly refer to the world outside the village. Quechua is the more suitable language for use at home or among kin, as it refers directly to moral, friendly, insider relationships.

The implicit meanings in Quechua and Spanish and in their combination obviously have implications in terms of women's lesser bilingual competence and consequent lesser authority in all matters that link the village to the wider social context of the outside world. In theory the linking of bilingualism to efficacy in certain political tasks has no negative implications for women. Women can remain forceful and authoritative in other spheres. As Quechua speakers and as women, they are the guardians of indigenous culture and exemplify the source of moral attachment, while men as bilinguals stress their Spanish competence in negotiating inter-community, even inter-household status.[9]

However, the prestige of bilingual discourse emerges in response to the weakness of the Quechua sphere. Women are very aware of this. Their lack of Spanish competence evokes feelings of inadequacy and inferiority and a sense of exclusion from certain levels of prestige within their community. So why the reluctance to use their Spanish? The reason appears to relate to the fact that femininity as a value in terms of which individual women can construct positive subjective identities is very closely connected to the inner world of the family and the community. It is by raising children and by interacting effectively in kinship networks, however wide, that women both value themselves and are valued. The importance of the role of women as mothers and nurturers is emphasised in the dominant images of femininity from both inside and outside the community. It is virtually impossible for women to have access to contraception, but both church and state institutions celebrate motherhood, and indeed women gain adult status from the birth of their first child. This femininity is closely connected to a Quechua-speaking social world and cannot easily co-exist with alternative, more urban images of women as autonomous and oriented towards the Spanish-speaking world. Autonomy and individualism are not necessarily attractive options for these women.

Dominant notions of masculinity, however, present no such conflict for men. Men can legitimately both be autonomous and express an affiliation to the moral relations of kinship, because their most valued achievement is a mediating role between households and between communities.

This pattern of difference is common in many cultures. The question it raises here is why women feel inadequate in their sphere of social life, why they interpret their own actions in a way that validates male experience at their expense. Bilingualism works for men; why do women not have an alternative, more positive concept of their use of Quechua?

To answer this question we have to take into account the fact that the notions of power, hierarchy and language which I have been describing are essentially experienced in a racial, not a gendered idiom. Spanish and Quechua are primarily understood as indicators of ethnic (and by implication class) status. Bilingualism essentially deals with the problem of colonial, i.e. racial, domination. In the following section of this paper I describe the ways in which gender is used as a metaphor to express other power differences; and I suggest that the use of this gender metaphor allows men to negotiate the ambiguity of their racial status, but at the expense of women. To do this, I look at a particular set of rituals which not only use a gendered idiom, but which explicitly connect representations of gender to the use of speech and silence.

The rituals to which I refer and which occur on various occasions in the ritual calendar of Ocongate all involve men dressing up as women and enacting female roles in ritual dramas. The occasions on which these events occur are: (1) the festival of the Immaculate Conception of the Virgin (8 December), (2) the festival of Saint Isidore (15 May) and (3) the Corpus Christi pilgrimage to the shrine of the miraculous Christ of the Snow Star (May/June).

The drama of the first festival involves a man dressing up as a soldier and another man blacking his face and dressing as a woman, a *mestiza*. Considerable entertainment for the onlookers is provided by this visual spectacle, but is increased when the soldier makes love to the 'woman', attempting to kiss and fondle her. The 'woman' attempts to evade the attentions of the man but remains silent throughout her ordeal.

At the festival of Saint Isidore teams of bulls are brought into the village square in an enactment of the ritually and materially important maize-sowing. Men, ideally dressed in traditional *bayeta* clothing, direct the bulls, while other men dressed as women place the seed in the ground. The character of the overseer, the *mandón*, mounted on a horse, directs the operations which are constantly disrupted by two other men, who represent the Awkis and whose task it is to place the fertilising ash on top of the seeds that the women have placed in the ground. However, they actually spend their time noisily molesting the 'women' and the onlooking crowds. The men and 'women' involved in the act of sowing do not react to the antagonism of the Awkis.

There are several ritual personae, either female or ambiguously male/female, performed by men during the festival for the Christ of the Snow Star. The *ukukus*, or bear dancers, carry an ambiguous symbolism in many respects (Allen, 1983). They fulfil various functions: they are the guardians of authority at the shrine, acting as a kind of police force, making sure that pilgrims behave with appropriate decorum; they are buffoons who entertain the pilgrims with their antics; and they act as general dog'sbodies in the various dance groups to which they are attached. Their ritual status is on the one hand high and autonomous – they lead an independent pilgrimage onto the glaciers above the shrine where they keep an all-night vigil – and on the other hand low and dependent, in that they are the servants of their particular dance troupes.

Finally, concerning the *ukukus*, I suggest that their gender is also ambiguous. As they march round the shrine, brandishing their whips and keeping order, and when they climb the glacier and risk death on the freezing ice, they are unmistakably fulfilling masculine roles, imposing order and demonstrating physical strength and endurance. However, they also spend a considerable amount of time begging from the people in high falsetto voices, brandishing small images of themselves, little *ukuku* dolls which they claim are their babies and for whom they need money or food. The language register they use for this begging is very similar to a preferred female register of request (rapid, high-pitched and with distinctive intonation). Finally, there are both the "'external go-betweens' between the spectators and the dance group, and 'internal go-betweens', between the dancers and themselves" (Poole, 1985:15) – a combination of the ideal behaviours of men and women.

The Qolla dance troupes who represent alpaca herders from the *punas* of Puno have among their number a female role, the *imilla* who is quite frequently danced by a man, although the Ocongate Qollas always use a woman for this role. On their return from the shrine, a ritual battle is enacted between the Qollas and another dance group, the Chunchus, who represent the inhabitants of the jungle and are distinguished by their feathered headdresses and *chonta* sticks.[10] On one occasion (the festival of Exaltation, 1987) the male dancers of the Qolla group dressed themselves as women, putting on homespun skirts and adopting the high-pitched falsetto voices of the *ukuku* dancers. The ritual battle centred on the depiction of sexual activity between the Chunchus and the Qollas, but most particularly between the Qollas themselves, until finally all the Qollas had been killed by the *chonta* sticks of the Chunchus, which had been used to represent the phallus in the antics performed throughout the fight. The Qollas were extremely active and noisy, in stark contrast to the female figures of the first two festivals I have described.

An interesting point of similarity in all these male representations of femininity is that the symbolism associated with the 'female' characters is as closely related to ideas about indigenous identity as it is to those about gender. In some cases the female characters are unambiguously female indigenous peasants, and in the festival of the Virgin the 'woman' appears with a black face and in clothes which mark the wearer as *mestiza* and thus more closely connected to an Andean than to a Hispanic identity, especially in contrast to the soldier. The 'women' in the Saint Isidore festival directly represent indigenous peasant women, wearing homespun clothing and performing the same functions that a female peasant would perform while sowing maize. Similarly the Qollas wore homespun skirts to identify themselves as indigenous women, and whatever the ambiguities over the gender of the *ukukus*, there is no doubt that they represent an indigenous presence among the huge variety of ritual figures portrayed in the Corpus Christi festival.

These ritual female characters are also closely connected to depictions of sexuality and implied notions of fertility. The jokes that surround the performances of the female characters at the festivals of the Virgin and of Saint Isidore always concern their having silently to put up with explicit sexual advances on the part of the male characters. The Qollas also engaged in explicit representations of sexual intercourse. The *ukukus* have a less explicit connection to sexuality, but the general symbolism of their characters firmly connects them to ideas about natural fertility and regeneration in that they are themselves supernatural figures associated with the animate powers of the local landscape.

Gender is a potent metaphor for other levels of social relations. It is an extremely strong representation of difference, and is also a concept which here succinctly juxtaposes both the idea of indigenous fertility and that of conquest or submission. Femininity as a concept has long been used as an image of defeat and power difference in the Andes. The Inka conquest hierarchy described ruling lineages as male while conquered peoples were conceptually female. Such a representation of gender obviously parallels the representation of a Quechua monolingual identity, with which the female is also associated. In what ways does the male representation of silent, as opposed to vocal, femininity relate to these other structures of gender and race?

The silent female characters are represented as extremely passive in the ritual dramas. The female character in the Virgin drama simply allows herself to be bothered by the soldier for the entertainment of the crowd. The female sowers in the Saint Isidore festival play an active role in the sowing, yet in the ritual as a whole it is the characters of the Awkis and the overseer who actively generate the ritual activity; the overseer orders the silent male peasants, on whose actions the women's sowing is dependent, and the Awkis make a huge amount of noise molesting the female sowers.

Referring back to the possible ways in which silence could be interpreted, I would suggest that this portrayal of passive feminine silence is not a portrayal of feminine power. Given that the male characters these 'females' are made to interact with are both representatives of outside power, the soldier (state) and the Awkis (animate landscape), I also suggest that it is improbable that their silence communicates respect. Thus we are left with the options which again connect femaleness with racial oppression – silence as both subordination and resistance. These female ritual characters thus appear to harness the metaphor of gender to express the subordination and insecurity of the local population in the face of both the state and the animate landscape.

To turn now to the other female characters, the Qollas and the *ukukus*, these characters are female in a far more ambiguous sense than the others, and the symbolism that attaches to them is thus somewhat more complex. Both have certain silent passive characteristics. The Qollas end their ritual drama lying silent, feigning death, heaped on top of each other in the village square – a very direct image of silent conquest. The *ukukus* are also silent in their subordinate role as dog'sbodies, where they occupy a very low rank in the dance group hierarchy. The strength of these characters is represented partly through their masculine characteristics and partly through their noise. In both cases their noise is confrontational and demanding, and in the case of the *ukukus* the falsetto register they employ is unequivocally female. Thus we are not simply faced with a male/female opposition that can be equated to a noise/silence opposition. While silent passive indigenous resistance is female, noisy active indigenous confrontation combines the male and the female.

The female thus invokes the negative aspects of racial identity while a male/female combination presents insider identity as an altogether more positive concept. Finally, I come to the question of why men are used to represent these female characteristics.

It appears that the combination of the male and the female that the male performance provides stops the dramas from becoming simply a representation of female – and by extension, indigenous – humiliation. It permits the expression of these sentiments without the experience of them in the enactment of the role itself. Men and women say that men have to act the parts because if women were to do so, then the male characters would have to be more restrained in their behaviour. In that case the gender interaction which I have analysed here simply would not occur. Such was indeed the case on one occasion when I witnessed the festival of Saint Isidore and the Awkis paid no attention to the female characters who sowed the seed. This was not without regret;

people said the festival was much better when the Awkis could molest the 'women' by pulling their skirts up over their heads. Paradoxically, then, the male cannot interact with the female and create the necessary male/female combination unless the 'female' is a male.

Conclusions

I come finally to some conclusions on the original question of why women speak less Spanish than men. A traditional theory of complementary and separate spheres might suggest that the best hope women have for some degree of autonomy and authority in the local community would be through their involvement with spheres of activity that relate more directly to the autonomous powers of the landscape in order to construct an identity that did not rely on validation from the male-dominated, outsider-oriented public sphere. Women's insistent monolingualism could be interpreted in this light. Their monolingualism does perhaps offer a degree of protection in so far as it isolates them from the Spanish-speaking state, or rather constitutes a statement of non-collaboration and lack of interest in this sphere of power. However, as we have seen, women themselves feel dissatisfied with this monolingual option.

I have tried to show how Quechua monolingualism is associated with subordination, oppression and ignorance and that this is an image associated with race and colonial domination and is one with which both male and female monolinguals identify. Their Quechua on its own is not sufficient to secure them a valued place in the contemporary world. Their monolingualism offers them no distance from the negative evaluation of their indigenous past.

The animate landscape, the physical focus of indigenous identity in terms of which Quechua holds positive connotations, is a source not of female power, but rather of indigenous power. Indigenous power in turn is an ambiguous concept that embraces the possibilities of regeneration as well as those of defeat. Men attempt to avoid the implications of the association between a Quechua identity and the subordinate status of a conquered people through cultural practices which involve articulations with the Spanish-speaking world. Their bilingualism is an example of such practices which reinforce the positive image of masculinity in which men act as mediators between the inside world of kinship and community and the outside world of finance and knowledge. The dominant image of femininity places women firmly inside the community, even if this is understood as the larger community of the business/trading networks. Speaking Spanish does nothing to validate this position, yet neither does association with the Quechua sphere offer women a strong and positive female identity. Where human gender is represented in relation to this sphere, women are at best the silent partners of men, at worst the objects of male ridicule, often only represented through the burlesque figures of disguised men.

All human beings construct their subjective identities in terms of the discursive representations which surround them and which constitute their social world. What I have tried to show in this paper is that while bilingualism offers a possibility for a degree of local autonomy and authority to indigenous men, it does not offer the same possibilities to women. Male representation and subsequent cultural association of femininity with the silent, dominated aspect of indigenous identity in fact constitutes a male appropriation of the alternative prestige culture at the expense of women.

These male representations, which are also crucially the central indigenous representations of female gender, make it far more difficult for women than it is for men to escape the implications of racial defeat. An appeal to non-indigenous cultural symbols such as speaking Spanish does not cancel the negative side of Quechua culture for women, because femininity itself is so strongly associated with the notions of defeat and subordination. Women cannot negotiate the ambiguity of insider indigenous status through *language* as men can, because as women they themselves embody their position. Their disarticulation thus has to be more far-reaching than the use of verbal symbolism.

Nevertheless more and more women are learning Spanish, in recognition of the connection between bilingualism and positions of authority in the community. However, they are simultaneously aware that such changes in language use have more to do with confronting power structures than with actually acquiring such authority.

Authority must to some extent be based on the ability to communicate – that is the ability to be heard, for your message to be understood and accepted. Language in itself does not guarantee communication. If women's Spanish already has an overlay of other meanings – as illustrated by the woman who was told so violently that her language came out of dog shit – even a woman's Spanish can impede her ability to communicate. Thus it is in those areas of Peruvian life where women have begun to organise and find a political voice that they have registered the experience of a changing relationship to their language. They say that they become more aware of language as they come across their language as an obstacle in their political practice, as they become aware that part of their oppression was an alienation from language, not in the sense of being forced to speak a male language, but in the sense that as women they had been excluded from communication in the language of power.

Notes

1. This article is based on three periods of fieldwork in the village of Ocongate, the first in 1983–5 (funded by the Economic and Social Research Council), the second in 1987 (funded by the British Academy) and the third in 1988 (funded by the Nuffield Foundation). Earlier drafts of the paper have been presented to the XIV Congress of the Latin American Studies Association, New Orleans, the Women's Studies seminar at the Charles Center, Williamsburg and to the London Institute of Latin American Studies workshop on Andean discourse. I am particularly grateful to Meryl Altman, Cecilia Blondet, Deborah Cameron, Cecilia McCallum and Maria Phylactou for their comments and suggestions. I would also like to thank my former colleagues at Liverpool University who supported all the research on which this paper is based.

2. Peru is divided into twenty-three departments, in turn subdivided into provinces and districts. Ocongate is a district capital in the Province of Quisipicanchis, Department of Cusco.

3. The escalation of guerrilla activity in the Cusco region in the mid 1980s led to a dramatic decline in tourism in this area.

4. Quechua influence on local Spanish is particularly evident in the following aspects of speech: intonation (for example, Quechua has no rising intonation for interrogatives), accentuation (Quechua has a firm rule of accentuation of the penultimate syllable), phonetics (Quechua has three vowel phonemes while Spanish has five, which leads to a correspondence of e/i and o/u sounds in local Spanish), grammar (distinctive variations in local Spanish include a lack of number and gender concordance, generalisation of rules for conjugating verbs which produces 'regular' forms of standard Spanish 'irregular' verbs, distinctive uses of the gerund and the pluperfect which follow Quechua grammar and syntax), lexical borrowings and calques.

5. *Mestizo* was originally a term used to refer to people of mixed race, while the Spaniards referred to the indigenous population as Indians. In contemporary Peru these terms carry complex and ambiguous meanings. They refer primarily to cultural and class distinctions rather than racial difference. In the context of a small town such as Ocongate, those with money or political influence, with some education and/or urban contacts are referred to as *mestizo*. Nevertheless, despite the fact that the terms denote distinctive cultural orientation and experience, they are also used to naturalise and validate social hierarchy through an appeal to racial difference which firmly distinguished the *mestizo* from the indigenous peasant, the *campesino*.

6. See for example Daly (1978), Lakoff (1975) and Spender (1980). Useful overviews of this literature are provided by Cameron (1985), Coates & Cameron (1988), and Graddol & Swann (1989).

7. Bourdieu, despite his sophisticated demonstration of how such values are maintained, does not provide a clear account of acquisition (Bourdieu, 1977).

8. Labov is apparently unaware of those cases where women can and do embody the prestige of vernacular culture. See for example McCallum (1990) and Harris (1980).

9. Harris's work on the Bolivian Laymi provides a comparable case for Aymara speakers (Harris 1980).

10. '*Chonta*' (Sp.) '*Bactris ciliata* is a small palm tree with a hard black elastic ebony-like wood growing in the montana below 1,200 metres. In Inka times it was used for making spears and other weapons, and it was an important trade item from the tropical forest people to the highlands' (Sallnow 1987:309).

References

Allen, C., 1983, 'Of bear-men and he-men: bear metaphors and male self-perception in a Peruvian community' in *Latin American Indian Literatures* 7(1) 38–51.

Bourdieu, P., 1977, *Outline of a Theory of Practice*, Cambridge: Cambridge University Press.

Brown, P., 1980, 'How and Why are Women more Polite: Some Evidence from a Mayan Community' in S. McConnell-Ginet, R. Borker and N. Furman (eds), *Women and Language in Literature and Society*, New York: Praeger.

Brown, P. and Levinson, S., 1978, 'Universals in Language Usage: Politeness Phenomena' in E. Goody (ed.), *Questions and Politeness*, Cambridge: Cambridge University Press.

Cameron, D., 1985, *Feminism & Linguistic Theory*, London: Macmillan.

———, 1988, 'Language and Sex in the Quantitative Paradigm: Introduction' in J. Coates and D. Cameron (eds), *Women in their Speech Communities*, London: Longman.

Coates, J., 1986, *Women, Men and Language*, London: Longman.

Coates, J. and Cameron, D., 1988, 'Some Problems in the Sociolinguistic Explanation of Sex Differences' in J. Coates and D. Cameron (eds), *Women in their Speech Communities,* London: Longman.

Daly, M., 1978, *Gyn/Ecology: the Metaethics of Radical Feminism*, Boston: Beacon Press.

Graddol, D. and Swann, J., 1989, *Gender Voices*, Oxford: Basil Blackwell.

Harris, O., 1980, 'The Power of Signs: Gender, Culture and the Wild in the Bolivian Andes' in C. MacCormack and M. Strathern (eds), *Nature, Culture and Gender*, Cambridge: Cambridge University Press.

Harvey, P., 1989, 'Genero, autoridad y competencia linguistica: participación politica de la mujer en pueblos andinos', *Documento de Trabajo* no. 33, Lima: Instituto de Estudios Peruanos.

Labov, W., 1972a, *Sociolinguistic Patterns*, Philadelphia: University of Pennsylvania Press.

———, 1972b, *Language in the Inner City*, Oxford: Basil Blackwell.

Labov, W., P. Cohen, C. Robins and J. Lewis, 1968, *A Study of the Non-standard English of Negro and Puerto Rican Speakers in New York City*, US Office of Education Co-operative Research Project 3288–1.

Lakoff, R., 1975, *Language and Woman's Place*, New York: Harper & Row.

McCallum, C., 1990, 'Language, Kinship and Politics in Amazonia', *Man*, vol. 25, no. 3 (412–33).

Milroy, L., 1980, *Language and Social Networks*, Oxford: Basil Blackwell.

Nichols, P. 1984, 'Networks and Hierarchies: Language and Social Stratification' in C. Kramarae, M. Schulz and W. O'Barr (eds), *Language and Power*, Beverly Hills, California: Sage Publications.

Poole, D., 1985, 'The Choreography of History in Andean Dance' (unpublished manuscript).

Sallnow, M., 1987, *Pilgrims of the Andes: Regional Cults in Cusco*, Washington D.C.: Smithsonian Institution Press.

Spender, D., 1980, *Man Made Language*, London: Routledge and Kegan Paul.

Trudgill, P., 1972, 'Sex, Covert Prestige and Linguistic Change in the Urban British English of Norwich', *Language in Society*, 1: 179–95.

4

Casual Chat and Ethnic Identity: Women's Second-Language Use among Buryats in the USSR[1]

Caroline Humphrey

This paper is about the way in which a sense of ethnic identity may be discovered through analysis of informal *genres*, such as casual chat. Of particular interest is the aspect of informal conversation that consists of taking someone into one's confidence. The example used here is a Buryat peasant woman of the Siberian *taiga* forests, 'chatting about everything', as she says.

As Lévi-Strauss remarked about myth or Geertz about 'common sense', we can also recognise casual chat, however different the culture is from our own. We know it by its informality, its lack of focus, its haphazard reiteration, as 'topics of conversation' crumble away in the compulsion of people saying what they can't help saying.

Before going on to discuss casual chat as a *genre* I provide some background information about the tiny group which forms the subject of this paper – a few hundred people living in the 1970s in two villages to the west of Lake Baikal. I believe that they are typical of many such isolated and far-flung communities all over Siberia, and very possibly in other parts of the former Soviet Union too, e.g. the Altai, the Karelian north, or the Amur River region. Ethnic identity in such groups has been conditioned by two dramatic shifts in relations with the Russians, first in the 1930s and then later at the end of the 1950s and beginning of the '60s. In other words, recent inter-ethnic relations are to a large extent a result of Soviet transformations and deeply tied to Soviet social aims. The appearance of bland public Russification during the Brezhnev period, to which this paper refers, hid undercurrents and ambiguities; casual chat in a bilingual situation, I suggest, is an important *genre* by which to understand the subtleties of identity.

The Nizhneudinsk Buryats, who arrived in the seventeenth century as refugees from internal wars in Mongolia, are clearly ethnically distinct from the Russians: they look Asian, speak a dialect of Mongolian, and

65

used to have a way of life based on livestock and hunting, with a little agriculture. In terms of their relations with the Russians, the interesting point is that Russians likewise first appeared in this region around the same time as Cossak adventurers, or later as exiles and poverty-stricken peasants looking for land. This meant that these rural Russians did not assume a condescending, colonialist attitude to the Buryats, but on the contrary they learned the Buryat language and even spoke it amongst themselves. They learned techniques of livestock raising from the Buryats and adopted certain items of Buryat clothing, tools and the like. The Buryats for their part had no need to learn Russian, since all local Russians spoke Buryat and were the mediators between the Buryats and the outside world. The Russians were peasant farmers and lived separately from the Buryats. Although elsewhere Buryats fiercely resented Russians taking over their land, here it seems that during the nineteenth century relations were generally friendly. There was a complex barter system linking the Russians and Buryats to another tribal group, the Tofalars, who were mainly hunters. The Tofalars obtained the furs which were necessary to pay taxes, traded them to the Buryats for livestock products, and the Buryats used the furs to pay taxes and obtain tea, sugar, flour, tobacco and manufactured goods from the Russians. All of this barter took place using the Buryat language. To this day, many of the Russians of the very oldest generation speak Buryat fluently.

However, the situation changed dramatically in the 1930s with collectivisation. Buryats were forced into collective farms together with the Russians, and these farms were run using Russian agricultural methods and with the aim of producing goods useful in the Russian cultural system of consumption. The transhumant Buryat livestock economy was broken for ever. The Buryats were now displaced, low-grade, workers on these farms, often still living in outlying isolated brigades, unfamiliar with the new aims, and their own local knowledge peripheralised or useless. Young Russians ceased to learn Buryat. But the Buryats on the other hand did not learn any more than a working smattering of Russian. Buryat children languished in the lower classes of the village schools, hardly ever acquiring the linguistic competence to do well. These farms were still without electricity, machinery, newspapers, telephones, clubs or cinemas.

It was not until the late 1950s, when the farms were amalgamated into larger units, when Buryats were moved to new houses to live alongside Russians, when farm work began to be mechanised, and there was access to Russian means of communication, that things began to change. By the late 1970s when the conversation to be discussed was recorded, the spheres of work, school, administration, newspapers, cinemas and clubs were operating only in Russian. Almost all Buryats, except young children and socially isolated people of the oldest generation, were fluent in Russian.

From studies of everyday speech it is clear that the Nizhneudinsk Buryat dialect has itself been strongly affected by Russian. Large areas of technical vocabulary do not exist in Buryat. But more than this, Russian everyday expressions and even word order have appeared in Buryat speech, indicating that Russian habits of thinking are now ingrained in the Buryat population. Indeed, sentences in one person's speech may shift from a basically Buryat grammatical structure, peppered with Russian words, to a Russian structure interspersed with Buryat vocabulary, and there are many terms in common use which one could hardly say belonged to either language. For example, in the sentence, 'My father works as a brigadier' the word 'brigadier' is Russian, but it is given an instrumental suffix in Buryat, this instrumental, however, being a Russian, not a Buryat grammatical necessity in such a sentence.

Numerous works by Soviet sociologists and linguists indicate that the Buryats are by no means the only ethnic group in this kind of situation. When I was in Buryatia I found, among Buryats meeting each other from different regions, an endless surprise and fascination with the variations in how things are said. Although there is an official standard Buryat based on a particular Eastern Buryat dialect, this is not in any sense 'truer Buryat' than the other dialects, all of which find themselves under increasing pressure from Russian. This situation is what we would expect to find with dispersed ethnic groups, never themselves unified, living in a centralised political economy in which centripetal links are strong, while those between the groups on the periphery are weak or non-existent. There was no central religion, such as Islam in Central Asia, to form a bond between all Buryats. Many groups of Eastern Buryats were Buddhists, but this did not include Western groups such as the Nizhneudinsk Buryats. Furthermore, even the major groups of Buryats have never been subjects in a single political-administrative unit of their own. They now live in three Buryat administrative regions which are not territorially adjacent to one another. Numerous small groups such as the Nizhneudinsk Buryats do not even live in one of these but in the Irkutsk oblast, surrounded by a sea of Russians. So, in these circumstances, with religious and political forms of community absent, what sense of identity remains?

Casual chat has perhaps been neglected by anthropologists as a *genre* because it is so personal and unstructured: surely casual conversation can only tell us about *these* people at *this* moment, when what we want is to know are larger, more general facts. I shall suggest, on the contrary, that casual chat, like other *genres* such as myth or the novel, although these have different values for analysis of identity, gives us a particular insight. This arises from two aspects of the *genre*. Firstly, chat, gossip (Haviland, 1977) and similar *genres* are relatively unstructured precisely *because* they are the social activities of reacting to people and events, haphazard and unexpected as these may be, and of evaluating them in relation to theories of the world. In other words, they allow us a window into the relation between 'reality' or context and people's views of the world.

Secondly, in conversation people mean more than they say, and to understand them we have to go beyond what is spoken aloud to what is unsaid but assumed. As was pointed out long ago by Bakhtin, what is assumed but not spoken is not some unknowable something located in the unconscious of the individual speaker, precisely because such a thing never could be assumed. To quote: 'Assumed value judgements are therefore not individual emotions but regular and essential social acts' (Voloshinov/Bakhtin, 1976: 100)[2]. Furthermore, and this takes us to the heart of the question of identity, people cannot see themselves in an absolute sense, but constantly refract their view of themselves through the values of others. 'Self-awareness ... is always a matter of gauging oneself against some social norm' (Voloshinov/Bakhtin, 1976: 76–77).

To recap Bakhtin's argument briefly, we must start with his theory of the self. The self is not a subject or an essence in its own right, as in Romantic philosophy; that is, it is not a source of sovereign intention, but can only exist 'dialogically', in a relation with all that is other, most importantly other selves. Understanding of anything takes place from a point of view, and my point of view must be different from yours because I am not you. What you can see, and I cannot see, is precisely myself. Thus, as I cannot see the self that I am, I must see it in the eyes of others. This refracting of the world through the values of others continues all our lives. The self, therefore, is not a static given but a project. So Bakhtin argues that the self finds itself in the sum of its discursive practices. He says,

> any instance of self-awareness (for self-awareness is always verbal, always a matter of finding some specifically suitable verbal complex) is an act of gauging oneself against some social norm. Social evaluation is, so to speak, the socialisation of oneself and one's behaviour. In becoming aware of myself, I attempt to look at myself, as it were through the eyes of another (Voloshinov / Bakhtin, 1976: 76–77).

Even if we do not agree with Bakhtin's notion of the self, which is opposed to that of Freud, for example, his vision of what goes on in dia-logical verbal activity is acknowledged to be an important insight for anthropology. It is true, as Gumperz' work (1982, 1984) shows, that a straightforward application of Bakhtin might run into trouble, since conversational misunderstandings reveal that the 'mutually understood' is not invariably shared. Nevertheless, the basic point still holds. Confidential casual chat assumes mutual understanding (which is its charm), and even if the interlocutor in fact makes mistaken deductions I accept here the idea that an attempt is still made on each side to discover the self through the other.

So what I am suggesting in this paper is that the process of realising self-identity as gauged against the assumptions and reactions of others, in relation both to the context of speaking and to social norms, is perceivable by outsiders in casual chat above any other *genre*. Whatever people label informal conversation as – 'being sociable', 'a real natter', 'a heart-to-heart' – its essence is the mutual evaluation of selves in the current flow of events.

Casual chat may be contrasted as a *genre* with gossip, which is fundamentally a conversation about third parties and about unusual or idiosyncratic situations. Gossip is implicitly judgemental. Analysis of gossip is therefore helpful in understanding social conventions, as it highlights the flouting of them. Casual chat, on the other hand, takes place in the realm of the utterly ordinary, the ongoing events with which we all live, but which we may nevertheless not be quite sure how to evaluate. Casual chat may refer to any topic under the sun, but its inner unity comes from the fact that it reverts constantly to the self.[3] Of course informal conversation will not indicate everything there is to know about identity, but it does reveal things we could discover in no other way. This was particularly important in a country like the former Soviet Union, where social life was pervaded with suspicion in most contexts. There were marked distinctions between formal and informal language, and between the guarded and the unguarded (or at least, relatively so) expression of what came into one's head.

This paper discusses the casual talk of a Buryat woman, a farm-labourer, with a Buryat linguist (see below). The talk was recorded by the linguist, Darbeyeva, in the early 1970s when she toured Buryat villages to investigate the effects of bilingualism on local dialects (Darbeyeva, 1978). Darbeyeva herself is a Western Buryat, from the same region though not the same locality as the speaker, but was separated from her by a wide social gap, being a highly-educated professional linguist. I am afraid that this text has many disadvantages from the methodological point of view: it is distant in time and place, second-hand, does not record intonation or gestures, and worst of all contains no record of Darbeyeva's reactions. What we have is simply one woman, the farmer, chatting on. Darbeyeva's book makes it clear that she herself did not speak during this section of the conversation, but she must have smiled, nodded and so on, and of this we have no record. The advantage of this text is that it is an accurate record of the words and also happens to be a concentrated expression of features which I aim to explain.

Darbeyeva's interpretation of the bilingual situation of this conversation is to characterise the first language, Buryat, as having a 'genetic' function, because it is passed on within the family and is used at home by the entire population of the Buryat village. Essentially this function does not change, which is why these small languages have survived. The second language (Russian) she characterises as having a socio-political function. It is used in a discontinuous way, for particular purposes, at times of contact with Russians, or in discrete situations (such as at school, in the cinema, or when reading the papers). Not everyone speaks it: pre-school children and old women do not know Russian – they live in a world where it is not needed. Unlike the first language, it is subject to changes in function through history, and to the decline or expansion of functions. I do not disagree with this formulation, but I think that the situation is not so simple, partly because even when 'speaking Buryat' people use much Russian interspersed with it, and partly because of the relationship between speaking Buryat, identity, and gender. Minority languages often became gendered with the imposition of Soviet state power, and speaking Buryat has become associated with women.

This requires a short discussion of gender in Buryat and Soviet society. Buryat rural society was still in the early 1970s organised around the localised, exogamous patrilineage (Humphrey 1983). Women were 'brought in' at marriage as wives; daughters were 'sent out' to marry elsewhere; the whole organisation of marriage was still to a great extent in the hands of male elders. Even if girls could decide whom not to marry, the idiom was still that the older generation had a duty to find a wife for its sons. The ideology was that the woman injects life or vivacity into the strength of the patrilineage. Buryats had a saying, 'Our women are Tungus, our men are Buryat', the Tungus being the wild hunters and fishermen of the forests, and this untrue statement had, I think, to do with the idea of incorporating an autochthonous, unsocialised and yet essential quality of wisdom into the male lineage. This is seen in many cultural forms (songs, stories, epics, plays at the theatre) in which the in-coming daughter-in-law has to prove herself by cleverness and intelligence (Hamayon and Bassanoff, 1973). The father-in-law sets her tests, which are above all verbal tests or tricks, like riddles. This identification of women with mastery of language and intelligence, as contrasted with the strength and virility expected of men, can be seen in people's names. In Mongolian culture names are made up of words designating desirable qualities. An example of this, analysed by Roberte Hamayon (1971), is the Buryat family of the 1940s in which the son was named Tractor and the daughter Hypotenuse.

Buryat women are identified with an intelligence which is controlled in a way by men, but which also turns into what is 'inner' about the community. It is consonant with this that, in ethnic relations, Buryat women, to a far greater degree than men, are expected to keep up traditions in dress, cooking and demeanour. Women are subject to blame if they marry outsiders, such as Russians, but men are less so, since the in-coming wife is transformed by the marriage and especially the bearing of male children. Earlier this century even in-coming Russian wives sometimes used to wear Buryat dress. In the period of this study, though the use of Russian had greatly increased, it was women who were most at home in using Buryat, and this can be seen as the result of the definition of Buryat as 'inner' and Soviet as 'public' in the Brezhnev period.

Let us now examine what the woman farmer said. We are in an isolated village, deep in the Siberian forests, where Russians and Buryats live and work side by side. The Russians know the village as Kushun; the Buryats call it Shugul. The speaker is talking in Buryat dialect, heavily interspersed with incorrect Russian. Because the two languages are so interlocked in this text (e.g. Buryat grammatical endings on Russian words) it is impossible to give an accurate rendering in English of the language choice, but to give some indication I have italicised in the translation those words spoken in Russian. Dots indicate pauses. Brackets show pronouns inserted by Darbeyeva or myself where they are absent in the Buryat, or other necessary explanations.

> When I myself go *hay-making* [I] feel very good (lit. whole inside). Varvar goes to school in the *nine class*. We say '*nine*' directly, but in the south people say 'ninth'... Oh, Katya was very *affectionate* to [her] *husband* ... Our Buryat people live surrounded by Russians ...
>
> Which *date* did *he* go away from here? ... Our language here is very hard and rough, cut up in bits like wood. [It] is tending more and more towards Russian. People to the south speak differently to us. Bilberries grow only in the valley. Yesterday Varvar went down there. It is full of *workmen* from the town, there are more of them than trees in the forest.
>
> The sky clouded over and it started to drizzle (lit. pee, urinate). So I didn't go to the *hay-making*. Then the sky cleared. Then it thun-

dered... Really, [I]'d missed the chance to go... [He] said [he] would come back. The moon waned. Now it is already full moon... The Buryat people are very shy. Don't [you] give way to people, don't submit!

Twelve quid [i.e. roubles, C.H.] has become too little. [You] have to buy tea, salt, this and that is needed. *Everywhere [you] turn*, [you] need money, *at every step*, money. Let it rain, *they've already got the hay in and that's it.* [I] *keep a dog*, if only to have a living being making a noise. *Before the collective farm* we never used to be formal with one another [i.e. use name and patronymic as Russians do, D.]. If [you] don't trust one another, *how can [you] live*? If [I] get divorced, I'll lose my name. [He]'s set up house [i.e. got a woman, C.H.] *in every settlement, and she accepts him all the same.*

First I did go up the hill, but [I] couldn't find any. Even mushrooms are necessary for large *families*. We really are chatting *about everything*. It is an ordinary *table*, not a *round* one. [He] said [he] would put in some work to fix it if [he] could. *At the dairy there are six milkmaids working.* One of them is a Russian tart. [She] can speak Buryat, but [she] won't. *We gather up the silage by hand.* P.S. said [he] would mend the old combine. In the morning the *brigadier* gives out the work, and *he* [the book-keeper] gives the details, *who, where*. [He] mows with a *tractor mower*. But I have to dig up the *potatoes* by hand. We live as we can, by our strength. [I] must go, the cattle are coming in. This little girl is very angry-natured. If someone is going to be a good person, [one] can tell it from childhood. Here, among us, we don't use the names of the parents-in-law, [we] call the mother-in-law 'Mum', and *in the same way* [we] don't use the names of *older brothers*.

Take that child to [her] *mother*. My boy was *such* an affectionate person. I bought him a *cap*. 'Granny, tell me a story', [he] used to say. Here, we have no *bad-natured* people. The world is wide. Everywhere, everywhere, people go on living.

Our first task must be to explain the Buryat semantic categories with which the two women, the speaker and Darbeyeva, operate. Many of these are unspoken and assumed. Clearly, it is impossible in a short paper to do this fully, so I shall limit myself to some of the more important categories.

Time It is the evening ('I must go, the cattle are coming in'), and the insistence on the agricultural regulation of time is a refrain throughout this talk. In Siberia the provision of hay and silage for fodder during the winter months is today quite crucial. To be done when the weather permits, hay-making pulls everyone in as a social duty, irrespective of age, sex, or job. Perhaps it is because of this internalised necessity that this woman feels 'whole inside' when she is out at the hay-making. Nevertheless, the fact that Buryat-Mongolian pastoralism used to be extensive and transhumant, without preparation of hay, is reflected in her use of a Russian word (*pokos*) for hay-making. Similarly, she thinks in terms of the old Buryat kind of time-reckoning, by the moon waxing and waning: 'He said he would come back. ... Now it is already full moon.' But the European calendar has entered her world, and the word 'date' (*chislo*) is rendered in Russian. In a longer time-span, it is not the Revolution but before and after the *kolkhoz* (collective farm) which is the important turning point for her.

Space Space is local space, the valley full of workmen where bilberries grow and the hillsides where mushrooms may be found. Beyond this, to the 'south' (*uragsha*, Bur.) live other Buryats who speak differently. This is an important expression deriving from the Buryat and Mongolian habit of orienting all living space by reference to the sun. Dwellings are always oriented to the south, and the term for this direction also means in front, forwards, in the vanguard, active, progressive, happy and successful. The reciprocal *xoito* means northern, back, secondary, cold, following, and after. The word for 'south' is derived from *urai*, meaning both previous/earlier in time and in front / before in space. Time and space are thus tied together in a way which is perhaps intuitively strange to the European mind.[4] The past, to which are linked also the family (*urag*) and the idea of flow (*uradxal*) is warm and happy and in front of us. In the present text, the 'people of the south' (*uragsha ulat*) refers to the main body of the Buryats, the dominant groups whose dialect forms the basis for literary Buryat, and from whom the Nizhneudinsk folk are cut off by miles of swampy forest, rivers and Lake Baikal itself.

Social Categories The category 'Buryat' is unproblematical, prefixed by the speaker usually with 'our' and clearly the group she identifies with, but this cannot be said for the Russians. She refers to Russians in two ways. *Orot* is a Buryatisation of the standard Mongolian *oros* (plural *orod*, Bur. dialect plural *orooduud*). The other term, *mangut* or *mangad* (dialect *manguut*), on the other hand, is used in reference to Russians as far as I know only by Buryats, and essentially is the word for monster. *Mangut* appear in their original meaning in Buryat and Mongolian folk-epics as huge, hairy, many-headed, supernaturally powerful enemies of the hero. They also have the unfortunate disability of a loose lower jaw, so they make funny 'wa-wa' noises and cannot talk properly. Perhaps it would be wrong to read too much into the use of this term. *Mangut* can be used in a more or less neutral way, as in 'He speaks Russian (*Mangar*) well'. But standard Buryat-Russian dictionaries do omit the term. Certainly, the stories which the little boy asks his granny to tell him would have *mangut* in them, figuring as monsters and nothing else.

All the other social categories in this text – workers, brigadier, milk-maids, the collective farm, the dairy, the settlements (where 'he' has his girlfriends) and even the family (which needs mushrooms) – are given in Russian. It is as though the speaker is surrounded by Russian social institutions, and what is Buryat appears only as a substratum, in the interstices.

Naming In Mongolian and Buryat culture the name is so closely associated with the personality that it comes to stand for it. The word name (*nere*) means reputation and authority, that is, something honoured and hence transcending the day-to-day *persona*. Everyone has to have a different name expressing some desired combination of qualities and their own individuality. Older and respected people are virtually never addressed by name, to the extent that their personal names almost become a secret (Humphrey, 1978). Buryats operate with two sets of names, public Russian ones and private Buryat ones. Mongols and Buryats say '*Nere xugaraxaar yas xugar*' – 'Rather than damage your name it is better to break your bone', the 'bone' representing the idea of male heredity and the clan. This complex of ideas is what our speaker is referring to when she mentions the prohibition on naming the parents-in-law and elder brothers. And it is the dread of losing her reputation that she is talking about when she says she will lose her name if she gets divorced. All of this must be assumed to be understood by Darbeyeva, as it is shared by all Buryats. Unspoken assumptions and values make links in what at first sight seems a series of more or less fortuitous statements. The speaker assumes Darbeyeva will understand who are the unspoken subjects of sentences, in particular the 'he' who crops up again and again.

What can we learn from this text about ethnic identity? Briefly, the Buryat woman is self-conscious about her use of language, but sticks by her mistakes. The 'roughness' of contemporary Western Buryat is contrasted with Eastern Buryat and seems to be attributed to Russification. Later on in the text the Russification of kinship terms of address is linked with loss of faith or trust, and the word the speaker uses (*etegel*) is a religious term, virtually deleted from Buryat official Soviet-type language in this kind of context. The woman feels surrounded by numberless Russians, like trees in the forest. Buryats are shy, and to venture into the valley full of Russian workmen is to step out of the local world. But despite this we have a sense that the speaker has definite social rules she will hold on to (and make the little girl do too), and that there is a certain passive resistance in the air, as when she tells Darbeyeva, 'Don't submit!'

Let us now look at the language choices this woman makes. The Nizhneudinsk Buryats, like many other bilingual peoples such as the Finns in Sweden (Haugen, 1973), are cut off from the living and developing source of their own language. A primary use of Russian is therefore to fill in colloquial gaps, as we see from our speaker's use of handy expressions – for example, 'everywhere you turn', 'at every step', 'just so as to'. Russian words are also used for things which to the Buryats are culturally Russian, such as potatoes, class, date, workers, settlement and hay-making. A further batch of Russian words came to the Buryats through Soviet institutions: collective farm, dairy farm, combine-harvester, brigadier. To none of these can we attribute any particular individual value on the part of the speaker, since local Buryat equivalents do not effectively exist.

However, there are some expressions which in the abstract might be put in Buryat, but which in this context are felt by the speaker to be dominated by Soviet Russian values, for example, work *rabootat* (in the dairy), or repair *rimantiiravakamna* (the combine). At times, talking about the world of work, the speaker moves entirely into Russian: 'They've already got the hay in and that's it' (*'Pokoos uzhe ubraali fsoo'*). We have noted already that social categories are given by this speaker almost entirely in Russian. If work and social groups are Russian, it seems that what remains as Buryat are more elusive things, attitudes and values.

I interpret this text, and others given by Darbeyeva, to show that when the speaker uses more or less pure Buryat in referring to Russians she is identifying herself positively thereby with a Buryat point of view: 'We Buryats live surrounded by Russians' (*'Mani baryaadut segeen manguut soo huuna'*), or 'Don't give way to people!' (*'Kunde bapta!'*). The cultural distancing effect is emphasised by the derogatory words she chooses: *Manguut* (monster) for Russians, or later on, *izi* (tart) for the standoffish milkmaid. This is what we should expect. But when, on the other hand, she uses more or less continuous Russian to talk about a Buryat situation, perhaps she is expressing her personal alienation from the event. When she is speaking about someone who must be her husband: 'He has a woman in every settlement, and she accepts him all the same' ('*Kazhnom stayaanka gerleet yirne, anaa fso ravnoo yigoo prini-maat*'), the alienation is emphasised by the use of the Russian third person pronoun 'she' (*anaa*) to refer to someone who might well be herself. Russian is used to distance herself from things she finds hurtful. Another example is the use of Russian for 'bad-natured'.

In this text there are many indications of the speaker's values, of her generation and class, which are not shared with young urban Buryats such as Darbeyeva. It is interesting, for example, that the speaker uses the Buryat word for 'horse-herd' (*aduuhan*) to talk about what must be cattle: horses do not come back in the evening, but cows do. In Buryat and Mongolian culture the horse, the prime domestic animal, used to stand for all livestock. But after the 1930s Buryat collective farmers were not allowed to keep private horses, though they could keep cattle. A younger farmworker or urban person like Darbeyeva would probably have said 'cows' if that was what she meant.

Bakhtin saw just this sphere, the assigning of values by linguistic choices, as a struggle against the necessity of given social interpretations. 'Each word ... is a little arena for the clash and criss-crossing of differently oriented social accents. A word in the mouth of a particular individual is a product of the living interaction of social forces' (Voloshinov/Bakhtin, 1973: 41). Among different speech *genres* we might expect to find the aspect of 'struggle' least present in casual chat where speakers are likely to have much in common with one another. At a political meeting, on the other hand, conflict over meanings is overt and frequently itself discussed. But even in intimate conversation what Bakhtin called the 'multi-accentuality of the sign' is present. Here we do not know how Darbeyeva participated in the rest of this conversation. But we can assume that she would not use 'peeing' for raining, 'horse-herd' for cows, 'monsters' for Russians, nor perhaps the rustic *solkhoboosh* for rouble. She might avoid *etegel* (religious faith) in the sense used by the speaker, and almost certainly she would not refer to a local milkmaid by the rude word *izi* (tart). What the speaker is doing by using these words is manipulating the rules of the game of polite conversation with outsiders. She presumes on the deeper identity, as a woman and a Buryat, between herself and Darbeyeva in order to bring about a complicity, a complicity involving Darbeyeva in her own backwoods, anti-Russian values. We know that she is self-conscious about her crude dialect. What she implicitly needs is a reaction which validates her attitudes and sympathises with her lonely situation (cf. the dog, kept as a 'living being to make a noise').

The language of the text indicates that there are some cultural rules which the speaker feels sure of, 'Before the collective farm we never used to be formal with one another. If you can't trust one another, how can you live?' or 'Here among us we don't use the names of the parents-in-law'. But there are other moral values where she seems uncertain, chiefly relating to the husband, who may divorce her, and who keeps re-emerging in the text as though the thought of him cannot be kept at bay.

What I have been suggesting in this paper is that in the present kind of casual chat, which involves taking another into one's confidence, what is at issue is the relating of individual experience to presumed cultural values by means of the interlocutor as sounding-board. The text I have used shows clearly that this is not simply a case of linking events or 'given' context to accepted social rules. While we could take the weather, the hay-making, and the collective farm as 'given' context and the little girl who comes in as an event, it is the speaker herself who introduces the problems of poverty, the errant husband, or the rough language of the backwoods. In other words, she establishes her own contexts simply by talking. By raising such topics of conversation in the tone, the order, and with the vocabulary she does, she evokes her own attitudes and draws her interlocutor into relationship with them. Because they may or may not be shared, this gambit raises unspoken questions: what, in her culture, is shared with Darbeyeva, and do they really have common values *vis-à-vis* the Russians?

It is certain features of casual chat as a *genre* – the erupting of unbidden topics, the way they create semantic and value-laden contexts, the constant reference to ongoing events, the intentional relation with the interlocutor – which reveal, beyond the ordinary sense of what has been said, everything that the speaker allows to let fall about herself.

Identity revealed in this way is always to some extent relative to the interlocutor. Clearly the speaker is talking to Darbeyeva in a way she would never adopt with Russians themselves. By doing this she raises between them the Buryat culture which she assumes they to some extent share, but this 'to some extent' is a vital matter for the Buryats. All the crucial social divisions among Buryats emerge in this little talk: the isolation of far-flung groups, the dialectal diversity, the difficulty of keeping up with mainstream Eastern Buryat cultural development, and the great difference in way of life between the collective farmers and the intellectuals. Similarly, it is unlikely that the speaker would have talked in this way about her husband if she was conversing with a man. She was implicitly engaging Darbeyeva's sympathy as another woman. Was it with compassion or with a wry smile that Darbeyeva reacted to the speaker's 'Don't you give way to people, don't submit'? The very admonition itself suggests that it would have been the former reaction.

Notes

1. This chapter was written in the mid-1980s, before the USSR was dissolved.

2. V. N. Voloshinov is the colleague under whose name it is now thought that Mikhail Bakhtin published some of his most important ideas. The texts relevant here are Voloshinov (1927) and (1929); see discussion in Clark and Holquist (1984).

3. It is possible that there are differences between cultures in the extent to which gender stereotypes encourage men and women to refer to the self in casual chat. In many cultures, including our own and the Buryat to judge from Darbeyeva's texts from male informants, men, even in very informal circumstances tend to talk about outside 'topics' and refer to themselves more indirectly than women.

4. It has been helpfully pointed out to me by Ketaki Kushari Dyson that this relation between time and space may be more widespread that I had supposed. She notes that there are similar examples in Sanskrit and the Indian languages derived from it, and she points out that I had forgotten the English case of the word 'before'. The positive and negative evaluations given to time/space categories in Altaic languages such as Mongolian are, however, vestigial in the Indo-European cases.

References

Clark, K. and Holquist, M., 1984, *Mikhail Bakhtin*, Cambridge Mass.: Harvard University Press.

Darbeyeva, A. A., 1978, *Vliyaniye dvuyazychiya na razvitiye izolirovannogo dialekta, na materiale mongol'skikh yazykov* (The influence of bilingualism on the development of an isolated dialect, on material from Mongolian languages), Moscow: Nauka.

Geertz, C., 1983, 'Common sense as a cultural system' in his *Local Knowledge*, New York: Basic Books.

Gumperz, J. (ed.), 1982, *Language and Social Identity,* Cambridge: Cambridge University Press.

Gumperz, J., 1984, 'Communicative Competence Revisited', Report of the Cognitive Science Program, University of California, Berkeley.

Gumperz, J. and Hymes, D. (eds), 1972, *Directions in Socio-linguistics: the ethnography of communication*, New York: Holt, Rinehart and Winston.

Hamayon, R., 1971, 'Pourquoi un Mongol doit-il être nommé?' *Turcica*, 3, 1971, Paris, 143–52.

Hamayon, R. and Bassanoff, N., 1973, 'De la difficulté d'être une belle-fille', *Études Mongoles*, 4.

Haugen, E., 1973, 'The Curse of Babel', *Daedalus*, vol. 102 no 3.

Haviland, J., 1977, *Gossip, Reputation and Knowledge in Zinacantan*, Chicago: University of Chicago Press.

Humphrey, C., 1978, 'Women, Taboo, and the Suppression of Attention' in S. Ardener (ed.), *Defining Women*, Tavistock, London: Tavistock; 1992 Berg (reprint).

_____ , 1983, *Karl Marx Collective: Economy, Society and Religion in a Siberian Collective Farm*, Cambridge: Cambridge University Press.

Voloshinov, V. N. (Bakhtin), 1973 (1929), *Marxism and the Philosophy of Language*, trs. Matejka and Titunik, New York: Seminar Press.

_____ , 1976 (1927), *Freudianism: a Marxist Critique*, trs. I. R. Titunik, New York: Academic Press.

5

Women and Second-Language Knowledge in Rural Soviet Georgia[1]: An Outline

*Nina Chinchaladze and
Tamara Dragadze*

Since in Georgia the native language is seen locally as the conveyor of the talent, psychology and traditions of the nation, it is a very complex subject to write about briefly. The position of women in Georgian society as a whole is also relevant because they have been seen for centuries as the guardians of literacy and the agents of social control in village life (Dragadze 1981, 1988).

The main issue associated with second language and bilingualism in Soviet Georgia is the question of the Russian language, a vehicle of colonial policy there. Georgia, an independent state for the best part of two millennia, was annexed to the Russian empire in 1801 and after a brief period of independence it was re-annexed for a second time in 1921, this time through forced incorporation into the Soviet Union. Under the Russian tsars in the nineteenth century, a system of education for a minimum of two years was promoted throughout Georgia, usually around the village church where education was in Georgian. The nobility, however, were able to have more access to education, mostly in Russian and were also able to learn French. It is interesting to note that a Russian traveller reported that if Georgian boys among the aristocracy went on to higher education it was more because of the insistence of their mothers than their sometimes almost illiterate princely fathers. The Georgian language, which suffered a certain demise, became prominent again at the end of the nineteenth century with the revival of nationalism and the Georgian movement for independence. Nevertheless, the Georgian language was developed and preserved mainly by the peasantry, and Russian was the official state language in which the gentry and aristocracy had a main stake.

After the 1917 Revolution in Russia, the Georgians seized the opportunity to declare independence. The first step was to reinstate Georgian

80

as the official state language, to open a university and several high schools, all of which used Georgian as the language of learning. When the Bolsheviks invaded Georgia in 1921 they were reluctant to banish the Georgian language again, and it has remained the official state language of Soviet Georgia even though, in 1978, quite a political struggle was needed to maintain this.[2] Georgia and Armenia alone were able to retain their own alphabets throughout the Soviet period.

Over the years, Russian has acquired an ambivalent status. In Georgia during the Soviet period as a whole, Russian has been the vehicle for communicating with non-Georgians including many foreigners from the West. It represents progress because scientific and general knowledge has been controlled from Moscow and transmitted in Russian. Russian in the Soviet communist system has been the vehicle for career promotions. The command economy, with so many factories and economic activities managed in Moscow, has also been dependent on Russian-language knowledge.

In Georgian villages, where the tendency is for men to travel and for women to be stationary, it has always been the men who have had to use their knowledge of Russian in daily life, and women have not needed it at all.

The Two Case Studies

The two villages in which we did fieldwork were Tsinsopeli (Chinchaladze) and Ghari (Dragadze). The first was only 3km. from a main industrial town, whereas the latter was in a mountainous area of north-western Georgia but which had a developed tradition of schooling and learning.

Tsinsopeli (with a population of approximately 4,290 in 1990) is in Imereti Province in Western Georgia, 180 km. from the capital Tbilisi and 3km. from Chiatura, a mining town producing manganese with around 68,719 inhabitants. Children went to school in Chiatura where there were residents of various nationalities for whom the lingua franca is Russian. The town had two Russian schools, but nobody from the village went to them; all chose the Georgian ones instead. In Tsinsopeli village, the inhabitants were all Georgian, and women hardly needed the Russian language in their day-to-day lives. The study of Russian from the second year in school (age eight or nine), both in the village school and in Georgian ones in the nearby town; had been compulsory for two or three generations. Yet women, although dedicated to helping their children with their schoolwork, did not usually spend much time on Russian; the reluctant fathers helped half-heartedly. There was nationwide resentment when, in 1985, there was a decree from Moscow that the learning of Russian should be intensified throughout Georgia. Despite the decree, local knowledge of Russian was not good, particularly because women as the chief educators were neither enthusiastic nor competent. Only men through obligatory military service were exposed to the necessity of learning Russian, unless they migrated for seasonal labour to Russia. Their knowledge of the language tended to be selective and largely superficial. Georgian, in contrast, was a language which had to be perfected to gain social acceptance and prestige.

The second village was Ghari, in the province of Ratcha. It had a population of approximately 450, and as it was 4 km. from the district town centre, there were opportunities for employment in the tertiary services as well as in alpine agriculture. In Ghari village there was one school that catered for primary – and middle – school ages, but for the last two years (ninth and tenth year) children had to study in one of the two schools in the nearby town. With a virtually completely homogeneous population, Georgian was the only language used in the region except for the compulsory Russian lessons. State farm accounts had still to be provided in Russian, and although clerks and accountants coped well with the linguistic demands of their jobs, their speech in Russian was less fluent than their written competence. The Communist Party local elite had been trained in Russian-language political schools and occasionally communicated in Russian. Otherwise there was little Russian to be heard in the region, although the increasingly libertarian television programmes beamed from Moscow were watched by local youths with interest.

Women in Ghari village were presented with a dilemma. They felt inadequate to help their children with their Russian lessons, and like the rest of the Georgian population whose national consciousness had been heightened since the massacre by Soviet Russian troops of innocent demonstrators in April 1989, they were reluctant to show any interest. On the other hand, competition among school-leavers for jobs or education was very high in Georgia and presented great difficulties to the villagers, many of whom lacked patronage or income deemed necessary to achieve success for young people. Because of the keen ambition of most villagers for their children to have higher education, some reported that they felt tempted to accept the offers of Russian visitors from remote provincial Russian universities to educate their sons there in return for relatively modest bribes. Their daughters, however, whom they felt they could not send so far away, had to be coached intensively and have money set aside for them in order to acquire the more demanding and expensive training and education in Georgia. Education for girls, although they are expected to marry in their early twenties, is deemed to be very necessary both for income-generating purposes and for developing their female identity as home educators. In Georgian educational institutions the Russian language had a certain amount of importance for examinations, though less so than the correct usage of the Georgian language itself and other subjects.

Discussion

Census data and other investigations for the Soviet period have tended to indicate a higher level of knowledge of Russian than might really have been the case in the Union republics, since it was so positively assessed till recently by the Communist authorities and Russification was associated with assimilation and progress.

The role of women in bilingual environments such as that of rural Soviet Georgia has been significant. Women travel less and are more integrated into local indigenous life than men, who have more encounters with all-Union institutions such as the army or migratory seasonal labour drives. Thus women are less likely to practise their Russian language knowledge even if they studied relatively well in school. This was the case both in Tsinsopeli, where in the neighbouring town of Chiatura visiting villagers would daily meet Georgians and non-Georgians, and in Ghari, where there were few Russians in the whole region. On the other hand, women's role in all rural Georgia as educators, as guardians of literacy and civility, allocates responsibility to them for their children to succeed in school, an ambition of particular importance in the traditions of Ratcha. Their authority in this field is undermined because of their lack of skills in Russian, although in fact several significant exceptions among women were encountered during fieldwork.

In Georgia's drive towards independence from the Russian-dominated Soviet Union, an ambition shared by rural and urban people alike, a positive appraisal was given to the eschewing of the Russian language which symbolised the imposition of Russian imperialism. Women have been praised for this, for remaining untainted by Russification in rural localities. Yet neither the Georgian economy nor its further education system could support self-sufficiency, especially in poor rural areas outside the important networks of patronage and relative wealth which are thought to secure jobs and places for study. Higher education or work in Russia has in the past provided a temporary alternative which, although dreaded by mothers whose sons took advantage of it, had till recently offered an outlet for rural people to fulfil their needs.

Now changes are taking place, with less casual employment available in Russia, fewer offers of higher education there and at the end of all study a virtual collapse of obligatory army recruitment. In 1990–91

Georgia had one of the highest rates of draft-dodging in the Soviet Union, with families no longer willing to expose their sons to the risks of serving in the Soviet Army which used force against minorities including the Georgians.

Viable alternatives for the compulsory teaching of Russian have not yet been put in place in schools by the two successive governments in Georgia. Under the first elected nationalist government in 1990–91, women were exhorted to have more children to increase the size of Georgia's indigenous population, and as is usual in Georgian tradition nationalist rhetoric was used for stressing women's traditional role as educators and propagators of the Georgian language and culture. However, from 1992 onwards people are aspiring to a variety of bilingualism where a western language, English in particular, would replace Russian, and much optimism is being expressed for this to reach rural areas and not to be confined to sophisticated city-dwellers. However long-term these aspirations may be, it is women who will bear ultimate responsibility for the language education of their offspring.

In Soviet Georgia as in some other colonial cases, women's role was crucial in maintaining the high standards of indigenous language teaching and practice in a bilingual environment. Independence has brought the government the possibility of evading Russian domination and of making new choices of political and trading partners. The transition to a market economy is a further factor which will undoubtedly affect women's roles in rural society in Georgia. Given the country's geopolitical position, however, it is unlikely that women will revert to complete monolingualism, in view of the increased mobility that economic development will bring and their role as rural educators, which will in all probability be maintained in the foreseeable future.

Notes

1. This paper was first drafted in 1989, before the October 1990 elections swept the Communist Party away from power in Georgia and before demonstrations and further elections put a new government in power in the now fully independent Republic of Georgia.

2. Street demonstrations, unusual at the time and carrying a high risk of bloodshed, took place in April 1978, to protest at Brezhnev's proposal that Russian should be the state language in all the Union republics.

References

Dragadze, T, 1981, 'The Sexual Division of Domestic Space' in S. Ardener (ed.), *Women and Space*, London: Croom Helm; 1993, Berg (reprint).

Dragadze, T, 1988, *Rural Families in Soviet Georgia,* London: Routledge.

6

Women and Linguistic Innovation in Brittany

Maryon McDonald

Introduction

Brittany is the home of a much-publicised Celtic-speaking minority, and the general image that has been created is one of a world sadly threatened with imminent disappearance. Breton language and culture have been defined as disappearing now for over a hundred years. One of the points that will emerge in the following paragraphs, however, is that Breton culture could be said, in many ways, to be thriving.

In the publicity which Brittany has received, it has often been the women who have been metaphorically summoned on to a national and international stage and required to be the most authentic repositories of Breton culture. Some of the problems and the ironies of this are contained in the ethnographic material presented in this paper. A more general point is that the images both of Brittany and of women have been similar, with minority identity and gender constructs drawn into mutual support. This is true both of their nineteenth-century romantic construction and of a more modern desire for 'liberation' – both in what is generally known as the Breton movement and in the women's liberation movement – from these very same constructs. In the nineteenth century, Breton identity and femininity were drawn up out of a common oppositional symbolism in which French/Breton and men/women were painted in very similar colours. Then, in the twentieth century, and especially since the late 1960s, Breton identity has been aligned with the oppositional symbolism of feminism. The following paragraphs expand on and illustrate the ironies and problems of these alignments.

Two Worlds

I first began research in Brittany at the end of the 1970s, and some of the material presented here draws, therefore, on a period which some would consider to have been the hey day of political counter-culture in France. I spent a year, first of all, in the regional capital of Rennes, studying, meeting, travelling and demonstrating with members of the modern Breton movement. This movement is devoted to the 'defence' of Breton language and culture, and in the political arena it is a movement of broadly 'autonomist' or separatist ambition. After over a year of participation in militant activity, I then moved to a small peasant village called Kerguz, situated in the centre of Finistère, which is the most western and traditionally the most Breton-speaking *département* of Brittany.

In a sense, my research spanned two worlds: the world of the militants of the Breton movement and the world of the peasants. Each of these worlds has a view of the other and each has its own means of resolving any contradictions posed by the other. The militants of the movement are educated urban outsiders, who are seen as such by rural populations even if they might summon up rural origins for themselves. Since the early or mid-1970s, a few militants have been living in and around the Finistère village of Kerguz (which had a population of 32 when I first moved there). In Kerguz, which is situated within the parish and administrative commune of Plounéour-Ménez (population 1,245), the two worlds have met in a quite concrete way. Most members of the Breton movement are, and always have been, well educated, often to university level, and almost all have been well-schooled in French.[1] The peasants of Kerguz are native Breton-speakers, and have had relatively little schooling. This is an important, if not surprising, difference between the militants and the 'people' on whose behalf they claim to speak.

The French Context

France is a country with large indigenous regional minorities, and there has been no strong desire in the past on the part of France's central authorities to summon these minorities into official existence. In comparison with that of Great Britain, the history of France appears as one of insecurity and frequent constitutional change, and much of the political reflection which, in Britain, could have been invested in conjuring internal minorities into existence was concerned in France with the existence of the French nation itself. France has been occupied by foreign forces, enemies and allies, four times in the last two hundred years, and, from a combination of external interference and internal self-consciousness, has tried to define its way over the same period through two monarchies, one consulate, two empires, five republics, one definitive revolution, the Paris Commune, the Vichy régime and the disturbances of May 1968. Faced with this succession of external threat and international upheaval, Paris has never been sufficiently sure of the integrity of France to wish into existence other identities within it: that would have risked rendering even more problematic the nature of France itself. On the contrary, France and the Jacobin State have given to the world a model of directive centralisation. Unable to tolerate the theoretical or actual possibility of variety within its boundaries, the French state allowed no comfortable political space that a minority could occupy.

The French language and French national identity have been inextricably linked, and it is only in relatively recent times – since the new, self-consciously international context of the post-Second World War years – that the cause of promoting any regional language or dialect has become respectable in national political debate rather than being cast as dangerously reactionary or seditious. And it is only since the 1960s and 1970s that the cause of a regional language such as Breton has moved from being the property of political reaction to being the property of the political left. This occurred under a broadly right-wing regime, giving the national left an oppositional ticket and the possibility of co-opting the vote of the minority enthusiasts. Decentralisation was also on offer. The groups and societies that make up the Breton movement tend nevertheless to take a definitional distance from the national parties of the left and try resolutely to remain un-French. Moreover, many would not see the decentralisation of France as in any way synonymous with their own vision of an autonomous and distinctly un-French Brittany. At least part of this vision derives from a wistful and provocative comparison with the position of other Celtic areas such as Wales and Scotland. However, the internal structure of the United Kingdom might readily permit such areas a political autonomy and nationhood in a way that the French context would not.

Femininity: A Political Imagery

In France, femininity as an ideal image of woman, her nature and her place, became firmly established in the nineteenth century and particularly during the reign of Louis-Philippe. Much of the structural imagery involved in the feminine/masculine duality (with all its positively or negatively evaluated correlates of irrationality/rationality) was carried on from the elite salons of the eighteenth century. The dominant political opposition groups of the nineteenth century – the camp of republicanism on the one hand and of ultra-Catholic and aristocratic legitimism on the other – both sent their ideal woman back to the home and to wifely and maternal duties, but not without a certain charm and glamour. The fighting women of the Revolution were placed in parentheses, and by the 1830s, under Louis-Philippe, the *citoyenne* of the 1789 Revolution had already become, once again, *Madame*.

This femininity then gathered to itself the moral and spiritual values of sentiment, intuition and prudent tradition in opposition to anything perceived thereafter as rationalism's excess. The notion of woman as the guardian of morality and tradition was not entirely new, but the dualities involved began, from the 1830s onwards, to take on a coherence they had never had before. In romantic accounts of the old province, Brittany became an untouched and 'virginal beauty' (Souvestre (1835–7) 1971: xiv–xv), and femininity was further draped over Brittany when philology constructed Breton as a Celtic language. Priests and aristocrats appropriated an increasingly common metaphoric of femininity and masculinity to oppose Celtic and Latin, and to describe and define a Breton language and culture in moral and political opposition to the self-consciously rational and increasingly secular French world that threatened their own status and influence (see McDonald, 1989: especially Chapters 6 and 14).

By the end of the nineteenth century there was a recognisable metaphoric of 'femininity' amongst the bourgeoisie in France, as well as amongst the clergy and the fading ranks of the aristocracy. There was also an educated conflation of this femininity and Celticness. From some members of the Breton aristocracy and clergy, who are now seen as founders of the Breton movement and who saw themselves as moral and spiritual guardians of a distinctly Breton world, we have Breton language and culture turning an oppositional and metaphorically feminine face to France. The sentiment that divided and opposed Breton and French, and Brittany and France, in this way was one conceived by well-educated men in the context of French internal politics.

However, Brittany has been officially part of France since the early sixteenth century, by which time some form of French had already been the language of power and nobility within Brittany for a few hundred years. Since at least the 1789 Revolution, when the French Republic was first established, the Breton population has, in one way or another, been living a certain Frenchness. In order to understand the Frenchness and the evaluations of Breton lived by women in Brittany we have to return to the wider context and look briefly at the question of education. Here we find both women and Breton invoked in the quarrel of Church and State, a clerical/republican battle that has so dominated French political life.

Women and Education

Where formal education for girls existed in the nineteenth century, it was overwhelmingly religious education in church-run private schools, and especially so in Brittany. [2] And yet women had, by all parties, been allotted the prime role of wife and mother, the great moral and educative force of the nation. Jules Ferry, the ardent republican who brought compulsory free lay education for both sexes to all parts of France in the 1880s, was driven in 1870 to speak of women's 'secret and persistent support' for the old order, for 'the society that is passing and which we are going to chase out forever'. He went on: 'The Bishops know full well that he who holds sway over the women holds all, because he has influence over the children and secondly over the husbands. That's why the Church wants to hold on to the women (but) democracy has to choose, on pain of death: either the women belong to science or they belong to the Church' (cited in Prost, 1968: 268–9).

Ferry might well have added that they either learn some French or continue with only Breton. It was of constant concern to educationists and politicians, right on into the early years of this century, that Breton women might know little or no French.[3] More boys were schooled, and they also had military service where the national language was learnt. Girls meanwhile usually had only poor-quality religious schools, if any, and often knew only Breton pious works. Women were under the Church, and under the influence, too, of self-consciously Breton clerics who were known to fear the 'invasion' of French and sin in single focus. In the republican camp, therefore, it was feared that women in Brittany were in danger of being isolated, and moreover of not bringing up French citizens.

Since the 1789 Revolution France had made the French language the very definition of the French nation, of that 'single and indivisible republic', and in a spirit of 'liberty, equality and fraternity' the authorities had set about securing the simultaneous spread of French, of rationality and of citizenship.[4] Confirming republican fears of Rome, of 'superstition' and reaction, however, the Breton movement, increasingly clerical, went on into the twentieth century to conflate the Breton language, faith and salvation into an ever purer, isolated, rural simplicity that was, for them, Breton culture (Elegoët, 1979). On the one hand, nineteenth-century school inspectors urged more and more schools for · girls in Brittany, both to combat this clerical hold and to get French and 'civilization' into Breton families.[5] On the other hand, Breton linguistic scholars, who had come to join the nobles and clerics, protested angrily as more and more Breton women and their children were turning to French, an evaluation they saw as imposed from Paris and encouraged by the then proliferating 'maternal' or nursery schools (anon., 1895).[6] In 1886, there were an estimated 1,300,000 Breton-speakers; today there are an estimated 500,000. There has therefore been an overall drop of more than 60 per cent in the number of Breton-speakers, but the population of Brittany increased by over 4 per cent over the same period and the population of Finistère has similarly risen by an overall 13.6 per cent. It is not simply a matter, then, of life-long Breton speakers having died off. It is more a question of a significant switch to French. And it is not the case that this adoption of French has been any straightforward imposition from Paris.

In the departmental archives of Finistère there is evidence that as early as 1831 for example, the local Breton education committee, with Breton-speaking members, was refusing a larger space to Breton in Finistère's schools, even though the government was offering it.[7] Later on local Breton republicans were actively complaining of still too much Breton in the schools.[8] Significantly, in 1846 a Breton municipal education committee happily reported that a woman teacher had begun educating their local girls; they reported that the pupils were introducing into the families a 'healthy morality' and 'the habit of using French', and that all this had brought 'a certain polish which softens the savagery and natural roughness of the peasants' (cited in Ogès, 1934: 143).

Travelling tradesmen and relatively wealthy and well-respected horse-dealers helped to bring new ideas, republicanism and a smattering of French to even the most isolated upland areas of Brittany – including Plounéour-Ménez – from the Revolutionary period onwards (Ariès, 1948: 54–5). The Léon, a former diocese, has traditionally been the most clerical and most Breton-speaking area of Finistère. Plounéour-Ménez has been part of the Léon. However, just after the Revolution, one Léon commune was already wanting a government girls' school, but complained: 'we have no female teacher; no woman yet dares to show herself as a republican' (year VI; cited in Ogès, 1942: 133). Things have changed since.

During my first summer living in rural Finistère, I went to a Breton-language Mass in the old Cistercian Abbey of Le Relecq, a hamlet near Kerguz, and also in Plounéour-Ménez. Apart from the occasional Breton hymns, Mass is usually celebrated in French. This once-a-year Breton Mass has been mounted by a section of the diminishing Léon clergy, more out of Catholic nostalgia and devotion than any radical language militantism; and they also have an eye on the possible attraction of newcomers and tourists. In a *commune* which, like so many others in France, has been actively involved in its own version of national Church/State battles, church buildings have been neglected by the municipal council, and any funding from collections at services is very welcome to the priest. The bishop of the diocese came along for this Breton Mass: he delivered an impassioned sermon in Breton to a full congregation, mostly women, and many of them no longer practising Catholics but there for this special occasion. The bishop complained that Brittany was no longer producing its traditionally high quota of boys and girls for Holy Orders. He blamed it on the mothers: they were not bringing up their children properly. Quiet smiles appeared on several faces, and I afterwards had coffee with a group of local women, who spent some time ridiculing the sermon, and doing so in French. Amongst these women was the wife of a former mayor of the *commune*, whose own father had been mayor before him, and the conversation involved some self-consciously republican family pride. The mayors and municipal council of Plounéour-Ménez have long boasted their own form of political radicalism (a 'red' politics), which is best defined as anti-clericalism, and the *commune* has seen well over a hundred years of willing education of its girls in French.

Related evidence of local sentiment and ambition was offered when a new priest took up office in the parish. This new priest had just returned to Brittany after many years' mission abroad. Unlike his predecessor he had in an earlier era been actively involved in the Breton movement. One of his first actions now was to increase the number of Breton hymns at weekly Mass. The local faithful quite liked this, noting at the same time that he had also reintroduced the old Latin *credo*. However, this priest then tried to deliver his weekly sermons in Breton and was met with swift reaction. Notes were delivered to his presbytery from local women, expressly asking him not to speak Breton. With sadness, he explained to me that: 'it is almost as if Breton smells of cow-shit [*kaoc'h saout*, Br.] to them. They think they are ladies [*Mesdames*, Fr.].'

Femininity: From Cow-Shit to Finery

Aristocratic and bourgeois notions of ideal femininity were not evident amongst the early nineteenth-century peasantry. In the 1830s educated travellers to inland Brittany, including the Plounéour-Ménez area, reported that women there seemed to be less valued by men than their animals and were the submissive vassals of the peasant men (see Brousmiche (1829–31) 1977, II: 205; Ariès 1948: Chapter 1). Although we might grant the peasant world its own unacknowledged, autonomous construction of male/female difference here, we can certainly allow that life on the land was hard and very different from the life of town ladies. Peasant women would barely have recognised the symbolism of femininity that was opposing them and their men to France.

By the end of the nineteenth century, however, the production of crude home-spun home-woven cloth for local use or for the linen trade had virtually gone, and had given way in some areas to the making of lace for the delicate garments of elegant Parisian ladies (Ariès, 1948: 34). Breton women were not slow in making new fashions part of their own world. In 1920s a visitor to Saint-Pol-de-Léon, the cathedral town of the old Léon diocese near the north coast, noticed that the women there had abandoned the dark traditional costume of their mothers, with its apron and discreet white *coiffe*, and were 'all flaunting themselves in lavish city attire; their legs, pinkened by flesh-coloured stockings, are perched on high-heeled shoes' (cited in Ariès, 1948: 59).

It is perhaps no coincidence that such fashionableness should have been evident in a town near the coast. The coastal areas and the towns in general had long been a pole of attraction away from the land and the interior, creating a demographic density around the edge of Brittany and a relative sparsity inland. Since the eighteenth century especially, government finance had helped to create relative wealth and security nearer the coast, in maritime and administrative interests. A popular scorn for the land was progressively manifest in the nineteenth century, in migrations to the coast and sometimes outside Brittany also, including to Paris. Migrations became permanent emigrations in the second half of the century, with visits home that increasingly framed the towns, the coast, security, finery and French as a single powerful pole of all that the peasant condition was not.

The flight of both men and women from the land was well under way in the 1930s,[9] but it was overtaken by a predominantly female exodus from agriculture after the Second World War. Since the end of the nineteenth century there had been a growing aspiration to be a housewife, or a town lady, or anything but a peasant's wife (cf. Weber, 1977: 174). This trend was now accentuated, particularly as the length of girls' schooling was beginning to catch up with that of boys. From the mid-1950s to the mid-1970s, the rate of female emigration from the land rose steadily, surpassing the figure for men, both for Brittany overall and for Finistère alone (see Trégouët, 1978). Plounéour-Ménez is still an agricultural commune in land use and in external image and self-image, and agriculture is still by far the largest single occupational sector. By the mid-1970s, however, only 18 per cent of the total population, or 46 per cent of the active population, were actually working farms, whereas a little over a decade before these proportions had been 37.5 per cent and 72.3 per cent respectively. Over the same period there was an overall drop of almost 18.6 per cent in the population of the commune, and yet there were significant increases in nearby and less agricultural communes all the way up to the nearest town of Morlaix, near the north coast. Of the young aged 15–24 years in Plounéour-Ménez in

1962, one and a half times as many girls as boys had left by 1968.[10] The economic area of the *pays de Morlaix*, which includes Plounéour, shows an increase over the same period of almost 11 per cent of women working in the tertiary sector (and 1.7 per cent of men; SEMENF, 1976: 49). In the village of Kerguz itself villagers can conjure up a time in living memory when over one hundred people were still living off small plots of land; there are now only three farms and two active peasants' wives. Each has sisters who have moved away and married salaried men. Another woman recently persuaded her husband to give up their farm and take a job in Morlaix. She is now a proud housewife, working part-time in a shop, and has elegant clothes and a new house with modern furniture, amenities and the general organisation of space that peasant homes lack. She would frequently show off her new home to visitors and point out in careful French the welcome difference between her new life-style and the 'hard, dirty' life she had previously known on a farm and which she so hated.

Femininity and French have arrived, and together they can speak a sophistication that is other than peasant work. The comment of the new priest which I cited earlier is already suggestive of the reality of these values in local life; such values do not necessarily manifest themselves in overt action of the kind involved in actually taking variously plaintive or hostile notes to the presbytery. Rather, they present themselves through the unreflecting proprieties of daily behaviour.

Women can define their femininity, and men their masculinity, through the language they use, and language-use has its correlates in social space. The fields and certain bars tend to be male domains, and in all-male company of a certain age Breton is the usual language of communication. Sanctions against the use of French here include a fear of being thought 'stuck-up' (*fier*, Br.). Contrasting with this world of rough and ready masculinity are certain female domains such as the special *salon* or parlour set aside in many farmhouses for guests. Sanctions against the use of Breton here are tacit but still forceful; Breton is not used at polite tea-parties.

In the militant world, the choice of language is a self-consciously political act, and the Breton/French linguistic difference is, for the movement, a political opposition. At the local level, amongst native speakers of Breton in daily life, language choice is not a political statement and the Breton/French difference is not a political opposition. Local speakers could choose to make these things explicitly political, and especially so in the context of a country in which language, identity and politics have been so strongly associated. However, in the daily round language choice has more to do with local and familial structures of identity or social status – including gender, age and occupation, for example – than with any self-consciously political statement of French or Breton identity.

Village women in Kerguz commonly speak Breton to their husbands and other men, and both Breton and French when helping the men in the fields. One locally-born woman has returned to the village with her husband after a working life as a domestic in Paris; her husband, from a nearby village, worked on the railways there. Anna speaks Breton to her husband but likes to speak French as the voice of sophistication in the village, including when helping out in the fields. Whatever her life was like in Paris, Anna is glamour in the village. She soon installed a bathroom, toilet and central heating in her house, none of which the other local women had. When the men are out drinking rough red wine, playing *boules* or working with the machines, women like to visit each other for coffee and sweet cakes in the afternoon. This has long been a rather special, and now distinctly feminine, thing to do. Anna prefers tea to coffee, and often declines the cakes, as she is slimming. She prefers dainty savouries anyway. The other women admire her sense of refinement and allow her to conjure up, in French, a world of fashion and ladylike good taste for which this female Breton world allows ample space.

Such afternoon conversations over tea and coffee move between Breton and French. When the men are present at evening gatherings of the whole village, such as occur at New Year, the women sit together at one end of a long table with their sweet cakes and sweet wine and speak predominantly in French, and the men pack together at the other end in a haze of cigarette smoke, eating cheap *pâté* and drinking hard liquor, playing dominoes or cards, and speaking predominantly in Breton. While Anna at one end speaks French to the women, her husband at the other end speaks Breton to the men.

A sense of finery and fashion as the prerogative of the women is well established. Often peasant women buy all the clothes for their husbands and unmarried sons, including their best Sunday shoes. Peasant men take some pride in saying that they couldn't care less about what they wear, not because they do not dress up when appropriate, but because men can, symbolically and actually, leave such things to women. Such a male/female distinction extends also to what is, in local self-perception at least, the relatively novel notion of romantic love: 'The women like that sort of thing', the men say. In order to halt the exodus of women from the rural areas in the 1950s and 1960s, Catholic groups worked hard in Brittany, as elsewhere in France, to try to publicise the idea that love and romance could exist in a peasant setting (see, for example,

J.A.C.-M.R.J.C. 1979: 72–3; here one sees somewhat unlikely pictures, produced in the 1950s and 1960s, of peasant men giving bouquets to their women). Marriage, traditionally an alliance between families and arranged by parents or a go-between with a keen sense of social status and an eye on access to land, had become, especially for the women, a matter of individual choice that could operate with rather different criteria. French terms had already come in: for example, an *akord* (/akɔrd/ cf. French *accord*) was an initial agreement after which a couple became *fianset* (/fi:aⁿsɛd/ cf. French *fiancé(e)*), or engaged. A girlfriend or a boyfriend, a relatively new status, is a *bon ami* (/bɔn ami:/ cf. French *bon(ne) ami(e)*). There is a more live and obvious Frenchness in this area, too. I was one day talking in Breton with a rather drunken group of ageing bachelor peasant acquaintances; suddenly, one took hold of my hand, much to the amusement of his mates, and kissed it and said '*Enchanté, Mademoiselle*'. Everyone laughed. 'Be quiet', he said, back in Breton now, 'just shut up – you're jealous. *Je fais la cour*'. It was generally agreed that he was 'a one for the girls'.

Liberation

In the meantime various forms of feminism have appeared in French educated circles. Simone de Beauvoir's work *Le Deuxième Sexe*, published in 1949, was keenly taken up after the wide protests and upheavals of May 1968. Femininity was denaturalised, declared to be arbitrary and a myth for the definition and pleasure of men whereby woman had become man's own incorporated 'half' (Beauvoir, 1949, I: 205–38, 313). Other well-known feminist writers in France went on explicitly to link their 'struggle' with that of the 'oppressed' and 'ethnic minorities' everywhere, including that of the Bretons in France (see for example, Halimi, 1973; Groult, 1975). Meanwhile the Breton movement itself espoused a more youthful and secular political radicalism after 1968, and had made feminism, the peasantry and Breton synonymous in a vision of a new 'alternative society'.

Feminism has also been felt within the ranks of the movement itself. Female student militants in Rennes refused to do any more typing for their male counterparts, and Breton Women's Groups were briefly set up in the towns. These groups disbanded largely because the cause of Breton language and culture and the cause of female liberation, whilst united in common opposition to the 'system', began to conflict when the definition was required to be positive rather than negative and when practical priorities had to be asserted. Different values of what it means to be 'Breton' – in this instance, Breton-speaking and feminist – which might unite the movement externally, in its appropriation of the popular world in opposition to all things 'French', can also come into conflict within the militant world when the context of definition, or just what is 'Breton' and what is 'French', is unclear. There have been militant women who have firmly declared that they want more front-line roles and would no longer be content just to marry a male militant (*un emsaver*) and breed Breton-speaking children (see 'War-du an istorekadur' in *Emsav* 1975: 106: 335–63).

This has not been an easy objective to realise, and it is noticeable that those few female militants who do have prominent roles in the movement are still those who have first done their duty as Breton-speaking wives and mothers. One of the leading Breton-learning manuals (Denez, 1972) has been strongly criticised in Breton-learning courses for its tendency to present women in traditional feminine roles; the women in the book are often engaged in nice housewifely duties, for example, cleaning, cooking and mothering for their menfolk, and they sometimes show great interest in the feminine frills of urban finery and fashion. The author's main defence has been that his book is simply describing life as it is lived. At the same time, all the characters in the book, of whatever age, gender and milieu, speak Breton and only Breton and are clearly committed to doing so.

To many female militants, learning and speaking Breton is liberation enough, but there are others who have gone a stage further in pursuit of Breton authenticity. A number of young women, sometimes with their partners or husbands, have moved back to the Breton countryside in a general back-to-the-land trend in France, and have become 'peasants' or 'artisans' in their own image of this popular world as an unconstrained, unbourgeois, and un-French naturality; they feel they have shed intellectuality and the system, they have learnt Breton, and they are living in studied and rugged ecological simplicity.[11]

I know of twenty-five or more such couples and sundry individuals who live in the area in and around Plounéour, some of them now working individual farms after having tried to set up a collective commune (or *communauté*) in the mountains. One young couple in Kerguz, keen on wholemeal foods and home-weaving, work a tiny vegetable plot, live in a tumble-down house, collect social security and have set up a windmill to generate electricity. Anna, their nearest neighbour, complains that the windmill is noisy and unnecessary, and regards all their bits of metal and old crocks as a sheer 'mess' that is marring the view of the smart, renovated frontage and garden of her 'modern' home. What Anna regards as 'mess' the young couple regard as 'recycling'.

Another back-to-the-country, militant couple in Kerguz are held in a little more respect. He is a psychologist commuting daily to a clinic in Morlaix; she is a teacher-turned-artisan, having taken a course in carpentry. Next door to them live a lively 67-year-old local widow called Thérèse and her 42-year-old unmarried son, called Iffig. Thérèse and Iffig still have some livestock and wood-holdings, but rent out most of their farmland since Thérèse's husband has died and her son now commutes daily to a job as a railway-workman further north. Thérèse has often shown me her hands: 'Look at them, all red, swollen and ugly'. Years of farmwork and helping her husband and then their son on their wood-holding have taken their toll. Many of the local women, including Thérèse, would often admire my hands: 'So white and delicate, like the hands of a town lady'. At first I was sceptical of such comments, which might easily be made in mockery; such scepticism, however, whilst not wholly inappropriate, was, I came to see, born of another world. When helping out in the fields or in the woods, I was seriously urged to put on gloves: 'Don't spoil those hands'. Meanwhile Thérèse's educated neighbour was gaining splinters, blisters and calluses from her carpentry – and yet she could, in her own Breton world, display her hands with a certain pride.

Such apparently diverse examples as old crocks and hands might serve to underline the simple point that the same mundane objects can have very different definitions and meanings when placed in different value systems. Similarly, acts which, within the female militant world, are perceived as displays of naturalness and liberation are often, within the local world, perceived as rude and embarrassing in polite female company (see McDonald, 1989 for further examples). Local Breton women are often felt to live an already feminist existence, and much about them, their life, their work, their language, is willingly taken up by the militant world as confirmation of this view. For example, the fact that local women in the rural world have usually continued to be known by their maiden name after marriage has been seen as evidence of the already feminist, liberated nature of the native-speaking female Breton population. However, the use of the maiden name does not conflict with or contest the civil use of the husband's name and it is usually by the title of *Madame*, plus the married name, that village women like to be publicly presented, particularly to strangers. Outside the contexts of kinship and locality the use of the maiden name easily feels, to these women themselves, parochial and old-fashioned.

Such a different evaluation, in the militant world and in the local world, of what might appear to be the 'same' objects, titles, acts or gestures clearly has linguistic or sociolinguistic correlates. Very different evaluations of the Breton and French languages, and of the

Breton/French language difference, are involved. However, local women can incorporate new enthusiasms, including enthusiasm for speaking Breton, without this assimilation of new evaluations being, for them, the political stand and the 'liberation' that militant epistemology and politics require it to be. Whilst enthusiasm for speaking Breton is, within the militant world, a political enthusiasm, responses to this enthusiasm by local women which involve them actually complying and speaking Breton rather than French, as the educated outsiders now require, are not in their own terms political acts. In their own world their compliance follows other channels, other structures of identity and evaluation. These popular values find no easy space, however, in the militant world which claims to represent them.

For those in the towns the inland mountain area of Brittany has long been a metaphor of true, surviving Bretonness, and when I left the regional capital of Rennes to go to the tiny village of Kerguz, up in the mountains, the militants assured me that this was a place where I would be sure to find straightforward, empirical evidence of Brittany's truly 'Breton culture'. In later conversations with militant friends I was warned not to be distracted by 'superficial' discrepancies such as consumer goods and French, which can be explained, and to persist with Breton in order to find the 'real' Breton culture to which they themselves aspire. The minority identity has, it is assumed, been historically overlain with external accretions that have brought false consciousness. Such accretions include femininity, finery and French. Views of this kind are not peculiar to the Breton militants, of course. The increased general interest in modern France in its rural areas has been linked to a decline in the agricultural population, and, coinciding as it has done with feminist sensibilities and peasant riots alike, it is perhaps not surprising that there has been a fast growth of social science studies focusing on rural peasant women (cf. Lagrave, 1983). Such studies tend to assert either that rural women are particularly dominated and oppressed, or that they have power and authority that other women do not have. Whichever view is required, rural women are and have been called on to support it: either they are the proper focus of feminist concern because they are particularly oppressed, or they are the proper object of feminist attention because they are already feminist, liberated, untouched by the femininity that modern feminism rejects. These theses are not necessarily contradictory, and in the ranks of the Breton movement, they become a question of all women in Brittany being properly liberated and Breton – as they should be once such external accretions as I have mentioned are absent or are taken away. Whether the women use French (=oppressed) or Breton (=liberated) can easily appear to the militants to be confirmation and justification of their own world and cause. The movement has a discourse which, no doubt well-intentionedly, invokes local women, but which these women are powerless to contest. There is little space in the militant world for accepting, other than as pathology or alienation, that Bretons have themselves valued and opted for French. In pointing this out, I am not seeking to challenge the authenticity of the militants' world, which is quite authentically Breton in its own way. If we talk of a popular Breton culture, however, then it contains, especially for women, a peculiar Frenchness that the militant world self-consciously rejects.

The popular world values French and education highly, and the women are particularly implicated here. Maternal responsibilities demand a special sensitivity to education, and a childless woman risks low esteem on a number of counts. When a woman is childless her womanhood is suspect, and when on top of this she is herself uneducated social respect can be hard to attain. Local evaluations that village women in Kerguz have of one another fully suggest this complex of values. Thérèse herself, for example, is highly esteemed amongst local village women, and this in spite of the thrifty simplicity in which she lives. She has a hard-working son, and for her age-group is regarded as relatively educated by local standards: she stayed at school until thirteen years of age, and she continues to read a good deal and takes a wide interest in current affairs. One of the other local women is regarded as particularly stupid, however; this woman has had relatively few years of schooling. It is said of her in the village, with some amusement, that when told of Kennedy's assassination, she simply asked: 'Kennedy? Is he from Plounéour?' This same woman is childless, and also readily speaks Breton to me and has problems with French. She is rarely invited to coffee by the other women (only once a year, it seems, at Christmas time); indeed, the other women often pointed out to me that they found her fat and uncouth, and on one occasion my attention was drawn to the fact that she has a moustache. One of her redeeming features, however, as far as the other village women are concerned, is that she keeps a pretty flower-garden. The fields are an ideally male domain now, and gardening of this kind is, by contrast, very feminine. Much to militant regret, the popular Breton terms for garden and flowers – *jardin* (/ʒaːrdin/) and *fleurs* (/flør/) – are, as in so many areas of ornateness and finery, taken from the French; literary and militant 'standard' Breton prefers *liorzh* (/liːɔrs/) and *bleuniou* (/blønju/), which, to the women of Kerguz, signify untended or overgrown land and wild blossom, respectively.

It would seem that just when the militants are aspiring to a certain ruggedness and naturality, to the countryside, the Breton language and some grass-roots Breton authenticity, the Breton women are looking to femininity, the towns and French. We might pause to recall here that 'femininity' was used by the early Breton movement to cast the whole of Brittany in opposition to France and to declare it distinctly un-French. The modern discourse of feminism might, revealingly, see this as the definition of Breton culture into a self-limiting and self-denigrating 'half' of an overall, French world. Indeed, this has been pointed out for the Scottish Gaels, defined into a 'half-world' by very similar structures (Chapman, 1978). The Breton militants, however, prefer to see the phenomenon as part of a general 'colonisation' of Brittany and of women by France and by men. It is striking, and equally revealing, that the imagery of femininity that cast the 'Breton' world in studious opposition to things French has, once translated into the popular peasant world, been a powerful motor of Frenchness. Further, women's double 'colonisation', in the militants' terms, by both French and men, has given them now a greater competence in, and access to, a world of refinement. Pursuit of this refinement has virtually emptied the countryside of young women, and in their own terms this was a form of liberation. For local women liberation has been measured not against some male-dominated bourgeois life but against the rigours and insecurities of the peasant life – that 'hard, dirty' life.

The Mother-Tongue

All this has left a striking toll of unmarried men in the rural areas. It is perhaps significant that a very common New Year greeting in the mountain areas is '*Bloavezh mat hag ur bourgeoise a-roak fin ar bloaz*', which might translate as: 'I wish you a Happy New Year and a lady wife before it's out'. Sometimes the only apparently available women are back-to-the-land enthusiasts who would like to speak Breton to their children. However, the local ageing bachelors tend to be in awe of these women's education, and it is a common sentiment amongst them that they would in any case be strongly opposed to any wife of theirs speaking Breton to their children.

The notion of the 'mother-tongue' is a widely evocative metaphor; from early philology to many modern education policies there has been some image of primitive primacy and primordial cultural attachment, and the notion has gathered an increasing moral imperativeness associated with the relationship of mother to child.[12] Although in the complex Breton bilingual world the concept has no easy translation, the Breton militants have invented a Breton term for it (*yezh mamm*), and have pleaded for almost a hundred years for Breton in the schools on the grounds of its being the 'mother-tongue' of Breton children. In the late 1960s and 1970s, they were still pleading this[13] but had been overtaken by popular evaluations of French, with Breton-speaking mothers speaking French to their children. The generational gymnastics that can now seem to be involved here, within any one family, usually have a wholly unreflecting symbolic rectitude of their own. In order to give the reader some idea of the familial sociolinguistic relations in which the local Breton-speaking mother might now commonly live, I have given an ideal-type, schematic summary in a note[14] (and for further details see McDonald, 1989). Militants now speak of a 'break in the chain' of generations, and by this they mean particularly the use of French by Breton-speakers of the generations that might include their own parents or grandparents. A few militants have been brought up in Breton by parents who were themselves members of the Breton movement. It is often the case that other militants who had, in their own childhood, occasion to hear and understand any Breton will have done so through close contact with their grandparents.

Breton-speaking children are now rare, and mothers now speaking Breton to their small children are usually militants who have themselves learnt or re-learnt the language. In 1975 an influential Breton manual stated quite simply that if Breton was no longer the mother-tongue, then they would have to make it so, and have Breton in nursery or 'maternal' schools ('*écoles maternelles*' in French) and get mothers to use it too (Gwegen, 1975: 267–73). In May 1977 a new militant organisation called *Diwan* ('seed') began setting up independent Breton-language nursery schools, with a strong sense of the power of 'maternal' schools (*skolioù mamm* in 'standard' Breton) to realise the image of a rightfully Breton-speaking childhood and a properly Breton-speaking motherhood. However, it was later calculated that of the 119 young *Diwan* mothers involved in 1979–80, for example, under 23 per cent felt they knew enough Breton to speak it to their children at home, and only 6.7 per cent were actually doing so along with their husbands; none of these mothers (eight in all) had themselves been brought up to speak Breton by their own mothers, and half of them came from outside Brittany. Moreover their own little children were happily speaking French amongst themselves in the *Diwan* schools. With an intuition of the scale of the problem, a 1980 Congress of all *Diwan* members urgently discussed the question (in a special 'Bretonisation' committee) of how to get more of the mothers to learn Breton and to speak it to their children at home. Mothers present, however, objected that they had jobs and no time to learn Breton, and there was a general female protest, too, that it was a chauvinist argument to expect militant mothers to bear the load; it could perhaps be the fathers' responsibility. Some hesitation and confusion followed. Proportionately more of the fathers in fact knew or were still learning some Breton, and it was gradually agreed that the fathers could help out. However, it was felt then, and still is, that the mother's language is all-important. The idea of '*langue paternelle*' caused some chuckles: 'father-language', it seems, does not easily replace one's 'mother-tongue'.

There are very many more men than women in the Breton movement, and the fluent Breton-speaking male militant has great problems finding a mate who will match his Breton fluency. The few female militants who have been brought up in Breton in older families of the movement (sometimes known, in the movement itself, as *ar mafia*, 'the mafia') have little trouble finding a partner or spouse within the movement's ranks, or they recruit from outside. However, their brothers, and male militants generally, have greater difficulty and cannot easily bring wives or partners from outside into the core of the movement. As I have already indicated, the demands are far greater on the women, expected as they are to become fluent Breton-speaking mothers. Relationships can break up over this issue, with the women leaving home and in some instances taking up a stand of freedom in disaffected hostility to all things Breton. There are also male militants, born of militant families, who have themselves decided to join the disaffected fringe and remain with their predominantly French-speaking partners. In such cases the men have commonly been accused, from within the core ranks of the movement, of being 'traitors' for taking up with such women. Militants have generally agreed (and reaffirmed more widely in, for example, an Inter-Celtic Congress held in Ireland in 1984) that the future of the Celtic languages lies with the women; they, it seems, were important agents in the advance of the majority tongue and they it must be who are to remedy the situation. As several women in rural Brittany have said to me: 'First they wanted us to speak French, now they want us to speak Breton.' This is, I think, an apt comment on a situation in which the power and centre of definition are always elsewhere.

In a curious and interesting way, the structural values of femininity, feminism, the peasant, and French and Breton have met and crossed. Such a crossing, or apparent contradiction, of values need not, however, cause conflict at the local level. Different values may simply be incorporated into existing structures and gather their own contextual proprieties. Jeanne is in her forties and a hard-working, Breton-speaking peasant's wife on the largest, most modern farm in Kerguz. She keeps her home spotlessly clean, visits a hairdresser in a neighbouring commune when she can, tries hard to be slim, and has great ambitions for her five sons, aged from seven to twenty. Paul, her eldest son, failed his studies, did his military service, and then 'dropped out', doing odd jobs elsewhere. In Plounéour, however, he met a very wealthy German girl named Katrin, who speaks good French and had dropped out of her own higher education at home to come and live in Brittany, where she joined up with the Breton militants. Katrin feels she is a liberated woman. One afternoon, Jeanne, well-groomed and in a smart dress, came to my door. She spontaneously spoke some Breton to me for the first time, and invited me to coffee. I went to coffee, still somewhat puzzled as to why Jeanne had spoken some Breton to me like that. Katrin talked, over coffee, of glamorous trips to America and of how she would show Paul the world. There were some hints of marriage. Jeanne looked proud at this prospect for her son. Katrin had a Breton-learning manual with her. 'Tell her how you learnt Breton,' said Jeanne to me excitedly. 'She wants to learn it too.' As if by way of explanation, Katrin then talked inspiredly of Atlantis, the Inkas, the Indians, of strange mysteries, of Woman, of Babylon, the Celts and the Beginning of the World. She smiled at her boyfriend and said what wonderful natural people these were, and there were suggestions that her parents might buy him a farm. Katrin was ready to be a peasant's wife. Paul, the 'peasant' now of his girlfriend's world, then tried, for the first time in his life, to stammer out a few Breton words. 'I never learnt it,' he said, 'my mother never spoke it to me.' Jeanne looked embarrassed, self-consciously tidied her hair, and busied herself with the coffee and cakes. 'I can help you learn some now,' she volunteered finally, as the dutiful mother who had always tried to do the best for her son. Katrin smiled, tossed her long, untidy locks aside, rolled a cigarette, and wiped her hands on her kaftan and fashionable dungarees. 'You must speak some Breton to Paul,' she said to Jeanne, 'so he can teach me.' Jeanne obligingly uttered a few Breton phrases, then changed into old trousers and overalls, and went off to milk her cows. Outside in the gathering dark her hair-do was slowly wrecked in the wind and rain, and I later heard her shouting a few words at the cows in Breton, as she usually did when taking them back to the fields in a totally different Breton world.

This is a world where a good mother, by definition, speaks nicely to children, but this can involve a structure of values so strong that in a peasant family up near a town on the coast, where I stayed for a week during my research, the mother spoke French to her two teenage daughters – and then Breton to cows but French to calves, and Breton to hens but French to their chicks, and Breton to pigs and sows but French to piglets. My stay with this family had been arranged for me by a militant group who like to send Breton learners from the towns to 'Breton-speaking' peasant families where Breton can be learnt in exchange for helping on the farms. However, all the families always, it seems, have great difficulty speaking Breton to unknown 'outsiders', and particularly the mothers, and especially so when the outsider is younger and female. The mother on the farm continually had to check herself in mid-French and make a conscious effort to speak Breton to me. She would laugh, say how odd and tiring it was but add that she had been asked to do it by a nice young local teacher; it seemed the young and educated were doing this sort of thing now. Towards the end of the course, however, she and other peasant women were shocked and upset to find that at a special dinner given by the militant organisers they were expected to stand for a Breton national anthem. The militant press cameras flicked furiously. This is just one obvious example of the general point that local women are summoned, metaphorically and actually, in the militant world into a political role, which, in their own terms, they are not performing at all. Putting it more extremely, we might say that local women can and do find themselves standing as radical feminists and Breton nationalists when, in their own terms, they might have imagined they were behaving in a way more evocative of sophisticated French ladies.

On the farm I have just mentioned I noticed that the mother spoke Breton to the dog but French to the cat, explaining to me that the dog was a 'farm dog' but the cat was a 'pet'. I will conclude now with a brief elaboration of this differential evaluation of animals. In its evocation of structures of values of the most banal and apolitical kind, it may serve to tie up various points already made in other ways in this paper. In a relatively undramatic way and without great upheaval women in Brittany have been able to take on first French and now the new image of 'Breton', and to incorporate in their lives issues which elsewhere have been a matter of great political debate and conflict.

The hamlet of Le Relecq no longer has any working farms and the population is ageing but relatively wealthy; some have been to the towns and returned and others made their money in the hey day of the horse trade. In Le Relecq the women are ladies, and these ladies have pets, dogs and cats or both. One especially hardy hunting man (a *chasseur*) in Plounéour is contemptuous of Le Relecq, with its wealth and 'useless pets' as he sees them, and what he sees too as 'hoity-toity' pretension. During my stay in the area two of the precious dogs were found dying from fox-poison. I tried to help by taking one of the dogs to a vet.

When Thérèse and Iffig, in Kerguz, heard about this, Iffig was openly surprised that 'so much fuss' had been made about a dog. Thérèse, I could see, was also surprised, but reproached her son, telling him, as she often did that he was ignorant and that it was no wonder that he had never found a wife. Iffig, in turn, would reproach her for having brought him up in Breton, and his mother would blush apologetically, and say that she realised she had done the wrong thing. Thérèse does know, however, about pets. Her nice neighbours have a pet dog and a cat; the cat, however, lives all the time in her house, where it is put to good use to catch very large rats. We were talking in French, and the subject came up of my stay on the farm where I had learnt some Breton and had heard the mother speak different languages to different animals, including French to the pet cat. Thérèse is getting used to the idea of young people wanting to learn and speak Breton – her well-educated neighbours do, for instance – and she was intrigued that the mother on that farm had dutifully spoken Breton to me. Her interest focused on the family: from my description, they were obviously well-to-do peasants, she concluded, with nicely educated daughters, and moreover they lived near a town on the coast. 'Those people are so sophisticated up there,' she said, 'unlike us savages here in the mountains.' She sighed and then picked up the cat. A somewhat straggly, rat-catching cat then found itself being gently groomed, stroked and petted on her lap, and spoken to in French. I had heard Thérèse regularly speaking only Breton to that cat over all the previous months, but when I enquired she paused and then was adamant: 'I always speak French to my cat,' she said to me finally, and she said this in a pointedly careful Breton, tailored to satisfy the enthusiasms of any town lady aspiring to 'Breton culture'.

Notes

1. The relatively high educational level and professional standing of members of the Breton movement, in comparison with the Breton population at large, is clearly set out in W. Beer, 1977.

2. In 1850, when the *Loi Falloux* introduced government girls' schools (previous laws having ignored them), under one-third of Finistère girls of school age were getting any education at all. Moreover there were three and a half times as many girls as boys in private religious establishments. (See Ogès, 1934: 134, 56; Taldir, 1935; for earlier periods see also Ogès, 1937, and M.A. and D.A., 1977: vol. 1.)

3. See Ogès, 1934: 19; Carré, 1888: 218, 222; Boucheron and Nonus, 1890 (1889): 37; M. Lamy (député) 16/1/1903, in *Journal Officiel* (Chambre: débats) 1903: 1: 24–34.

4. A questionnaire sent out by Abbé Grégoire in 1790 revealed that whilst under two-thirds of France could understand French only one-fifth could confidently speak it and over one-third knew no French at all (Chervel, 1977: 24). The wiping out of linguistic differences, although never achieved, was declared to be an 'integral part of the revolution' (Grégoire, 1794, cited in Gazier, 1969 (1880): 303). However, whereas French seemed in the new national framework,

to be the 'language of liberty', Breton on the other hand became associated with local royalist and clerical reaction, and then with the Girondins: it was said to be the language of 'federalism and superstition' (Barère 1794, cited in Gwegen, 1975: 33).

5. See: letters from the Primary Inspectors of Brest and of Quimper and Morlaix, to the Academic Inspection (Quimper): 3/9/1863 (ref: A.D.:T:I:79; Brest no. 847) and 31/10/1863 (ref: A.D.:T:I:79:1755).

6. This 'anonymous' pamphlet was written by the respected Celto-Breton scholar Vallée (see Taldir, 1935).

7. See A.D.:T:I:79:1054 (archival reference).

8. See, for example, A.D.:T:I:79:1877 file (archival reference) for correspondence concerning the commune of Ergué-Armel. A teacher was reported, by the local republicans, for using Breton texts as well as seemingly speaking Breton in class. Available Breton texts would no doubt have emanated from the clergy.

9. The hitherto excess population of Finistère, living off small parcelled plots of land in most instances, fell by 8 per cent from 1911 to 1931; the higher rate of births over deaths was absorbed and overtaken by emigration. If the Finistère population shows no more striking decrease, in spite of a falling birthrate, it is primarily because of a (related) internal attraction of the coastal area and increased activity there in all sectors. (On this general point see Ariès, 1948.)

10. Within agriculture itself in the commune there were about 58 per cent less women (aged 20–59 years) working on farms in 1975 than in 1962, and 52 per cent less men. All figures here are from the official census returns of 1962, 1968, and 1975. See also: Charpy 1972; C.R.D.P., 1976; I.N.S.E.E. 1980.

11. Finistère shows, in microcosm, two of Europe's great population movements: an emptying of rural communes to the towns and a fall in the population of larger town centres. There is a shift to the suburbs and outlying areas, which for Brittany means the countryside (see *Bulletin de conjoncture*: 1978, 1979, 1980, Préfecture, Finistère; C.R.D.P. 1976). Some younger people from the larger town centres of Brittany and elsewhere have moved right into the otherwise emptying and ageing rural communes of Finistère, and it is some of these young people that we are talking about here.

12. On the philological aspects here, see D. Droixhe, 1978 and Ardener, 1973 (1971).

13. See S.V. 1967, no. 11: 4, 7; and A.E.B. 1973: 51ff.

14. Generational differences in language-use could perhaps be summed up schematically in the following way:–

	Age
Generation 1 great-grandmother	c. 80 years
Generation 2 grandmother and grandfather	c. 50 years
Generation 3 mother and father	c. 25 years
Generation 4 child	c. 5 years

This might be in itself a fictional but nonetheless typical agricultural family inhabiting rural Finistère. Nearer the coast French might intervene earlier. (I am grateful to Malcolm Chapman for confirming this general picture from his own research experience on the southern Breton coast.)

Generation 1: Great-grandmother feels more at home in Breton than French, and Breton is usually a more appropriate language, in any case, for much of her daily round. She knows that her French is not as good as that of her descendants, and she also knows that French is the polite language to speak to strangers or to important visitors. However, she tends to use Breton more than she did, as her grasp of sociolinguistic proprieties begins to wane with age. Usually she speaks Breton to her daughter and son-in-law (generation 2), and they commonly respond in Breton.

Generation 2: Grandmother and grandfather use both Breton and French amongst themselves. Breton is often used when they are alone together or talking privately or of private adult matters (and do not want the children to hear), or when they are in informal situations with friends of their own age. They normally speak French to their children and their children's generation (generation 3). They use only French to their young grandchildren (generation 4).

Generation 3: Mother and father speak French between themselves, and to grandmother and grandfather (generation 2). They have heard a good deal of Breton spoken around them over the years, but it has not actually been spoken to them. Their parents (generation 2) have made every effort to bring them up as French-speakers, and have never wanted or expected them to speak anything but French. This generation (generation 3) is therefore able passively to understand much Breton, but does not really speak it. They might, however, use a limited amount of Breton in communication with great-grandmother (generation 1).

Generation 4: The child, and the brothers and sister if there are any, do not speak anything other than French. They are normally addressed by everyone in French. Should great-grandmother (generation 1) forgetfully address them in Breton, they might just, if alone with her, muster some sense from her words and respond in French. Their confusion is usually enough to jolt great-grandmother herself back into French and propriety. If parents (generation 3) or grandparents (generation 2) are present (a presence more likely to cause or contribute to, great-grandmother's own confusion in the first place), then the children are likely to look to them for help. The children will reply through these older generations.

There are several qualifying factors and complications that one could introduce here – including for example the fact that generations 1 and 2 will usually have cohabited whilst generations 2 and 3 will not; and if generation 2 is living in the family of the male partner (the 'grandfather' here) then the different uses of Breton and French between generations 2 and 3 may well have an extra edge of rivalry and exclusion, and affect also the language used within generation 2. It is not uncommon for mothers-in-law to use Breton to exclude daughters-in-law, for instance, and it has also been known in the past for daughters-in-law to use French, and only French, with everyone in the household to mark themselves off from mothers-in-law with whom they do not get on.

The kinship terms used here are obviously those of a British system. The appropriate Breton system is one in which both gender and educational level are important, and age more important than generation, in determining the terms used in kinship designation and, especially, address. Significantly, where the female gender is involved, and also when one moves nearer the coast, there is less lateral generalisation of terms and a more obviously 'French' terminology (see, on some of these points, Izard (1965), although he finds 'impoverishment' and a disappointing un-Celticness here – where local women would, no doubt, find sophistication.)

Abbreviations

A.D.	Archives Départementales (Finistère).
A.E.B.	*Amañ Emgleo Breiz* (a Breton militant journal).
B.S.A.F.	*Bulletin de la Société Archéologique du Finistère.*
C.I.R.R.E.E.S.	Centre Interdisciplinaire de Recherche et de Réflexion sur les Ensembles Economiques et Sociaux (Rennes).
C.R.D.P.	Centre Régional de Recherche et de Documentation Pédagogiques (Bretagne).
I.N.S.E.E.	Institut National de la Statistique et des Etudes Economiques.
J.A.C.-M.R.J.C.	Jeunesse Agricole Chrétienne – Mouvement Rural de la Jeunesse Chrétienne.
M.A. and D.A.	Maïté Albistur and Daniel Armogathe (1977, below).
SEMENF	Société d'économie mixte d'étude du Nord Finistère.
S.V.	*Skol Vreiz* (a militant journal for the teaching of Breton).

References

Albistur, M. and Armogathe, D. 1977, *Histoire du Feminisme français*, 2 vols, Paris: Editions des Femmes.

Anon., 1895, *La Langue Bretonne et Les Ecoles*, St Brieuc: Prud'Homme.

Ardener, E., 1971, 'Social Anthropology and the Historicity of Historical Linguistics' in *Social Anthropology and Language*, E. Ardener (ed.), ASA Monographs, 10 London: Tavistock.

Ariès, P., 1948, *Histoire des Populations Françaises*, Paris: Editions Self.

Beauvoir, S. de., 1949, *Le Deuxième Sexe*, 2 Vols., Paris: Gallimard.

Beer, W. R., 1977, 'The Social Class of Ethnic Activists in Contemporary France' in M.J. Esman (ed.), *Ethnic Conflict in the Western World*, Cornell University Press.

Boucheron and Nonus, 1890 (1889), 'Compte-rendu des Conférences d'Octobre 1889' (Carré), *Bulletin Officiel et Spécial de l'Instruction Primaire*, Académie de Rennes: Département du Finistère.

Brousmiche, J. F., 1977 (1829–31), *Voyage dans le Finistère en 1829, 1830 et 1831*, 2 Vols. Morvran.

Carré, I., (1888), 'De la manière d'enseigner les premiers éléments du français dans les écoles de la Basse-Bretagne', *Revue Pédagogique*: XII: 3

(15/3/1888).

Chapman, M., 1978, *The Gaelic Vision in Scottish Culture*, London: Croom Helm.

Charpy, J., 1972, 'Dénombrements de la population des communes du Finistère', BSAF: XCIX.

Chervel, A., 1977, *... et il fallut apprendre à ecrire à tous les petits français. Histoire de la grammaire scolaire*, Paris: Payot.

C.R.D.P., 1976, *Le Finistère 1800–1914 (les hommes)*, Rennes: C.R.D.P.

Denez, P., 1972, *Brezhoneg ... Buan hag Aes*, Paris: Omnivox.

Droixhe, D., 1978, *La Linguistique et l'appel de l'histoire (1600–1800)*, Geneva: Droz.

Elegoët, F., 1979, 'Prêtres, Noble et paysans en Léon au début du XXe siècle. Notes sur un nationalisme breton: *Feiz ha Breiz*: 1900–1914', *Pluriel*: no. 18 (Rennes).

Gazier, A. (ed.), 1969 (1880), *Lettres à Gregoire sur les patois de France, 1790–1794*, Geneva: Slatkine Reprints.

Groult, B., 1975, *Ainsi soit-elle*, Paris: Grasset.

Gwegen, J., 1975, *La Langue Bretonne Face à Ses Oppresseurs*, Quimper: Nature et Bretagne.

Halimi, G., 1973, *La Cause des Femmes*, Paris: Grasset.

I.N.S.E.E., 1980, *Annuaire Statistique Régional: Bretagne*, Rennes: INSEE.

Izard, M., 1965, 'La Terminologie de parenté bretonne', *L'Homme*, V, 3–4: pp. 88–100.

J.A.C.-M.R.J.C., 1979, *50 ans d'animation rurale*, Paris: Promo.

Lagrave, R.-M., 1983, 'Bilan critique des recherches sur les agricultrices en France', *Etude Rurales*, 1983, no. 92.

La Villemarqué, Th.-C.-H.H. de, 1963 (1867), *Barzaz Breiz*, Librairie Académique Perrin.

Markalé, J., 1976, *La Femme Celte*, Paris: Payot.

McDonald, M., 1989, *'We are not French!' Language, Culture and Identity in Brittany*, London and New York: Routledge.

Ogès, L., 1934, 'L'instruction primaire dans le Finistère sous le régime de la loi Guizot (1833–1850)', BSAF: LXI.

_____, 1937, 'L'instruction sous l'ancien régime dans les limites du Finistère actuel (suite)', *BSAF*: LXIV.

_____, 1942, 'L'instruction dans le Finistère pendant la Revolution (suite et fin)', *BSAF*: LXIX.

Prost, A., 1968, *L'Enseignement Primaire en France 1800–1967*, Paris: Colin.

SEMENF, 1976, *Le Pays de Morlaix: évolution et perspectives*, Morlaix: SEMENF, August.

Souvestre, E., 1971 (1835–7), *Les Derniers Bretons*, vol. 1, Brest: Le Portulan.

Taldir, 1935, 'Genèse de la campagne en faveur de l'enseignement du breton', *Le Foyer Breton*, No. 52.

Tanguy, B., 1977, *Aux origines du nationalisme breton*, vol. 1 (Paris: 10/18).

Trégouët, B., 1978, 'Agriculteurs: le dépeuplement des campagnes', *Octant* no. 3, September, Rennes.

Weber, E., 1977, *Peasants into Frenchmen*, London: Chatto and Windus.

7

The 'Death' of East Sutherland Gaelic: Death by Women?

Evi Constantinidou

In any language shift, some individuals will be in the vanguard, some will hold the middle ground and some will lag behind. Where the subordinate language is associated with a stigmatised group, language choices are inevitably charged. Anyone who adopts the dominant language will be viewed as something of a traitor to his original group.

(Dorian 1981:103)

We're too proud, Evi; that's why there's no more Gaelic in Embo.

(WR, female informant)

Studies of language-death/shift, as will be discussed below, indicate a special 'role' for gender in this social process. Yet because of much more politically significant conclusions on the subject, gender is usually relegated to a 'secondary study'. In this essay the role of gender will come out from the sidelines and be part of a 'mainstream' argument. I will seek and assess evidence concerning the role of gender ('en-gendered' decisions) in the transmission and eventual death of East Sutherland Gaelic (ESG). It is not the aim of this exercise to reach general and generalising conclusions about the relationship between gender and the fate of Gaelic (or any minority language). Resisting generalisations of this order is imperative on both theoretical and empirical grounds.

My empirical evidence was articulated within the 'world' of East Sutherland, and furthermore within the linguistically poignant world of a fishing village whose residents have in recent years been said to have upheld the last bastion of East Sutherland Gaelic (ESG). Even within the linguistic map of East Sutherland, the village had its own variety of Gaelic referred to by residents as Embo Gaelic.[1] My empirical domain therefore generates ethnographic examples limited to that area and its language. After all, 'Scottish Gaelic will not become extinct with the loss of East Sutherland Gaelic . . . In a regional context a language will have died' (Dorian, 1981: 104). The restricted scope of my argument, howev-

111

er, draws attention to the theoretical advantages of localising linguistic responses, even within an essentially academically united linguistic area.

There have been many scholarly comparative contributions to the Gaelic linguistic literature, notably by MacKinnon (1977), Durkacz (1983) and Withers (1984, 1988). Folk and literary value-laden oppositions set up to describe the relationship of the Gael (Gaelic) and English[2] become unchallenged goalposts of linguistic discussions and controversies.

ESG has a distinct 'saga'[3] within the linguistic history of the Highlands, especially different from the Gaelic of the West Highlands and Islands. There is an overlapping sequence of historical and geographical contrasts between the east and west coasts of the Highlands that permeates their linguistic history. These oppositions, even though arguably an academic and literary construct,[4] have infiltrated laymen's accounts of and attitudes towards the East and West Highlands.[5] Many a time I have been told by my informants (as well as by well-meaning strangers) that if I wanted to find the 'Real Gaeldom' (both linguistic and cultural), I should have gone to the west. For the social researcher the west is supposed to be fertile ground and the east a desert. The academic canvas of Gaelic therefore causes my account to be 'parochial', steering clear of generalisations.

This background is essential for my discussion of gender and the fate of Gaelic in East Sutherland because the relative academic obscurity of the east coast, a direct result of the above oppositions, enables the researcher to free herself from linguistic generalisations permeating accounts of the West Highlands and Islands. Nancy Dorian was the first linguist to look at and analyse the 'local' linguistic situation in East Sutherland (Dorian 1978, 1981). Her description of East Sutherland Gaelic as a legitimate dialect quite distinct from 'adulterated' or 'bad Gaelic' had a profound effect on both the people who lived there and the social scientists who wished to study the region. Her accounts created for social scientists like myself a vision of the sociolinguistic world of ESG speakers free from tempting generalisations about Gaelic in the Highlands and Lowlands (or Gaelic in the East and West Highlands) and in some respects set the stage in which 'en-gendered' decisions about Gaelic could be studied.

The Sociolinguistics of East Sutherland Gaelic

Compared to the sparsely populated west coast, the east coast of Sutherland is heavily populated. Statistics also indicate that the east has been substantially less Gaelic-speaking than the west, even though Embo (in

East Sutherland) possessed, until the middle of this century, a concentration of Gaelic speakers unrivalled in the 'Gaelic West Coast'. The loci of ESG are Embo, Golspie, Brora and Helmsdale. By the end of the nineteenth century the Gaelic-speaking populations of these townships were concentrated in their fishing quarters.

Golspie, Brora and Helmsdale were part of the Sutherland Estate, whose presence still looms over the landscape and history of the area. At the beginning of the nineteenth century these planned villages were notorious resettlement places of the Highland Clearances. Their fishing components are therefore part of the planning of the Sutherland Clearances (cf Richards 1982). Embo has a different history,[6] belonging at the time of the evictions to a different family, the Gordons of Embo, even though popular belief categorises it along with the other fishertowns of the area.

The fisher families were socially isolated from the non-fishers and tended to marry among themselves, while the rest of the population looked down on them. As Dorian (1978, 1981) noted during her visits to the area in the 1960s, to be bilingual in Embo at that time was an infallible marker of fisher origins (Dorian 1981: 60). The physical segregation of the fisher families is still noticeable even though fishing has long ceased in East Sutherland. There are East and West ends in Golspie and Upper and Lower neighbourhoods in Brora and Helmsdale: the West End and the Lower neighbourhoods are the areas associated with the fisher families. Embo is almost two miles from Dornoch, its nearest town, but is nevertheless perceived as its fishing satellite.

In Search of Gender

In East Sutherland, as documented by Dorian (1978, 1981), there was a linguistic lag between the fishers and the non-fishers. The fisherfolk started being bilingual in English much later than the rest of the population, and lost their Gaelic at a much slower rate (Dorian 1980, 1981). What made the death of ESG observable was the language's relative longevity. Its death was not a protracted one: it happened and was confirmed within the lifetime of individuals.

Expressing one's observations and conclusions in gender-language is not a straightforward matter; there are, as always, some academic 'smoke screens'[7] to lift. The gender-imprint in language-death does therefore require some detective work. Susan Gal (1979), writing about bilingual Austria (German/Hungarian), remarked that shifts in European languages have been construed as signs of linguistic and cultural assimilation to a national majority, and therefore have political undertones (1979:2). Christina Bratt Paulston (1986) also noted that: 'Language shift, especially if it involves language-death, tends to be an emotional topic, and maintenance an object of much wishful thinking' (1986:493). The 'moral' and 'political' undertones of language-shift make it rather difficult and/or unproductive to introduce 'en-gendered' observations into the sociolinguistic analysis of such sensitive areas.

Such undertones are endemic in academic and lay sociolinguistic literature dealing with Gaelic. The problem is that when we deal with language shift in a group discourse, gender is not a consideration. The speakers are assigned to uniform minority and majority languages or cultures and other considerations (such as gender and age) are usually relegated to the position of 'subcultural factors'. Gender enters sociolinguistic discussions as a 'sex variable'. Gender therefore was not, if we were to use mathematical language, part of the equation, but just another variable; yet part of the flourishing theoretical aspect of Women's Studies in the UK and the USA has been to create 'en-gendered' equations rather than present 'en-gendered' outcomes, footnotes and variables. As Maryon McDonald has recently written: 'It is to be hoped that anthropology is approaching the point where it can confidently declare such inability or omission [of gender] simply bad anthropology' (1989:312).

Empirically, 'gender' remains unavoidable in the context of language-death. Susan Gal found that: 'In studying language shift, I was studying the impact of large-scale historical processes on the minute details of intimate verbal interaction and of individuals' linguistic expression of their own identity. The macroscopic and the microscopic level of analysis dovetailed' (1979:1). When the microscopic and the macroscopic converge through the experience of individuals, as in the case of the death of ESG, they become conceptually and empirically indistinguishable. To ignore them would be not a regretful omission but 'bad anthropology'.

In the world of ESG the death of the language and the lifetime of individuals ran the same course, occupied the same semantic and physical space. In the local folk-model of language-death the death of Embo Gaelic is very closely identified in the late 1980s with the physical death of individuals. Therefore the focus of the discussion shifts from the group's responsibilities and actions to the individual's, whose gender is, if not the most significant, one of the most important markers of his/her actions.[8] Dorian's work exemplifies this individuality and gender-specific aspect of language choice. Most of her livelier quotations come from female informants, but whereas she analyses women's code-switching behaviour as different from men's, she does not question why some kinds of statement about language should be made consistently by female informants.

My analysis is 'en-gendered' in a different way. The 'sociolinguistics' are in some respects meta-sociolinguistics. This is not due to some perverse theoretical inclination on my part, but is a reflection of the ethnographic 'reality' I encountered in 1988–90. The days of ESG as a living language were officially over, and I had many more discussions *about* Gaelic with my informants than conversations *in* Gaelic. I tried never to define the linguistic medium of my interviews; I always tried to let my informants decide. Usually they chose to talk about Gaelic rather than in Gaelic.

East Sutherland Gaelic, a split second away from its extinction, had become a social and historical 'text' to be commented on, to be admired, to be recalled, but not to be lived. In some respects my informants were amateur anthropologists and linguists themselves. With the 'academic' pronouncement of their language as dead, they had acquired a certain linguistic self-awareness.

In the late 1980s I was presented with a version of 'life' that made use of this text. I encountered a series of paradoxes and contradictions in which gender was not a 'sex variable' but the fabric on which the tale of language-death has been embroidered.

There are several channels through which women pre-empted the fate of Gaelic in East Sutherland. Their language choice was not the only factor. There is no direct evidence, and there cannot be, for in the case of ESG there is no ethnographic present for that scenario. The reality I was faced with in 1988 is set in a different linguistic landscape, tainted not only by the passage of time and a sense that life goes on, and by the death of many of my possible informants, but also by the existence of a number of 'academic texts' declaring the death of their language (ESG).[9]

Like many historical studies, the endeavour resembles a criminal investigation seeking to bring a murderer to justice a number of years after the crime, when most of the witnesses are gone, and following a long serialisation of the case in a local newspaper.[10]

Ethnographic Encounters

My first encounter with the role of women in the 'death' of ESG was on a cold winter evening at the house of one of my main female informants. We usually had 'Gaelic lessons', followed by tea and cakes, talking about the 'old times', followed by village gossip and 'world' current affairs. The evenings we spent together were always very informative and pleasant. My hostess, a lively 84-year-old widow, had three daughters, two of whom lived in England and one in nearby Golspie. One of them was married to a man of Mediterranean descent, a fact that we both cherished in conversation (since I come from Cyprus).

My hostess's daughters were at best rather poor passive bilinguals according to their own classification. Their mother, in contrast, was a very enthusiastic informant about Gaelic and fishing in the village. Being one of my oldest informants, she was very aware that she really ought to have the best Gaelic in the village and often enquired anxiously about the Gaelic competency of some of my younger male informants. She could talk for hours about the beauty of the language, her all-Gaelic youth, her 'Gaelic-English' situation antics. She had what she called 'stories' about the Gaelic, which she generously shared with me.

Sometimes on the Fridays while I was there her daughter who lived in Golspie dropped in for a visit. One day she walked in during our Gaelic lesson and asked us to continue and not let her presence interrupt our 'work'. She sat down on the settee, and after a while when the discussion inevitably turned from Gaelic to talking about Gaelic, she suddenly announced: 'I have no Gaelic, *she* never taught *us* any.' 'It's true,' she continued defensively, glancing at her mother. '*You* never *did*! You wanted to keep the Gaelic to yourself, so we [the children] wouldn't know what you were talking about.' At this her mother faltered, for the outburst was destroying the image she had carefully constructed for me: of herself as someone who cared deeply about Gaelic and its survival. But she did not deny the 'accusation' and never expressed any regrets. She made a remark about Lassie (her dog) and got up to make some tea.

I had similar encounters with some of my other female informants. During a 'lesson', someone of the younger generation would come in, a daughter or a niece, and the tensions would surface. My informant might venture a remark to the younger one like: 'You don't have any Gaelic', or 'You are not interested in the Gaelic', or 'Evi's putting you all to shame'. This would be a rather innocuous comment paying an ambivalent compliment to me, their unlikely visitor and friend. The younger woman would reply, '*You* never taught *us*, it was all English you spoke to *us*.'

These events were the result of my being classified in an ambivalent way with regard to age and gender. As an anthropologist I was involved with people of all age-groups, but my perceived and declared interest in Gaelic placed me in a much older age-group. My 'physical age', however, was obviously nearer to the 'young ones', and created an ambivalence. This ambivalence generated events such as these outbursts, which gave me a genuine glimpse of the world of the Embonites. In the understanding of the younger informants, the non-transmission of Gaelic came down to personal decisions which were ultimately and purposefully made by their mothers. They were not willing to be accused of 'showing no interest', even though most of them probably agreed with their parents' decision in retrospect.

Until the 1940s the entire village was Gaelic-speaking, with the exception of the teacher and one or two incomers. In the 1930s someone even contemplated having a Gaelic-speaking teacher to safeguard Embo Gaelic: 'Embo, an entirely Gaelic-speaking community, surely deserves a qualified Gaelic teacher. The township offers the best field in the county for keeping the language in the fore. Gaelic is the first language of children in the community' (*Northern Times*, 6 October, 1932).

In the early 1930s there was also a controversy pertaining to the right of Embo children to a Gaelic education, which encouraged the emergence of value judgements about the Embonites' proficiency in both Gaelic and English. The correspondence columns of the local weekly newspaper, the *Northern Times*, were filled with letters, sometimes vehement, some defending and some putting down Embo Gaelic. The writers included both people from Embo (local and expatriate) and people from other parts of Scotland. The comments made in those letters in the 1930s carry a striking resemblance to comments made by my informants in the 1990s. It all started with a quite innocuous complaint about the allocation system of the Donald Mackay 'Gaelic scholarships':

> The people of Embo, young and old, are much interested in above [scholarships]. Embo is practically a hundred per cent Gaelic, and the people of this township will strongly object to the proposals ... by which the Donald Mackay bursaries are to be filched from their Gaelic boys and girls for the benefit of non-Gaelic applicants ... So long as Embo lads and lasses retain their Gaelic speech they can justly claim a full share of the £250 or £300 available annually from the Donald Mackay funds. The sturdy Gaelic people of Embo are proud of their ancient language and they delight in the use of it. They are not influenced by the snobbishness which prevails in other circles, nor do they suffer from that peculiar ailment, 'the Celtic inferiority complex' (Mrs Barbara A. Mackay, *Northern Times*, 13 August, 1933).

This letter prompted a war of words in which the 'Embo' linguistic performance was closely scrutinised. Some writers resented this:

> The gallant folks of Embo have lately received much attention in your columns. Their ancient and true Sutherland Gaelic and their English form of speech have been criticised and commended in turn. Your correspondents agree that Embo is 100% Gaelic. When the children quit the school buildings they revert to the language of home and fireside ... Our slogan should be: While men may come and men may go 'Keep Your Eye on Embo' (*Northern Times*, 7 September, 1933).

Yet criticisms persisted. Someone called W.A.S. from Glasgow wrote in one of his letters:

> Sir, I am convinced by the tone of Mrs Barbara A. Mackay's letter that the 'Gaelic question' can be a very thorny one. It is disappointing to find your correspondent a victim of supersensitiveness, and with a tendency to the use of sarcasm, as is evidenced by one or two remarks regarding the dialects of Cowcaddens and Bridgegate districts of Glasgow.
>
> My letter contained nothing that was liable to give the impression that Glasgow's dialect is entitled to a higher pedestal than either English or Gaelic as spoken in Embo ... Much has been said of the people of Embo being bilingual, but as one who has come in contact with people from almost every district in the Highlands, I find that the people of Embo have the most feeble grip of both English and Gaelic. There can be no doubt that an 'inferior quality' of Gaelic has a detrimental effect on English. There are parts in the west Highlands where the Gaelic is the predominant language, but most of the inhabitants are good English speakers. If there are a few who do not feel at home with English they cannot be charged with 'broken English'.
>
> There is no desire to under-estimate the sincerity of your correspondent when she takes up the cudgels in defence of Gaelic. Few they are, who are blessed to the same degree with parochial patriotism as the people of Embo, which in itself, if not allowed to run riot, is deserving of admiration. It, however, must be borne in mind that all the sincerity and parochial patriotism in the world forms no criterion of truth (*Northern Times*, 21 September, 1933).

I think that the above letter explains more by way of sociolinguistics than an academic treatise on the subject ever could. It sets the tone of the linguistic discussions about Gaelic for East Sutherland. Once more people jumped to Embo's defence, and interestingly the discourse moved away from linguistics. 'An Inverness lass', Nurse N.M, wrote from London:

> I should very much like to say a few words in favour of this little, much trod on village. I certainly think that Mrs Mackay is perfectly justified in becoming so indignant, not merely because of the suggested change in the clause and terms of the Endowment, but of the very inappropriate remarks made by W.A.S. True, W.A.S., the English of the village people could be a great deal better but, as Mrs Mackay says[,] what of the Glasgow English? And especially (as it is the most Gaelic speaking village in the Highlands) its English is no worse than any of the other villages. It's got its own peculiarities of speech just as Wick and Thurso, Elgin, Banff etc have their 'brogues'[,] which though perhaps prettier, are in no way perfect. It seems that W.A.S. is entirely without actual practical knowledge of the language, and he seems to have an entire absence of personal acquaintance with the people of the village. And he moreover, does not realise that half the charm of the people lies in their quaint Gaelic speech; and he has never heard a Gaelic choir, or a Gaelic congregation singing from the Psalms on a Sunday evening . . . I can

never understand why everybody seems to want to crush this little village. It is never given a chance. No proper water supply, no proper housing, no drainage system, no harbour for its livelihood; though promised[,] these things never materialise. Yet, you will find that it is always first to help any deserving cause . . . And you will find her sons in all corners and proud to belong to this little township (*Northern Times*, 28 September, 1933).

It was understandable then that the emphasis of my informants was placed on their inadequate linguistic performances. Their English was, by their own admission, rather poor: 'We were like a lot of foreigners then, the whole lot of us.' Most statements of this kind were made by female informants with children or nieces and nephews among the first generation of non-Gaelic-speakers. There are a lot of anecdotes in the village about their broken English, all of them recounted to me by women. A very characteristic one was narrated by a woman in her seventies who has lived most of her married life in England. She recalled the very first time her Plymouth-born husband met her grandfather (mother's father) in Embo. She said that afterwards he asked her, seriously, which country her grandfather had come from. She is a fluent Gaelic speaker, but she sees the passing of Embo Gaelic as a regrettable but inevitable development.[11]

The Embonites' foreignness did not lie in their ability to speak Gaelic but in their inability to speak proper English.[12] It seems that women were more acutely aware of this inability. Women because of their position in society are sensitive to issues of power which would include the 'language of power', and the power struggle of languages (Bratt Paulston 1986, MacDonald 1987). Part of my aim here will be to disentangle statements about the position of women from statements about the power of groups. I will try to show the local intricacies of the relationship between Gaelic and gender in a community which rarely claimed more than a few hundred speakers.

The Embo women's awareness of their 'poor' English and consequent 'foreignness' must have stemmed partly from their occupational lifestyle, which took them to many fishing ports in Britain as herring-gutters and therefore brought them into contact with a Britain to which they wished to belong linguistically. Fishing was part of a wider cultural experience which, however much it was associated with the Gaelic-speaking population in coastal East Sutherland, belonged also to a different experiential milieu. Rovinsoe, Balta and Lerwick in the Shetlands; Stronsay and Stromness in the Orkneys; Fraserburg, Peterhead and Aberdeen on the East Coast; Eyemouth, Berwick, Shields, Scarborough, Grimsby, Yarmouth and Lowestoft; Wick, Scrabster, Stornoway, Castlebay, Mallaig, Oban and Isle of Man: these names feature strongly in the geographical discourse of these women. This is the Great Britain of the fishergirls. Most of them had never been to London except on the trains carrying them to the south coast. Great Britain was for them a series of ports connected by rail links. They felt they belonged to this 'movement of people' and succession of places as much as to their beloved village in the Highlands. They were isolated by British onlookers as 'a race apart, a race made for gutting', as my informants recalled. Yet on further questioning they did not identify this 'race' with the 'Gaels' or the 'Highlanders' or even the 'Scots'; the discourse of the answers was one of 'sturdy fisherwomen', with Norse origins.

Was the death of ESG really caused by women? We have evidence that it could have been. At one stage after the 1930s Gaelic was not transmitted to the younger generation. The preceding generations had been monolingual in Gaelic before reaching school, where they were introduced rather abruptly to English. The generations of children following the Second World War were denied Embo Gaelic. In their eyes they were denied it not by the state but by their parents.

It also seems that the decision not to transmit Gaelic was in fact made by women. The first generation of poor passive bilingual or non-Gaelic-speakers was produced at a time when the search for employment caused the sexual division of labour to acquire a geographical dimension as well. Male and female workplaces required differential migration which involved families living apart for months at a time. The children either stayed with the grandmother at the village or more usually followed the mother around the herring fishing ports. Later on, with the demise of the herring fishing industry, the women started working at the hotels in Dornoch, and a lot of men joined the Merchant Navy.

Why did the women decide not to teach their children Gaelic? This is a straightforward question, and one that this innocent anthropologist did not ask. In the Gaelic sociolinguistic literature it was not an issue.[13] MacKinnon (1977) in his survey of Gaelic in Scotland did note that young women with children afforded the *least* loyalty to Gaelic. How can we explain this 'least loyalty'? The very use of the word loyalty reflects negatively on women in the language domain. It is quite characteristic that when women are brought into the linguistic scene they are ascribed negative value, and at the same time are denied any determining role in the language-death or shift.

Some of my most reliable male informants have noted that women were more 'fickle' with Gaelic and quite unpredictable in their linguistic behaviour. They would reply in English when you spoke to them in Gaelic. In the household where I was staying, it was more likely for the women to switch codes than the men. Sometimes the men would stick to Gaelic despite the change of code by women and furthermore pointed out to me, with a sense of academic conspiracy, that it was their sisters who were changing the code.

As has been noted by MacDonald (1987) and others, women are more sensitive to the presence of a third party not speaking their own language. This is related to their own perception of the relative strength of their native language. In Embo I was given many examples of linguistic *faux pas*, mostly by women who did not always hold to this code of basic courtesy, as they called it, but were much more aware than men of breaking it.

In the stories recounted to me, women were caught out using Gaelic when basic courtesy dictated the use of English. For example, two Embo women working at the hotels in Dornoch indulged in gossip about the head waiter in Gaelic as they were cleaning his room in his presence, and got caught because the man was from Lewis and 'had the Gaelic'. Another story had two Embo waitresses speaking rudely about a couple of tourists who were taking their time with their meal, only to be asked for the bill in Gaelic. Gaelic was never safe, even in rather unlikely situations. In the presence of Canadian soldiers in the Second World War the girls would be exchanging secrets about their boyfriends in Gaelic before they discovered that the soldiers 'had' some Gaelic since their folks went to Canada from the Highlands. Gaelic, however, did not always ensure friendship between the people who used it. A so-called 'crew',[14] each member now in her eighties, would remember with resentment the fact that in the gutting stations they would be singled out by other Gaelic-speaking women as 'having the Gaelic', i.e. as possible intruders into the privacy of their Gaelic conversations.

The men's 'Gaelic stories' were mostly about how they could make fun of their foreman in Gaelic without his ever realising, or could create a camaraderie in faraway Australia with other homesick sailors. For women, therefore, 'getting caught' was a recurrent theme that does not appear in the men's stories. In the female world Gaelic contexts of privacy could be breached, whereas in the male world privacy could be achieved and maintained by means of Gaelic.

I believe that the Embo women's attitude to bilingualism is not an attitude peculiar to their being Gaelic speakers as such, but an offspring of their attitude towards their fishing past. I was told many stories in which the women had thrown away and burnt many of the old artefacts and furniture cluttering their home. 'We were no wise!' For them at that stage these were not antiques, but 'rubbish', a bond with a fishing past from which they would rather break loose. Of course, throwing away artefacts regarded as rubbish was a widespread phenomenon before the rediscovery of such items as antiques. What is unique in this case is that there was a time-lag; these things were already antiques elsewhere in Britain when the women of Embo were throwing them away as rubbish. The same pattern had appeared in their language loyalties and use (Dorian 1981). This lag explains away Embo's sociolinguistic peculiarities; furthermore, it affords speakers and commentators a platform for value judgements about private language choices.

There are not many houses in Embo that contain conspicuous bonds with the beginning of this century. 'Gaelic' was part of these 'old things' now turned 'antiques' which have come back to haunt them. In Embo there used to be all the social connotations of being a fisherman associated with specific areas, a specific language and a specific past.[15] Young women especially went through a process of redefining themselves (soon after the Second World War) by getting rid of all the visible symbols of their status. Their children lived in a different world, a world that had undergone a thorough spring cleaning.

But why were women more aware of these symbols? In all my interviews with women I was struck by the amazing objectification of their pasts. The descriptions of their experiences, however individual, had a generic tone. This was evident in narrations of the life-histories of the fishergirls, quite a high percentage among my informants. To help me recount their life-stories, I was offered books about the fishergirls, newspaper clippings, pictures of other fishergirls at other times and places. I then realised that I was looking at a written 'oral memory' which was in itself confining the women in an inarticulate group. By the same token these women with their muted memories were trying to tell me something. They were symbols of the fishing industry in its heyday and in its decline[16], the markers of the separateness between the fishers and the non-fishers. Given the local social hierarchy and the discrimination against the fishers, it was perhaps not altogether surprising that the women were less 'loyal' to Gaelic, which was associated with the fishertowns and destroyed their chances of social mobility locally. It was the women who were turned down for positions in the shops because of their background and the way they talked, whereas the men usually took up manual work in which their background did not matter.

Discussion and Conclusions

Was the death of East Sutherland Gaelic caused by the attitudes of women in the 1930s? The answer, I think, cannot be found solely with reference to the issue of bilingualism: it is an integral part of the world in which the Embonites were living. We need to unravel this world and to understand the ambivalent position of women within it.

First, these women were part of a group which was defined from the outside: 'the fisherfolk', 'of the fishertown'. According to Nancy Dorian it was almost as if this was a 'negative ethnic identity'(Dorian, 1981). Characteristically, late last century a registrar insisted on entering 'Fishertown' as the place of birth of an Embonite. The people protested that there was no such place, but the entry and many others like it found their way into the book. Secondly, these women were part of an ambivalent Gaelic Scotland. They were haunted by the literary image of the Gael as a noble savage, proud to speak his mother-tongue. On the local level the romantic image of Gaelic had no currency, being subsumed into a local stratification which associated Gaelic and fisher[17]. There was no positive value in speaking Gaelic, no moral or material reward. Thirdly, within the fisher group the women were salient symbols. They populated postcards and fishing museums as colourful fisherwives, industrious herring fishergirls, careless mothers with the (oh so many) dirty children. The linguistic situation afforded these women decisions. Their decision *not to transmit* Gaelic was itself, retrospectively, a muted one. It was not articulated in a public domain. Public debates around the time of the creation of the first non-speakers of Gaelic did not mention anything amiss within the village. The event has also been practically erased from local memory. It does surface, but only in the anomaly of the presence of a 'foreign' anthropologist learning Gaelic.

What I want to draw attention to here is not only the importance of gender in bilingualism, but the need to examine each case in the light of all its individual peculiarities. The preoccupation with the locality is not a way to forgo any responsibility towards recognition of larger processes at work, like education and social policies, but it does help us to place in the picture what is in many ways the most significant point of view, that of the 'native speaker', whose gender is significant in his/her world view and in his/her (linguistic) decisions.

Sociolinguistics and Life

Mairi, who had moved to Canada when she was newly married and in her twenties, only to return to Embo senile and in her eighties, has become a symbolic figure in the village. Her daughter, who accompanied her to Embo, said that she knew every single stone in Embo before she arrived there for the first time in 1975, but she knew no Gaelic. Her mother, senile during my fieldwork and a few months away from her death, spoke only Gaelic now, and the daughter could not understand a word. This is not a study of dementia and language, for I know nothing of the medical reasons for this, but nor did my informants. Her situation was perceived as one of great poignancy, a summary of many lives lived in Embo with an added paradoxical end. She was a 'fishergirl' in her youth, migrated to Western Canada to work in the salmon fishing and returned to die in Embo, cared for – as everybody admitted, in the good old way – by her daughter, until Gaelic came as a wall between them.

Notes

1. The differentiation between the different 'kinds' of Gaelic in the area was made by Nancy Dorian (1978, 1981). I am using the lay idiom of 'kinds' of Gaelic because whatever the academic linguistic term, this is the way that my informants described their linguistic map. When my informants pointed out to me the difference between their Gaelic and Golspie and Brora Gaelic, they were communicating to me Dorian's results which she had freely discussed with them.

2. These oppositions and their use in the creation and propagation of the 'Gaelic Vision' have been discussed by Chapman (1978). These value-laden oppositions included such evocative pairs as 'primitive/wild' vs 'civilised', 'traditional' vs 'modern', 'oral' vs 'written'. All these oppositions are based on a perceived time-lag between the Gaelic culture and the English culture, between the Highlands of Scotland and the Lowlands. It is therefore not surprising that there should be a link between the political aspirations of the Scottish and the popular image of the indigenous and 'true' Gael.

3. The use of a non-Gaelic Norse metaphor such as a 'saga' to describe the 'story' of ESG is not accidental. A 'saga' according to The *Concise Oxford Dictionary* is a 'medieval Icelandic or Norwegian prose narrative, esp. one embodying history of Icelandic family or Norwegian king; story of heroic achievement or adventure; series of connected books giving the history of a family etc.; long involved story [ON, = narrative, cogn. w. SAW]' (7th edition 1982:921). A saga therefore expresses the textuality and the narrative continuity of a story, qualities manifest in the recounting of the death of ESG. This metaphor also expresses the 'non-Gaelic' element of the category of space and people that have become the vessel of ESG; 'Northern Scotland' and 'Gaelic Scotland' are, after all, competing definitions of the same geographical space.

4. W. J. Withers has recently published a scholarly and diverse account of the historical construction of these oppositions in *Gaelic Scotland. The Transformation of a Culture Region* (1988).

5. Dorian (1978) drew attention to the perceived contrasts between the East and the West Highlands by quoting a letter to the *Northern Times*, the local newspaper, which remained unchallenged in a context in which letters to the editors are usually contested by fellow-readers: 'Our county is divided into two for all practical purposes – east and west, and the west is recognised in the Highlands as a Gaelic speaking area' (*Northern Times*, 7 June, 1974).

6. The Old Parish Registers indicate the presence of several families of fishers in the area going back to the 1750s long before the planned evictions took

place. There is genealogical continuity between the original people in the Old Parish Register and the fisher families in the area for the next two centuries.

7. A far more eloquent term has been given by Edwin Ardener (1975): 'muting', 'absence of words/worlds'. I am a bit apprehensive of using the term now, more than ten years later, not because it is not suitable or old-fashioned, but because by now 'muting' should only be an aspect of culture and not an attribute of the social sciences.

8. The discourse of groups and the discourse of individuals in the social sciences do not necessarily invalidate one another. One may therefore wonder what is the purpose of this exercise. I am arguing that it is only by using the discourse of 'choices' that the 'academically muted' gender will enter academic discussions about language shift/death.

9. The close association, both concrete and symbolic, between the lifetime of individuals and the time-scale of the academic language-death of ESG will not be discussed in detail here.

10. I did not go searching for a crime, and through the flow of life in East Sutherland there is no smell of a corpse. The 'crime' occurred in the phrasing of my questions.

11. This woman conducted most of her thinking in Gaelic. She could not use Gaelic with her husband, and chose not to use it with her children. For her, Gaelic was very much alive, but instead of Gaelic being the language of private life, of the fireside and the community, her public linguistic sphere had expanded to include her husband and children, whereas her private linguistic sphere included just herself. When she visits her Gaelic-speaking sisters and brothers they might exchange the occasional Gaelic sentence, but usually the conversation was conducted in English.

12. The Embonites were once more being defined from a centre alien to them. Their self-categorisation as 'foreign' is the result of the paradox identified by Edwin Ardener (1987); people are not only defined by their social space, they are also the defining consciousness of that space. The outside 'label' has been given an internal reality.

13. Academic muting occurs on two levels: on one level language-death is an emotive issue and one which should not be needlessly burdened with personal decisions, and on another level 'muting' further hinders 'en-gendered' questions.

14. The herring fishergirls worked in groups of three, two gutters and a packer. The three women were usually relatives or close friends and worked together for many herring seasons.

15. Where mobility was possible, it was mobility through space. Almost all the women who married outsiders moved away, whereas men were more likely to stay in the village with their spouses.

16. In the good old days they were the fishwives, conspicuous in their trips around the towns and crofting areas, carrying heavy creels full of fish and with masses of 'dirty' children with them. During the rise of herring fishing the limelight shifted to the fishergirls, the seasonal migrant workers from fishing communities in Scotland gutting and packing the herring. Pictures in books about

fishing in Britain are often mostly of women and fishing-boats. The women are quite aware of this, and they do enjoy visiting the abundant fishing-folk museums dotting the coast of Britain.

17. As Mertz wrote about Cape Breton Gaels: 'Although we cannot make a simple correlation between . . . prestige values and language shift, there is no doubt that the difference in status between Gaelic and English played a role in shaping the interpretive filter through which Cape Breton Gaels understood their linguistic situation'(1989:109).

References

Ardener, E., 1972, 'Belief and the Problem of Women' in S. Ardener (ed.), 1975
———, 1975, 'The Problem of Women Revisited' in S. Ardener (ed.), 1975.
———, 1987, '"Remote Areas" – Some Theoretical Considerations' in A. Jackson (ed.), 1987.
———, 1989, 'The Voice of Prophecy' in M. Chapman (ed.), Oxford: Basil Blackwell.
Ardener, S. (ed.), 1975, *Perceiving Women*, London: J. M. Dent.
Bratt Paulston, C. 1986, 'Social Factors in Language Maintenance and Language Shift' in J. Fishman et al., (eds), 1986.
Chapman, M., 1978, *The Gaelic Vision in Scottish Culture*, London: Croom Helm.
Dorian, N., 1978, *East Sutherland Gaelic*, Dublin: Dublin Institute for Advanced Studies.
———, 1980, 'Linguistic lag as an ethnic marker', *Language in Society*, vol. 9, pp. 33–41.
———, 1981, *Language Death: The Life Cycle of a Scottish Gaelic Dialect*, Philadelphia: University of Pennsylvania Press.
——— (ed.), 1989, *Investigating Obsolescence: Studies in Language Contraction and Death*, Cambridge: Cambridge University Press.
Durkacz, V., 1983, *The Decline of the Celtic Languages*, Edinburgh: John Donald.
Fishman, J., Tabouret-Keller, A., Clyne, M., Krishnamurti, Bh. and Abdulaziz, M. (eds), 1986, *The Fergusonian Impact: Volume 2, Sociolinguistics and the Sociology of Language*, Berlin: Mouton de Gruyter.
Gal, S., 1979, *Language shift: Social Determinants of Linguistic Change in Bilingual Austria*, New York: Academic Press.
Jackson, A. (ed.), 1987, *Anthropology at Home*, London: Tavistock Publications.
MacDonald, S., 1987, 'Social and Linguistic Identity in Staffin, Isle of Skye', unpublished D.Phil. thesis, Oxford University.
McDonald, M., 1989, *'We are not French!' Language, Culture and Identity in Brittany*, London: Routledge.
MacKinnon, K., 1977, *Language, Education and Social Processes in a Gaelic Community*, London: Routledge & Kegan Paul.
Mertz, E., 1989, 'Sociolinguistic Creativity: Cape Breton Gaelic's Linguistic "tip"' in N. Dorian (ed.), 1989.

Richards, E., 1982, *A History of the Highland Clearances*, London: Croom Helm.

Withers, W. J. C., 1984, *Gaelic in Scotland: 1698–1981*, Edinburgh: John Donald Publishers.

_____ , 1988, *Gaelic Scotland: The Transformation of a Culture Region*, London: Routledge.

8

French: No One's Language, Therefore Everyone's Language: Convent Speech in Lower Zaïre

Joan F. Burke

Introduction

This paper presents field data on language accommodation gathered during the period 1980–88 while I was living and working in Lower Zaïre. It focuses on a group of Catholic sisters numbering about one hundred women, over eighty of whom are Africans. My principal research interest was the social reconstruction of the Catholic sisterhood by African members who draw on both Kongo institutions and the colonial-missionary experience. Language usage, though not the primary interest, turned out to be very important for the purpose of identifying the basic operating models of social relations within the group. Language has also helped elucidate how the sisterhood is perceived, both by the sisters themselves and by the Zaïreans in general.

The sisters of Notre Dame de Namur first went to the then Congo Free State in 1894, one year after the arrival of the Jesuits, to whom the evangelisation of the Lower Congo had been entrusted by the Propaganda Fide in Rome at the request of King Leopold I. The priests had solicited the help of the sisters specifically to work with young girls and women. This was clearly stated in a letter of Father Van Hencxthoven, Jesuit Superior of the first group of missionaries, when he wrote back from the field to his Provincial Superior in Belgium, 'Without them [sisters], without the education of young girls, the conversion of Congolese families is absolutely impossible. It is largely because of the lack of religious women for the education of black girls that the work of our former missionaries was so long hampered and rendered almost fruitless in the . . . Portuguese regions of the Congo'(*Précis Historiques* 1893:509). As in the very beginning, the sisters still mainly work with young Kongo girls and women. They serve in primary and secondary schools, techni-

128

cal education, teacher training, rural dispensaries, outreach health education programmes and in basic development with village women.

The first sisters sent to the Congo Free State were mostly Belgians – both Flemish and Walloon – with some Germans, Dutch and Irish. The second generation were almost entirely Belgian. Since 1969, a few Americans have joined the Zaïre Province.[1] The Jesuits, with whom they worked until the 1970s, were Flemish.[2] Today Zaïrean priests staff practically all parishes in the diocese where most of the sisters live. By 1988 approximately three-quarters of the sisters were themselves local women. But for one exception, they live in communities of three to ten members, spread out in rural areas of Lower Zaïre between 120 and 700 kilometres from Kinshasa. The combined administrative centre and formation house is a community of thirty sisters located in an area on the outskirts of the capital. Because all these communities are multicultural, they give us insight into women and second-language use.

Languages in Zaïre

There are approximately 250 different languages in Zaïre: some are linguistically related while others are totally distinct. Most would be classified as Bantu languages. Four local languages are officially recognised because of their importance: Kiswahili, used in the eastern part of the country; TshiLuba, spoken in the southeast; Kikongo in the west; and Lingala of the north. The latter, which was the market language used extensively along the River Zaïre (formerly Congo River), is of increasing importance since it is the lingua franca both of the army and of the capital, Kinshasa.

In the region where I did my research the local language is Kikongo, spoken by approximately three million people. The Kongo are the largest linguistic group in the country. Different groups of Kikongo-speakers are found not only in western Zaïre, but in northern Angola and the southwest of the former French colony of Congo-Brazzaville. To my knowledge there was no newspaper or journal in general circulation, nor has literature been published in Kikongo since independence in the area where I was working. Before that time there used to be a printing press in Kisantu set up by the Jesuits, which had a considerable output. As would be expected, most of the publications were of a religious or educational nature. However, the press also promoted the study of the Kikongo language and literature. At least one regular journal existed at the time: *Ntetembo Eto*, started in 1901.

As in the rest of colonial Belgian Congo until the late 1950s, teaching in almost all schools was done in the local language. From the outset, the missionaries had seen education, not only as part of Belgium's civilising role in the Congo, but also as a means of evangelisation. It was in these terms that one of the first missionaries explained the importance of the local language to the Superior General back in Namur, Belgium: 'We have to ... teach the local language so that the Congo children may better understand and relish religious truths when they are taught in their own tongue' (Sister Teresa de Assomption, letter dated 1 May 1898, cited in *Précis Historiques* 1898:452). Because of this preference the language of the classroom was Kikongo until nearly the eve of independence. Throughout most of the colonial era other factors reinforced this early choice of the vernacular over one of Belgium's national languages.

Because of the situation in the *métropole*, the Belgians were particularly conscious of the importance of the cultural question, which they closely linked with the *question linguistique* there. The small country of Belgium had often been trampled over by the larger continental powers of Europe. Following the First World War the principles agreed upon at Versailles calling for a respect for minority rights and self-determination rang truest among the Flemish-speakers, who felt aggrieved by what they perceived to be cultural domination by the French-speakers of Belgium, the latter including the aristocracy among the Flemings themselves, referred to as *Fransquillons*. During the latter part of the nineteenth century, northern Belgium (Flanders) experienced the rise of a strong wave of Flemish nationalism and regional consciousness. This had its effect in the colony and the importance that missionaries placed on local languages. Most of the missionaries, the largest single occupational group among the expatriates in the Belgian Congo, were Flemish.[3] Markowitz, in his study of missions in the Belgian Congo, has remarked that 'the most vocal missionary proponents of linguistic and cultural revival among various Congolese tribes were Flemish' (1973:157).[4]

Towards the end of the colonial period political pressures in the Belgian Congo eventually prevailed upon the missionaries to adopt the teaching and promotion of French. Until the mid-1950s nearly all educational institutions as well as most medical facilities functioned under the auspices of missions – mostly Catholic. This arrangement was an integral part of Leopoldian, and later Belgian, colonial policy, which had been officially established by the signing of a Concordat between the Congo Free State and the Vatican in 1906. The policy of giving a monopoly to the church in this way not only ensured these services to the population, but also, even more importantly for the government, virtually guaranteed a presence of Belgians across a territory that was far too extensive for the comparatively small home country to administer directly through civil servants.

When a socialist-liberal government came to power in Belgium, favouring the development of *écoles laïques* (state schools, which also tended to be anti-clerical), Catholics in the colony felt very threatened. Sister Léonie de l'Assomption, who had worked in the Congo since 1910, wrote in 1955: 'Every effort is being made to set up a system of state schools... All missionaries are very distressed by the measures the government wants to take with regard to our own schools' (*Congo Débuts 1894–1906*:117). Later, when she described the years 1957–60, her notes reflected the chagrin of the missionaries at the adoption of French in the schools: 'The big question for the moment is the study of French. One never hears the end of it. No one is any longer at this point satisfied with only the strictly necessary' (*Congo II 1920–1960*:2).

At this time the schools in the colony were obliged to follow the established state curriculum as in the *métropole*. With this shift, French gained the ascendancy over local languages. Former missionary Sister Maria Vandeputte wrote of the time, 'the setting up of official schools [i.e. state schools] spread the taste for studying French; subsequently, programmes of study were turned upside down to make French obligatory from the first year in primary school' (1980:79). The missionaries perforce complied, although they regretted the change. At the primary level, French was introduced gradually as a second language; in secondary schools it became the medium of instruction.

Once independence came, French was proclaimed the official language of the country, which added to the importance of French in the schools. Many of the nationalist movement leaders saw that the earlier, almost exclusive, promotion of local languages in education was divisive since the country had no common language for all its citizens.[5] They were also quick to point out that the lack of a more widely recognised European language effectively limited their access to higher education. At the time of independence there were hardly any Congolese with university degrees, apart from clerics.[6]

Linguistic Profile of the Sisters in Lower Zaïre

The majority of the sisters, including the expatriates, grew up with a mother tongue other than French, the official language of the country since independence.[7] Most of the Zaïreans are Kikongo speakers from villages in Lower Zaïre. A smaller group are Yaka, whose language is for the most part understood by the Kongo and *vice versa*. One professed sister is a Mutetela from the Kasai, a distinctive region as are its languages. She does not speak Kikongo, nor do the younger professed and the novices from the capital Kinshasa and from Brazzaville across the Zaïre River, where Lingala is the mother tongue. When I left Zaïre in 1988 the expatriate sisters could be classed by their first languages into three almost equal groups: Flemish, French, English. The one German Swiss had lived most of her adult life in French-speaking Belgium before going to Zaïre. In sum, among the nearly one hundred sisters of Notre Dame in Zaïre, only seven are native speakers of French. For the others, French is a second or even a third, language. In this sense, for the majority of the sisters 'French is no one's language and can therefore serve as everyone's language.'

Since all of the communities are ethnically mixed, the adopted formal language of the community when the sisters are among themselves is generally French, which serves literally as a lingua franca. French is normally used among the sisters for prayer and worship, at meetings, and in table conversation. Informally the Zaïrean sisters, and some expatriates[8] in conversation with Zaïreans, frequently revert to Kikongo. The fact that there is beginning to be a number of African sisters who do not easily understand the Kongo language has caused some to question the extent to which it should be used in community. Many seem unconscious, however, of how the use of one language may exclude members who do not understand it. In my own experience, although a few sisters may occasionally feel themselves to be victims of this kind of exclusion, neither Zaïreans nor expatriates cause this intentionally.

Several factors affect the range and fluency of the sisters in both French and Kikongo. The most significant factor in the case of the Zaïrean sisters is their age. As noted above, until the late 1950s the language of instruction in the schools of Belgian Congo was the vernacular. A consequence of this preferred use of Kikongo is that the older Congolese are distinctly disadvantaged today in comparison with the younger generations who have had a formal training in French.

In 1979 the area handbook for the US Foreign Service, edited by Irving Kaplan, cited the statistics for general literacy in Zaïre as 20 per cent, and for literacy in French as 15 per cent (p.178). Although the more senior Zaïrean sisters have greater fluency in the French language than other women of their age, they certainly do not have as much command over it as their juniors in community. Those of this older group who joined the sisterhood before 1960 were first members of a local congregation, the Sisters of St. Marie de Kisantu. This wholly African diocesan congregation was founded by the Sisters of Notre Dame de Namur at the request of the local bishop in 1940.[9] Once the latter themselves began to accept African members in 1959, several of the first group asked to be incorporated into the order, and today they constitute the first generation of Sisters of Notre Dame. I often heard them say jokingly – but also with a degree of resentment, because of the resultant language limitations – that they were not allowed to study French in their youth because of the missionaries' fear that it would encourage them to converse with expatriate men! None of the older missionaries ever confirmed or denied this statement in my presence.

On the other hand the younger sisters, who were educated in French, although more fluent in that language than their seniors, cannot for their part claim the same command of the richness of Kikongo as the older sisters. Most have had no formal training in their local language since their primary school years. Because most came from rural Zaïre, they probably stayed in an *internat* while at secondary school, since there are relatively few secondary schools in the interior. By that very fact they were removed for much of their adolescence from the milieu in which they would have had more opportunity to hear the Kongo-esteemed 'art of speaking' which is used in clan gatherings and the settling of disputes.

Naturally, fluency in French is also affected by the individual sister's educational background. Even in the very early days women wishing to join had to have first obtained some kind of professional or vocational qualification. The majority entered the community with a teacher's certificate for either primary or secondary level. The first generation of sisters trained as primary school teachers in the three-year post-primary *école des monitrices*. It was not until 1948 that secondary schools as such were set up in the Belgian Congo. To become a teacher in more recent times requires four or six years of post-primary training in an école normale. A few of the candidates had a secondary school certificate or diploma in dressmaking. None had either a nursing or a post-secondary diploma. During the last fifteen years many of the younger sisters with the potential have been encouraged to pursue further training in institutes of higher education. These varying backgrounds of educational experiences naturally affect the sisters' competency in French.

For the expatriate sisters, the identity of their mother language and the nature of their formal linguistic training before they came to Zaïre are naturally relevant, but otherwise their command of both French and Kikongo is largely related to their specific sphere of work. For those serving in the rural dispensaries and village outreach programmes, Kikongo is the most used language. Whereas Kikongo is important for working with the students and their parents outside school hours, its use in the classroom is minimal. In schools French is the medium of instruction. For this reason the learning of French takes precedence over the local language for the sisters working in formal education who are not themselves native French speakers.

A Case Study[10]: Kongo Kinship Terminology Within the Convent (Internal Accommodation[11])

Join me for the moment around the dinner table at Nselo, where there is a small community of three Zaïrean sisters: Sr Nsimba is in her sixties, Sr Kizunza is in her fifties and Sr Nsoki is a youngish Superior in her early forties. It is market-day and there is the usual banter about the morning's buying and all the people met along the road and on the stalls. They are speaking in French.

Ya Nsoki, what were the prices like today?

Very high, *Ya* Nsimba. The merchants with lorries from Kin [Kinshasa] already made the rounds of the villages last night to buy up goods, so not much was available at the market.

Ya Nsimba, *Tata* Swana will be coming around this afternoon to see you.

Were there many students in class today, *Ya* Kizunza, or were they all playing 'hookey'? [translation of the French *jouer école buissonière*]

[There is a knock at the door; the oldest sister, Nsimba, has just risen to put the flask of tea on the table, so she goes to see who is on the porch. She calls back from the door:]

Ma Supér, it's for you.

[*Ya* Nsoki goes to the door.]

[Since all have finished eating, Sr Kizunza goes out to bring in the hot water from the fire, and Sr Nsimba gets up saying:]

Bampangi, let's do the dishes quickly since there will be many *baTata* and *baMama* who will be dropping by on their way home from the market.

Here I would point out a few common kinship terms of address that have been used in this conversation:

Ya/yaya	older sister or older brother (no distinction of sex)
Ma Supér	as an abbreviated form of *Mama Supérieure*, Mother Superior (N.B. Formerly, when titles were used in the congregation, 'Mother Superior' was strictly reserved for the Superior General.[12] Local superiors of communities were addressed as 'Sister Superior')
(ba) Tata/Ta	father, title of respect for an adult man
(ba) Mama/Ma	mother, title of respect for an adult woman
(ba) Mpangi	brother or sister (no distinction of sex)

Note: *Ba* is the plural prefix.

This vignette illustrates how the Kongo kinship idiom offers to the African sisters a repertoire of different social models that at varying times and in different circumstances may be observed as operative in the way in which the sisters relate to one another in the day-to-day life of the community. The constitution of the religious community is, of course, quite different from that of any Kongo co-residential group. Most obviously, all members are adult females. The sisters do not normally have any 'real' relationship to one another through belonging to the same kin group. They live multiculturally: Zaïreans, Belgians, Americans. The Zaïrean sisters themselves come not only from different regions of the country, but also from more or less dissimilar ethnic groups (Bantandu, Bampese, Bambata, Bandibu of the Kongo people; Bayaka; a Mutetela). The bonds that unite the sisters are based on their freely-chosen commitment to the sisterhood.

The extent to which and how kinship terminology is used may be a very revealing barometer of the sisters' social construction of what could be termed a micro-society, which itself reflects their given social environment and position in it as Kongo women. The relational language of kinship terminology serves as an analogy for the sisters, who express their perception of their religious community in terms of a kin group. In this they are both using and re-structuring existing Kongo models of social relationships.

What is of particular interest here is the degree to which the use of the described kinship terminology is accommodated not only by Zaïrean sisters when speaking French among themselves, but also by the expatriate members of the community. The following discussion will explore these as a case study of one group of women's use of a second language.

Kinship Terms Referring to Sister/Brotherhood

The table conversation of the sisters at Nselo exemplifies the frequent use of the term of address *Ya* or *Yaya*, older sibling, in 'inside' situations. This is common parlance within the community. It is the term of address which the older Zaïrean sister uses even when she is speaking to a younger member. In the lay Kongo kin group, however, a younger brother or sister would always be addressed by the term *nleke*. Among the sisters it is very rare to hear another called *nleke*. It is used when an older sister is correcting or offering unsolicited advice to a younger one.

Among Kongo *yaya* and *nleke* are terms that stress the importance of relative age within the generation group and signal behavioural expectations. Etymologically, *yaya* is a substantive that seems to be related to the verb *yaya* (to be honored, respected), and its derivative *yayidila* (to be cordially received). In addition to being the term of reference for an older brother or sister, it may also be used to directly address a grandparent with whom one is usually presumed to have an affectionate, though respectful, relationship. The noun *nleke* is derived from the verb *leka* which means 'to lie down, to be subordinate'. The strongest bond that joins persons together in a relationship of brothers and sisters (*bampangi*) is common membership of the same matriclan (*kanda*) and/or patriclan (*kitata*). Other kinds of commonality may also forge fraternal links, such as that of place (same village, *gata dimosi*) or a shared experience (e.g., classmates in contemporary society). Normally persons who are *bampangi* would be of the same approximate generation.

As might be expected within a religious community, the members frequently articulate a commonly held ideology of sisterhood (in the local French, *fraternité*). Obviously the different cultural groups understand that ideology with differing nuances – if not fundamentally, at least in its expression, as the following demonstrates. It is a case in which I tried to accommodate a French expression, but one that turned out not to be of any real meaning in the Kongo situation.

I first went to Zaïre in 1971, staying for two months. It was during a period of mounting tension within the country, especially between expatriates (mostly Belgian) and Zaïreans. The president was preparing to announce what would become a very significant 'policy of authenticity'. This was, in fact, presaged during my visit, in his changing the country's name: I had arrived in Congo, but would leave Zaïre. Among the sisters themselves there was also considerable tension. Parity between the numbers of Zaïrean and expatriate members had almost been reached. However, most of the posts of responsibility in the Province were still held by Belgians, including the Provincial Superior and Novice Mistress. Since almost all the expatriate missionaries present had arrived in the country before independence in 1960, it was not surprising that their ways of relating to the local population were not free from the colonial overlay: a mentality of superiority and paternalism. The examples that the Zaïrean sisters cited to me included: the Belgians' condescending language in addressing or referring to the Zaïreans,[13] their discouragement of Zaïrean sisters who wanted to pursue post-secondary and further professional training (which in fact most of the Belgians lacked), and the tight control of all finances by the expatriates. A verbal indicator of the tension between the cultural groups was the frequent use of the French expression, '*nous autres*' (we) . . . '*vous autres*' (you). Perhaps because I was an outsider and closer in age to the Zaïrean sisters, and also because I had been sent there from Rome on a fact-finding mission for the Congregation's Generalate (headquarters), the Zaïrean sisters spoke to me very freely of how, in community, they were made to feel inferior to the old-time missionaries.

Because of this prior experience, when I returned to join the Zaïre Province as a member in 1980, I made a very conscious effort from the outset always to refer to the Zaïreans in community as '*mes consoeurs*':

I meant this as an expression of my own understanding of sisterhood as a call to live with each other on equal terms as full sisters. I was initially aware that this language put some of my Belgian *consoeurs* ill at ease. Obviously it was not congruent with their own mode of relating to the Zaïreans. However, the intention of my use of the expression *consoeur* was lost on the Zaïrean sisters too. It took me quite some time to realise that this was not an idiom that was translatable, let alone meaningful, in their own experience. I recognised after some time that the Kongo model of sisterhood included the important acknowledgement of relative age. Persons who are *bampangi*, sisters, relate to each other as *yaya* or *nleke*. In social relationships, for the Kongo the quality of brotherhood, mutuality and solidarity are of far greater importance than strict 'equality'. Consequently an undifferentiating, levelling term such as *consoeur* in the Kongo community was inappropriate. *Bampangi* are joined to each other in a definite bond of fraternity, but not in an unqualified equality. Relative age always remains operative as a significant, differentiating consideration in such relationships.

Kinship Terms Referring to Successive Generations

In the table conversation in the community at Nselo, the sister who was familiarly referred to as *Ya* Nsoki was addressed as *Ma Supér* when she was called to the door. The term *Mama* – often shortened to *Ma* as is *Yaya* to *Ya* when used with a person's name – signifies that she is considered a member of the life-engendering generation. The identifying title for a man in this generation is *Tata* (or *Ta*). These persons would be *bambuta*, that is, elders in the sense of the 'life-givers'. The substantive *mbuta* derives from the verb *buta* which means 'to give birth, to engender'. On occasion, a person may address an older brother or sister as *mbut'amo*, 'my elder', or even *Ya mbuta* (big sister/brother); however, the term here emphasises that the person was born before the one speaking.

Most frequently *mbuta* identifies the individual as belonging to the preceding generation, and thereby having a recognised moral authority. There is a double source for this moral authority. Firstly, the elders stand in a position of greater ascendancy in the life-line passing through the clan from the ancestors. It is in their role of mediating the life of the living-dead to successive generations that *bambuta* derive their power both to bless (*sambula*) and to curse (*loka*). Secondly, the elders hold a moral authority because their greater experience of life should provide them with an accumulated, deeper understanding of ancestral wisdom.

The only sisters in community who are regularly referred to and addressed as *mbuta* are superiors, irrespective of whether they are

Zaïreans or expatriates. The two more common expressions are: *Ma Supér*, shortened form of *Mama Supérieure*; and *Mama nkuluntu*, 'first/eldest of mothers'.[14] It seems that the latter expression was introduced specifically for this context by the early missionaries. Until the 1950s the Jesuit Mission superiors in the region were addressed as *Mfumu* (chief) *nkuluntu*, and only then was it modified as *Tata nkuluntu*.[15] I have never heard the word *nkuluntu* used in the village milieu among the Kongo in the region where I lived. Very likely it derives from *nkulu muntu*, meaning 'ancient one'.[16]

The term *Ma Supér* is not a fixed form of address for the sister who is the superior, but is more usually employed when the speaker is treating her as an authority figure. In informal conversation and banter, even the Provincial Superior is addressed as *yaya*. This discriminating use of titles would certainly not obtain in common Kongo parlance. A chief, no matter what the occasion or situation, is always addressed as such with his proper title *Mfumu* (chief).

There are two other circumstances in which the sisters might use *mbuta* as a reference word for an older member. Both cases reflect strained relations between young and old. Firstly, if a conflict has developed between a junior member and a senior in community, the former may begin to refer to the latter as a *mbuta* with the clear implication that she is old and fixed in her ways with no understanding of the young. For her part, the older sister might remark that the younger one is but a *nleke* who has a lot to learn about respect. I never heard a sister refer to another by the strict term for the successive generation, *mwana* (child).

Secondly, complications and friction may readily arise in relationships between a young superior and members of the community who are older. If the junior who is *Ma Supér* does not make a special effort to seek the counsel of the older sisters, the latter may increasingly withdraw their active participation and themselves begin to speak in allusive ways of the *baleke* (young) who do not respect their *bambuta*. I never heard, though, any sister directly address a superior as *nleke*, no matter how strained relations had become.

Extension of Kinship Terminology to Expatriates

Kongo kinship terminology and its accompanying behavioural patterns are extended in varying ways to apply to the expatriate members of the Zaïre Province. The sisters in this category are few in number and come from two main groups with different histories. Consistent with Kongo logic, membership in the kin group includes the dead as well as the living. The ancestor class will be described last.

Many of the older Belgian sisters, some of whom have lived in the country for forty and even fifty years, are referred to by the Zaïrean members as *Mama*. But out of respect for the preferences of the sisters themselves when being addressed directly, the French '*ma Soeur*' is used. Three of these sisters were formerly, as Mistresses of Novices, engaged in the initial training of the first generation of Zaïrean sisters. Without a doubt, they are considered as *bambuta* since they were the mothers of these early sisters.

The Zaïrean sisters amicably address a few of the Belgian sisters in French as '*Tante*' (as English-speakers would use the familiar 'Auntie'). Most of these women are a bit younger than the above mentioned 'old-timers', but they are still clearly associated in the Province with the elders. They are sisters from Belgium whence came the 'founding mothers' to the then Congo Free State in 1894. Their long association with the *métropole* during the years of colonialism naturally reinforces their being classed as *bambuta* (life-givers). It is interesting to note that the Zaïreans frequently describe the periodically strained relations between their country and Belgium as: 'Our uncles are disputing again, but in time let's hope that they'll work out their palaver.' The 'uncles' mentioned here refer to President Mobutu, who describes himself as 'Father of the Nation', and the Belgian government ministers.

Two Belgian sisters are referred to with great affection as *Nkaka*, grandmother, although the sisters actually use this as a title of direct address only in one of these cases. The first sister has been in the country since 1939 and taught for years in the schools as a music teacher. The sisters respect her preference to be called *ma Soeur*. In the other case, *Nkaka* Tchi-tchi is very happy with the appellation.[17] She only came to Zaïre in 1962 when she was in her late forties, but has spent most of those years caring for very small children and babies left to be raised at the mission for some years after their mothers had died during childbirth in the maternity clinic run by the sisters. *Nkaka* Tchi-tchi demonstrates her affections more openly than most of her compatriots from Belgium, and enjoys both teasing others and being teased in the manner of the easy, familiar relationship between members of alternate generations: *nkaka*, grandparent, and *ntekolo*, grandchild. The root of the latter is *teka* (*tekele*), 'to flower', and its derivative *tekula* is 'to make flower or blossom'.

By contrast, the Zaïrean sisters in community usually address all the American and a few Belgian sisters as *Yaya*. Most of these women came to the country some years after independence when they themselves were in their twenties and thirties. There were then already a number of young Zaïrean sisters in the Province. Because of the similarity in their age and probably because their training and background were different from those of the earlier generations of missionaries, these sisters had an easier rapport with the Zaïrean sisters from the outset. I did not hear any of this group referred to as an *mbuta*. This includes the one American sister who agreed to serve as a superior and was later also a provincial councillor. She is not called *Ma Supér*, although the sisters hold her in great esteem: they generally call her *Ya Midi* (Emily). The Kongo idiom of sisterhood seems consistently to incorporate the Americans and the younger Belgians into the group as *Bayaya*.

In all these appellations the sisters respect each other's preferences. As in the village, one may not give a person a name, nor indeed give one person's name to another, as in the naming of a newborn child (*tombula zina*, 'to initiate with a name'), without the person's permission. Similarly, the Zaïrean sisters respect the preference of the few expatriates who prefer not to have the Kongo kinship terms applied to them. Nevertheless, behaviour patterns demonstrate how the Zaïrean sisters slot them into appropriate niches: *mama, tante, nkaka, yaya*.

The continued presence in the Province of sisters who are closely linked to the 'founding mothers', particularly the women referred to as *Mama* and *Nkaka*, is very obviously appreciated as a great blessing. In the villages, a sign of the favour of the *bakulu* (ancestors) is their gift of longevity to clan members. Such a person might be called a *nkulu-muntu* (literally, an ancient one), which has the implication that the person is a 'living-ancestor' among the people. Because of their closeness to joining the ancestors, these elders of the elders are regarded as having a particular power to protect the clan and promote harmony among all its children. Recently, when two sisters of this class, both in their upper seventies, left the Province to retire in Belgium, the Zaïrean sisters expressed their distress at the departure of women who had served the Province and their communities as *véritables paratonnerres* or 'true lightning rods'.

I have been present several times when Zaïrean sisters spoke with an obvious relish about the wonderful funerals they would give to sisters such as these! In Kongo villages the death of an *nkulu-muntu* is followed by a celebration markedly different from other burials, which are sombrely accompanied by loud wailing and mourning. By contrast, during a wake for those who die at the end of a long life, there is music and dancing: the villagers and the clan fête an 'ancient one' who has gone to his or her rest among the ancestors after being blest with longevity.

This celebration of the ancestors' blessing of their kin with longevity was touchingly expressed by a group of Kongo sisters on the occasion of the Fiftieth Jubilee of Sister Xavéria's arrival in Zaïre. She had served as the Novice Mistress (1957–62) for the local Sisters of St.

Marie. Members of this Zaïrean congregation presented to her, who had been a 'Mama' to them in their early days, a *luvenda* as a Jubilee gift. This is the traditional blanket brought by close clan folk to a wake and used by the family to wrap the body of the deceased before burial. The sisters wanted to publicly honour the missionary as a recognised 'living-ancestor', whose continued presence among them was a blessing, as would be her death when she would take their concerns with her to the ancestors.

During recent years there seems to be, particularly among the older sisters in the Province, a greater consciousness of and reference to the 'founding mothers' of the Congregation in Zaïre. This is in evidence on the anniversaries of the deaths of these sisters, when the community invokes the deceased in prayer. On such days, if there are sisters in the community who knew the missionary personally or had heard stories about her, they will recount anecdotes to the other members at a meal-time. In a few instances when word arrived from Belgium of the recent death of a remembered missionary, her passing was solemnised by the chanting of a composed litany that addressed her by name along with all the other 'living dead' of the Province who preceded her, such as,

Mama Tifwani, *utusambila.*

[Mother (Sister) Stephanie, pray for us.]

Mama Sofi, *utusambila.* (Josephine)
Mama Diza, *utusambila.* (Elisabeth)
Mama Vé, *utusambila.* (Xavéria)

This is very reminiscent of the spontaneous prayers and invocations said to the ancestors at the grave site when kin bury a member of the clan. In this way the ancestors are invoked to receive the sister among them and to pray for blessings on the living members of the Province. No doubt the sisters will eventually add Zaïreans to their number.

For the Kongo the more recently deceased kin are literally the more alive 'living-dead'. Stories of exceptional past heroes and the history of the clan's migration from ancient Mbanza Kongo in the time of the *Ntotila* (chief of the Ancient Kingdom of the Kongo) may be recalled at solemn gatherings. Apart from these, other distant ancestors are referred to generally as forebears. They are invoked as such without personal names. The more recent, 'known' dead who are still living in people's memories are invoked by name. Frequently in community prayer and discussions the foundress of the congregation, Ste Julie Billiart, is mentioned and invoked with great familiarity, even though she was a Frenchwoman who lived in 1756–1816. Clearly the Zaïrean sisters place great importance upon recognising her as the clan's *Ngudi Kisina* (literally original or root-mother, the foundress of the matriclan). She is addressed as *Mama* Zudi.[18]

Other Field Data

Vocabulary Domains Relating to more Frequently Employed Language

Here I shall briefly offer some field data on the frequent incorporation of words of one language into the other, as observed firstly within the religious community by the sisters, both Zaïrean and expatriate, and secondly among the general population.

Common Transfers of Vocabularies by the Sisters

Two vocabulary domains are frequently served by Kikongo words even when the speakers are using French. As already indicated, Kongo kinship terms applied to relationships within and without the community are often used with no attempt to translate them. This indicates that the operative model for most social relationships is in fact the kin group. Secondly, Kikongo words prevail in the names of commonly used household and table objects, including general food categories (e.g., vegetables, condiments, drinks).

On the other hand, the sisters often draw on French for terms specific to formal education and the health profession. Often these words will be transformed to accommodate Kongo language patterns, by adding vowels at the end of words, using Kikongo prefixes to form plurals, modifying letters that do not exist in the language (c, j).

Generalised Accommodation by the Local Population

The first partial word list given below (Table 1) suggests the types of words that are commonly heard in ordinary village discussions even when people are speaking in Kikongo. It is by no means complete. The second (Table 2) indicates Kikongo words that are commonly incorporated into conversations of Kongo-speakers using French.

The 'Art of Speaking'

The younger sisters, who have not had a nuanced education in their mother tongue of Kikongo, will on occasion recruit their older Zaïrean sisters to serve as public spokeswomen. This is particularly true when there arises a 'palaver' (conflict) that needs to be dealt with. More than once I saw younger superiors and headmistresses of schools invite a senior sister to serve as an *nzonzi* (facilitator) in a delicate 'palaver' involving personnel who work in the community, its schools, or its dispensaries. The young recognise that they are not as skilled in using and understanding proverbs which are such an important part of talking through and settling disputes. The younger sisters know that they are handicapped in speaking with *bambuta* in such situations.[19]

During my last years in Zaïre I also noticed that the younger sisters would frequently turn to their seniors to help them continue their traditional education, truncated because of their schooling. Even though almost all the younger sisters grew up as 'village girls', their understanding of much of Kongo folk knowledge – the traditional pharmacopoeia, clan history and traditions, the legacy of fables and proverbs – is far more limited than that of their elders. To some extent this ignorance of the young is in direct proportion to their education. Their eagerness to make up for this lacuna expresses itself in their willingness to spend many evenings listening to the older sisters sharing with them in the manner of *bambuta*. The young question the seniors about the ancestral ways. Significantly, these long discussions are almost always in Kikongo. Frequently this happens in the evening when the community is sitting around talking informally while shelling melon seeds or groundnuts, as women do in the late afternoons in the villages.

Conclusions

No doubt the former colonisers' own linguistic experience has had an impact on language usage in today's Zaïre. It certainly figured in the early missionary literature, which closely linked the use of the vernacular with the maintenance of local customs.[20] For both Flemish and Walloons, language has been a question of central importance in discussions of ethnic identity and self-determination in Belgium.[21]

The transfer of Kongo kinship terminology into the convent is a natural corollary of the kin group's being for the majority of the sisters the operative model of social relations. It suggests how they perceive their relationship with one another in the religious community, and the facility with which the different ethnic groups within the community accommodate the kinship terminology indicates the ease of social relations among the sisters.

The sisters' clear choice of French, the language of a small minority, as the common second language in community assures all members access to group life. It is the lingua franca for formal gatherings: meals, meetings, community prayer. The growing influence and use of Lingala, spoken in the capital and increasingly across Zaïre, coupled with the ever smaller number of expatriate sisters in the Province, may change the picture. It will be interesting to see if the community eventually adopts this nearly national African language as its more formal medium of expression in place of French. Because of the demography of the Congregation, the Zaïrean sisters recognise that English is of increasing importance for communication within the order, since two-thirds of the members speak English as their mother tongue. The five other Provinces of the Sisters of Notre Dame in Africa are all in English-speaking countries. Language preference is a marker of chosen identity with a given group.

The cited vocabulary domains and partial word lists demonstrate the situational quality of language choice and also how 'imported' words are adapted to be consistent with the 'receiving' language's own internal patterns (e.g., spelling, use of prefixes). This is in no way a new phenomenon for the Kongo. Many long-standing words in Kikongo clearly have Portuguese origin, such as: *mesa* (table), *nela* (window). In this Kikongo shows itself to be a dynamic, living language.

Table 1: Partial Word List Showing Common Incorporation of French into Kikongo (in more usual Kikongo-ised form)

English	French	Kikongo
lorry	*camion*	*kamio*
sweets	*bonbon*	*bombo*
bicycle	*bicyclette*	*bisikleti*
handkerchief	*mouchoir*	*musuadi*
jumper	*tricot*	*tidiko*
machine	*machine*	*masinu*
rail tracks	*rail*	*nlayi*
chain	*chainette*	*tieni*
slippers	*pantoufle*	*tuntufu*
trousers	*pantalon*	*pantalo*
wardrobe	*armoire*	*arumwadi*
pen	*bic*	*biki*
plane, scraper	*rabot*	*labru*
farm	*ferme*	*fermi*
armchair	*fauteuil*	*foteyi*
tiredness	*fatigue*	*fatiki*
bag, sack	*sacoche*	*sakosi*
handbag	*sac à main*	*sacrame*
government, state	*état*	*leta*
towel	*essuie mains*	*suime*
petrol	*essence*	*esami*
diesel fuel	*mazout*	*mazuti*
error, mistake	*erreur*	*aledi*
pin	*épingle*	*pengedi*

bishop	*évêque*	*pisikopo*
deacon	*diâcre*	*diakono*
jam, jelly	*confiture*	*konfitidi*
paper	*papier*	*papie*
Bible	*bible*	*biblio*
address:		
Sister	*ma soeur*	*maseri*
Brother	*mon frère*	*monfreri*
Priest	*Mons. Abbé*	*Tata Labe*
by no means	*pas moyen*	*moyen*
metal pot	*marmite*	*marmiti*
drinking glass	*verre*	*veri*
eye glasses	*lunettes*	*luneti*
French	*français*	*kifwalansi*

Table 2 Common Incorporation of Kikongo Words into French

Kikongo	English
fufu	anything that is powdery by nature (ex. flour, soap)
masa (water)	anything that is liquid (ex. water, oil, petrol, ink)
ngatu	perhaps
nkatu	used as a negation
fulu nkatu	there is no more room
gana mbote	say hello
malembe, malembe	gently, slowly
kiosi	cold
matadi makiosi (literally cold rocks)	ice
ndombe	anything that is dark in colour
mbisi (literally meat)	any condiments eaten with cassava
makaya (literally leaves)	any vegetable
nti (literally tree, wood)	chair or something to sit on
mafuta	anything greasy or oily (ex. margarine, diesel fuel)
nioka	anything having the form of a snake, including worms and spaghetti

Notes

1. Province in this instance is an administrative division within the Congregation which would have its own resident regional Superior, called a Provincial. Most decisions affecting the sisters living in such a region are made at the province level. Province divisions usually reflect national or linguistic boundaries.

2. Most were then withdrawn from the then more established Diocese of

Kisantu to staff younger dioceses of the interior that had fewer local clerics.

3. According to the historian of the colonial period, Vellut (1980:263), 83.6 per cent of the Belgian missionaries in the colonies of the *métropole* were Flemish. Cf. also Stengers 1989:202–03.

4. The mission historian points out the consequences:

the ethnocultural policies and attitudes of the missionaries contributed to political fragmentation along tribal and ethnic lines in the Congo...

Flemish parochial nationalism was often projected by Catholic missionaries on to the African setting ...

The Christian missions ... had nurtured the elite that was responsible for the nationalist movement, but they could not provide a focus for national integration. On the contrary, in many ways they fostered the disintegrative forces which have been at work in the Congo at various periods since independence, and which remain a potential danger (Markowitz 1973:157, 163, 164).

Cf. also Young 1965:129. Concerning the background of Flemish nationalism in the *métropole*, see Lorwin 1966.

5. Cf. Lemarchand 1964:133–43 for a critical assessment of educational policy in the Belgian Congo.

6. The first graduates of the University of Lovanium in 1958 numbered only eleven. At independence, there were thirty Congolese university graduates (Young 1965:95).

7. French is the language of instruction in formal education beginning in the third year of primary school.

8. Most of the missionary sisters have a speaking knowledge of Kikongo.

9. Diocesan congregation means an order under the direct jurisdiction of the bishop of the diocese. By contrast, the Sisters of Notre Dame de Namur, like most international orders, is a congregation of pontifical right. As such the latter has one of its own members as the major superior and thereby enjoys a certain degree of quasi-autonomy.

10. Cf. Burke (1990: Chapter 9).

11. For a discussion of how Kongo kinship terminology is applied to the Sisters outside the convent, see Burke 1990: Chapter 7 and Burke: (1993).

12. In some parts of the Congregation, until the 1950s, the Mistress of Novices was referred to by the title of 'Mother'.

13. Some of the Belgian sisters were more sensitive than others in their language use. Following a meeting of the superiors in the Province with the representative of the Superior General in 1958, the following was included in a series of Directives sent to the communities, 'The Congolese Sisters will no longer be designated "*petite Soeur, Soeur noire, Soeur indigène*". These terms must be suppressed' (internal document – Archives of Mother House in Namur).

14. *Nkulu* as an adjective means 'old', and by extension as a substantive 'ancestor'.

15. As early as 1901 the expression *Mfumu* is used in Jesuit missionary correspondence to refer to their superior (*Précis historiques* 1901:142). The first instance found of the similar use of *Mfumu nkuluntu* was 1907. The same letter

uses *Mfumu* for a priest (*ibid.*, 1907:242).

16. It is interesting to note that to the southwest among Manianga-Kongo the Founder of the Kongo Universal Church is addressed as '*Nkuluntu*' (MacGaffey 1983:206).

17. Her name is in fact Sister Maria Laetitia; but this is very difficult for Kikongo speakers to pronounce, so the usual rendering is Tchi-tchi.

18. Zudi: Kikongo rendering of Julie.

19. Cf. Burke 1988: Document dc travail, no. 5; Burke 1990: Chapter 14.

20. Cf. Fabian 1986; Lemarchand, 1965:563–4; Markowitz, 1973:157f; Yates, 1980.

21. Cf. Mallinson 1963; Lorwin 1966.

References

Burke, J. F., 1988, *Dossier: inculturation de la vie religieuse chez les Soeurs de Notre Dame de Namur*. Unpublished study commissioned by the Sisters of Notre Dame de Namur, Kimwenza, Zaïre.

———, 1990. 'The Sisters of Notre Dame de Namur in Lower Zaïre: A social and historical study', unpublished D.Phil. thesis (Social Anthropology), University of Oxford.

———, 1993, 'These Catholic Sisters are all *Mamas!*' in F. Bowie, D. Kirkwood and S. Ardener (eds), *Women and Missions*, Oxford: Berg.

Fabian, J., 1986, *Language and colonial power: The appropriation of Swahili in the former Belgian Congo, 1880–1938*, African Studies Series, no. 48, London: Cambridge University Press.

Kaplan, I., 1979, *Zaïre: a country study*, Washington, D.C.: American University.

Lemarchand, R., 1964, *Political awakening in the Belgian Congo*, Berkeley: University of California Press.

———, 1965, 'Congo (Leopoldville)' in J.S. Coleman and C.G. Rosberg (eds), *Political Parties and National Integration in Tropical Africa*, pp. 560–96, Berkeley: University of California Press.

Léonie de l'Assomption, n.d., *Congo Débuts (1894–1920)*. Manuscript, Archives of the Sisters of Notre Dame at the Mother House in Namur, Belgium.

———, n.d., *Congo II (1920–60)*. Manuscript, Archives of the Sisters of Notre Dame at the Mother House in Namur, Belgium.

Lorwin, V. R., 1966, 'Belgium: Religion, Class, and Language in National Politics' in R.A. Dahl (ed.), *Political Oppositions in Western Democracies*, pp. 147–87, New Haven: Yale University Press.

MacGaffey, W., 1983, *Modern Kongo Prophets*, Bloomington, Indiana: Indiana University Press.

Mallinson, V., 1963, *Power and Politics in Belgian Education, 1815–1961*, London: Heinemann.

Markowitz, M. D., 1973, *Cross and Sword: The Political Role of the Christian Missions in the Belgian Congo, 1908–1960*, Stanford: Hoover Institution Press.

Précis Historiques. Bulletin mensuel des Missions Belges de la Compagnie de Jésus. IIIe Série, tome troisième, XLIIIe de toute la collection.

Stengers, J., 1989, *Congo mythes et réalités: 100 ans d'histoire*, Louvain-la-Neuve: Editions Duculot.

Vandeputte, Sr Maria, l980, *L'Apostolat Notre-Dame au Coeur de l'Afrique, 20. partie: 1944–1980*, Manuscript, Archives of the Sisters of Notre Dame at the Mother House in Namur, Belgium.

Vellut, J.-L., 1980, 'Les Belges au Congo (1885–1960)' in A. d'Haeneans (ed.), *La Belgique: sociétés et cultures depuis 150 ans, 1830–1980*, pp. 260–5, Brussels: Ministère des Affaires Etrangères.

Yates, B., 1980, 'The origins of language policy in Zaïre', *Journal of Modern African Studies* 18:257–79.

Young, M. C., 1965, *Politics in the Congo*, Princeton, N.J.: Princeton University Press.

9

Language and Diaspora: The Use of Portuguese, English and Konkani by Catholic Goan Women

Stella Mascarenhas-Keyes

Introduction

The introduction of new ideas, religion, food, dress, technologies and such like into a society and the degree of resistance to or acceptance of them is an area of considerable theoretical and empirical interest. In the field of anthropological linguistics, the role of colonialism in introducing a second language into a speech community needs examination. A second language often becomes a language of imperial administration, but its vernacular as a first language is an area that has been little explored.

Although there have been a number of recent studies of language and gender (including Spender, 1980, Thorne and Henley, 1975), the role that women play in the maintenance of the vernacular and the shift to second-language use has not received attention. In this paper I shall attempt to redress this situation by examining the role Catholic Goan (CG) women played in the use of two second languages of European origin, Portuguese and English, and in the use of Konkani, the vernacular of Goa, descended from Sanskrit. In order to do this, the colonial context in which the two second languages were introduced into Goa is first examined. This examination highlights various facets of Portuguese linguistic policy which were directed specifically at Catholics[1] converted from Hinduism. As I shall show, a section of CG women played an important role in facilitating second-language acquisition. These women operated within the context of a changing local and global political economy which favoured international migration[2] from Goa. I shall focus on the contribution to the spread of second-language use that such women made formally as workers, particularly in the new profession of teaching, and informally as mothers pursuing the new ideology of what I shall

149

term 'progressive motherhood' which gained prominence from the turn of this century. The effect of women's choices on the use of Konkani is examined in the last part of the paper within the context of the colonial legacy and the community's ambivalent attitude to the vernacular.

This paper draws on data collected during intensive fieldwork in Goa in 1979–1981,[3] supplemented by personal knowledge as a native anthropologist (see Mascarenhas-Keyes, 1987b).

Portuguese Colonialism with Particular Reference to its Linguistic Policy

Goa is a small region of 3,400 sq.km. on the west coast of India. According to the 1981 census it had an indigenous population of approximately 1 million, of which 32 per cent were Catholics and 63 per cent Hindus. It was ruled by a succession of Hindu dynasties and by the Muslims until the conquest of the central areas (known as the Old Conquests) by the Portuguese from 1510, and of the peripheral areas (known as the New Conquests) in the latter half of the eighteenth century. Portuguese colonialism lasted until 1961, when Goa became incorporated into the Indian Union. English then replaced Portuguese as the official language of Goa. Konkani, which was suppressed during the colonial régime, has enjoyed a renaissance since 1961.[4] A referendum held in 1967 to determine whether Konkani or Marathi (also descended from Sanskrit) was the mother tongue of Goans favoured Konkani. It has been adopted by the government as one of the official languages of Goa, introduced into the school curriculum and approved as one of the modern Indian languages for degree studies (Gomes, 1987:313).

Portuguese colonialism, articulated by a predominantly monolithic approach by the state and the Catholic church, led to multiple changes in Goa. Goa became the administrative, political, judicial and ecclesiastical headquarters of the Estado da India which at one time stretched from the Cape of Good Hope across to China (Boxer, 1969; de Souza, 1979). Portuguese was imposed in Goa and the rest of the empire as the language of imperial administration. Roman Catholicism was the state religion until 1961, and Latin was the liturgical language.

Colonial policy led to the creation of two distinct religious communities, Catholics and Hindus, the former being predominantly resident in the Old Conquests and the latter in the New Conquests. It resulted in a cultural syncretism among the Catholics who were drawn from all sections of the population.[5] This syncretism was manifested in a number of ways (Mascarenhas-Keyes, 1987a:92–144; 1988b), two of which are relevant for this paper: retention of caste and adoption of western culture.

The pre-colonial system of stratification based on caste was retained, although in an attenuated form (D'Costa, 1977; Mascarenhas-Keyes, 1987a:125–33). This was expressed *inter alia* firstly by a hierarchy analogous to the Hindu *varna* ranking with Brahmins at the apex;[6] secondly, by a communal land-tenure system whose dividends were distributed in accordance with caste rank; thirdly, by a strong preference for marital endogamy, especially among the upper castes; fourthly, by the absence of a ritual concept of purity-pollution; and finally by the minimal association of caste with name, dress, diet, commensality observances and religious worship. Western culture was adopted by CGs under pressure from colonial policy[7] and in some cases voluntarily, and is characterised by Christian first names and Portuguese surnames, dress, diet, music, education and language. The position of women changed in a number of ways, for instance in the late age of marriage, celibacy, entry to religious orders to become nuns and improved property rights (Mascarenhas-Keyes, 1990a).

Portuguese linguistic policy in Goa had three main components: the active promotion of Portuguese, exposure to other western languages, and the suppression of Konkani. The first two aspects of this policy are discussed in this section, with the last one later in this chapter.

Roman Catholicism was an important vehicle through which western linguistic models were promoted in Goa. Since the sixteenth-century Portuguese concept of conquest included religious as well as political and economic domination, Goa (specifically the Old Conquests) was subject to considerable proselytisation. Intensive missionary penetration aided the incursion of western languages into a formerly monolingual speech community.

Since Latin was the liturgical language of the universal church, conversion implicitly led to exposure to this language, which increased the receptiveness of CGs to other European languages. The large number of women as well as men who joined the convents and seminaries learned Latin during their vocational training. Lack of knowledge of Portuguese among converts was seen as detrimental to adherence to the Catholic faith. Thus the Inquisition of Goa, which was set up in 1560 (Priolkar, 1961), attributed the retention of Hinduism among converts to the lack of observance of directives 'prohibiting the natives to converse in their own vernacular and making obligatory the use of the Portuguese language' (Rivara, 1858:207).

The measures to encourage the adoption of Portuguese included the following. Parish priests and school teachers were told by the Viceroy in 1684 to impart instructions in Portuguese 'so that in course of time the Portuguese idiom will be common to one and all to the exclusion of the mother tongue' (Rivara, 1858:183). The upper castes were given six months, other castes a year, to learn the language. Fluency was made a prerequisite to Christian marriage. It was obligatory for those working in public offices and military head-quarters to speak only Portuguese (Rivara, ibid:216). Attempts were also made, for instance in 1745, to make recruitment to the priesthood contingent on the proviso that the candidate 'knows and speaks Portuguese only' and that the same applies 'to his close relatives of both sexes' (Rivara, ibid:212). Since candidates to the clergy were at the time mainly drawn from the two upper castes, such attempts paved the way for the erosion of pride in the mother tongue among them. Although the multiple directives were not unanimously supported or implemented (Rivara, ibid:184), their existence is an important indication of the attitude of the colonial régime to Portuguese and Konkani.

As a Roman Catholic ecclesiastical centre, Goa housed various educational institutions at primary, secondary and tertiary levels. Since the curriculum was almost entirely western, western education became equated with a Catholic education. Portuguese was taught in schools in all the parishes (Rivara, 1858:191), and was also used as a medium of instruction in schools and colleges, initially as a sole medium, but later supplemented by the vernacular in primary schools (Varde, 1977:2).

The provision of education for females and males had gradually been expanding around the turn of the eighteenth century. This gave more and more Goans access to primary as well as secondary and tertiary education. From the mid-nineteenth century onwards compulsory education for both sexes was introduced and penalties imposed to ensure attendance (Rodricks, 1974:90–1).

Specific educational provision in Portuguese for females in Goa was established by the state in the mid-nineteenth century, and a small number of females attended single-sex and co-educational secondary institutions (Menezes Bragança, 1923:195–200). Various congregations of nuns who had a high pedagogic reputation also provided education for females (Moraes, 1972:136).

Access to tuition in European languages other than Portuguese was increased through state provision of Latin, English, German and French classes (Rodricks, 1974:87). The teaching of European languages was also available at general institutions such as the Professional Institute of Nova Goa, the Lyceums, and the Escola Nacional de Sexo Femino which catered for females only (Varde 1977:16–18). In addition a number of private language schools were established after the state encouraged such activity early in the nineteenth century (Rodricks, 1974:83).

English-language provision was promoted by the Portuguese government because it enhanced opportunities for job acquisition, and remittances from international migrants were crucial to offset the negative commercial balance (Almeida, 1965:268; Ribeiro, 1965:80). The greater employment opportunities in the British Empire led to the fact that by 1950 (when Goa was still a Portuguese colony) there were sixty-five private English-medium primary, middle and secondary schools with 13,477 students, compared to 10,944 at the Portuguese schools (Varde, 1977:90–1). Most of the English-language provision was under the Catholic church, and this was supplemented by private schools and tutorial classes run in the homes of fluent speakers.

Both Portuguese and English speakers enjoyed high status. Since fluent Portuguese usage was mandatory among ecclesiastics, the intelligentsia, civil servants and the military in Goa, it came to be positively associated with power, knowledge, white-collar and professional occupations. Western language speakers were regarded as more independent, ambitious and self-confident, and fluency connoted high educational level and socio-economic status, as also noted in Africa (Parkin, 1977:193). As English became the lingua franca of many countries and the major link language in the world (Conrad and Fishman, 1975), its prestige increased. The prestige of English, particularly in a non-English-speaking country like Goa during the colonial period, was strongly connected to the prestige of education.

Apart from Portuguese colonial policy and practice, another factor which influenced the acquisition of Portuguese and English by a large cross-section of the CG population was their geographical and occupational mobility.

The Goan Diaspora

The Goan diaspora has its roots in four major factors: firstly Goa's position as the headquarters of the Estado da India, which led to its having extensive extra-territorial links; secondly the lack of economic development in Goa during the colonial regime (Mascarenhas-Keyes, 1990b); thirdly the rise of British colonialism; and fourthly enhanced access to Catholic western education, which raised occupational expectations and a desire for a better quality of life.

International migration has come to be seen by most Catholic Goans in Goa as part of the life-cycle, with the probable return to Goa to spend the 'winter of our lives' (Mascarenhas-Keyes, 1988a). Goans, particularly Catholics, took advantage of employment opportunities within the Portuguese Empire, and thus many migrated to Mozambique, Angola, Macao and Portugal. Complementing the diaspora to the Portuguese

Empire was the subsequent much larger migration to areas encompassed by the British Empire in the nineteenth and twentieth centuries. Catholics also took up employment on shipping lines, such as B.I. and P & O., plying on international routes. Secondary migration, particularly from Africa, to the West and Australasia was stimulated by the political and economic changes that accompanied the end of empire in British East Africa in the 1960s and in Portuguese East Africa in the 1970s. Migration to the Middle East and especially the Gulf States gathered momentum in the 1970s when these areas experienced an economic boom with the discovery of vast amounts of oil. As a result there are CG communities in every continent, the majority in Anglophone areas.[8] This diaspora has led to the creation of an international Catholic Goan community (ICGC) which transcends geographical boundaries (Mascarenhas-Keyes, 1987). It comprises the multiple satellite communities, their families in Goa and returnees. This community covers a cross-section of castes, as the wide range of job opportunities available outside-Goa was not caste-specific. There was a demand for cooks (of western cuisine), waiters, butlers, western musicians, *ayahs* (governesses), technicians, white-collar workers, ecclesiastics and professionals. The demand for different categories of workers varied in different historical periods and in different geographical areas.

There was considerable scope for upward mobility for those prepared to acquire internationally marketable skills and to be geographically mobile; and it was greatly enhanced by a cultural ethos which emphasises 'coming up', an appreciation of western education and increasing financial means to invest in education. Such investment was aided by the fact that apart from nuclear families, there were very limited avenues in which remittances could be invested in Goa. Consequently international migrants and non-migrants with surplus funds invested their money in the education of their children. The intention was to educate both males and females, but where there were financial constraints, males were given priority.

Those who sought employment within the Portuguese Empire took advantage of the educational opportunities in Goa and Portugal, and one of the skills acquired was fluency in Portuguese. There were material advantages associated with learning Portuguese, as it enhanced the speakers' opportunities for employment in the civil and ecclesiastical bureaucracy, formal education and commercial activity. For those responding to the greater employment opportunities in the British Empire, fluency in English was indispensable (Fishman, 1975:114–15). Since English/Portuguese was an important requirement in the non-manual 'good jobs' CGs aspired to, it provided a powerful incentive to learn the language, a situation parallel to that motivating Israelis to learn English (Cooper and Seckbach, 1975).

Women played various roles within the diaspora. As Catholicism gave women access to independent vocations outside the family, many joined religious orders founded in the West to become nuns, complementing the large contingent of men who became priests. Some of the women joined convents within Goa, but a large number joined convents outside, initially in India. From these institutions they undertook educational, medical and other apostolates all over India, and overseas as well. Other women who participated in independent migration were usually of low caste, seeking employment as *ayahs* and domestic servants. A small number went into the teaching profession and had an important role to play in second-language use, as we shall see shortly. However, most women were associational migrants, accompanying or joining their migrant husbands, and any employment they undertook, which was rare for earlier generations, was secondary to their role as mothers. In cases where married women were unable or unwilling to migrate they remained in Goa, where one of their principal concerns was the social reproduction of the future generation of migrant labour, as we shall see shortly.

Second-Language Use by Female Workers

As a result of Portuguese linguistic policy, some categories of women acquired a western language. Initially this was Portuguese, but later as English-language provision became more widespread and more desired, linguistic competence in English was acquired. While knowledge and use of Portuguese was confined to a smaller number of women, in the case of English not only were the numbers greater but the women were also drawn from a wider cross-section of the Catholic population. The main reason for this was that the financial wherewithal to pay for education came largely from the remittances of international migrants, who were themselves drawn from a wider cross-section of the population. Most women knew only one western language, but some of the better-educated were familiar with both Portuguese and English. Some women mastered only conversational skills, while others also acquired reading and writing ability. These skills were used by three categories of female workers: traders, teachers and office workers.

Few CG women worked as traders, but some, such as fisherwomen, sold their catch in the urban markets. Since their clientele included Portuguese speakers, they mastered a degree of conversational skills.

Teaching was one of the major vocations which particularly attracted early generations of educated Goan women. Female teachers, some of whom were nuns, were employed in Goa, elsewhere in India and in Africa. Teachers in Goa belonged to two categories: those who taught in Portuguese-medium schools and those who taught in English-medium schools and private tutorial classes. As the educational provision until the twentieth century was greater in Portuguese, more women were employed in Portuguese-medium than in English-medium schools. However, as the demand for English-language education grew, the amount of educational provision increased, with a corresponding increase in the number of female teachers.

Goan female teachers were also widely employed in Bombay and other towns in India in schools affiliated to the Catholic church. The extensive provision of Catholic schools and colleges within British (and later independent) India was largely the outcome of a deliberate education policy (Moraes, 1972:166). A number of the teachers in the predominantly Goan parishes in Bombay were Goan women who complemented the staff team comprising priests (Colonias Portuguesas, 1912:186). These teachers taught not only local residents, but also children and teenagers one or both of whose parents were based in Goa. These parents capitalised on the more vocationally advantageous English-medium opportunities available in British India in order to circumvent the Portuguese government stipulation that a pass in a certain level of Portuguese was a prerequisite to English-language studies in Goa (Varde, 1977:90).

In the early decades of this century, as English-medium educational facilities with many Goan female staff became available in Goa, they came to be used not only by local residents but also by others living in Africa. In British East Africa Goans with Portuguese nationality were precluded from attending government schools (Nelson, 1971:223). A few small private elementary level 'tutorial' classes in English were run mainly by educated CG women, and secondary education was provided in the Indian subcontinent until equivalent facilities were established in British East Africa. In Nairobi in 1940, the Goan Overseas Association was able to establish an English-medium community secondary school, a trend which was subsequently replicated in other cities and towns to cater for the community (Nelson, 1971:223–7). Western languages, including Latin, and literature were given a prominent place in the curriculum. The staff team comprised a number of Goan women and men as well as European Catholic priests and nuns.

Despite the number of women who served as teachers, among the earlier generations of migrant CG women the overall numbers that went out to work were small. However, as succeeding generations of young women became fluent English-speakers, they capitalised on the tremendous demand for office workers in British India (D'Souza, 1975:253; Haward, 1980), Africa (Kuper, 1973:155) and the West (Mascarenhas-Keyes, 1979:28–33). In pursuing such vocations they followed the precedent of educated Portuguese-speaking women who gained white-collar employment in the Portuguese civil service in Goa and elsewhere in the empire (D'Souza, 1975:253). English fluency was supplemented by the acquisition of the universally recognised skills of shorthand and typing. The entry of English-speaking CG women into the nursing schools and the profession was facilitated by an appreciation of western medical models and practices. Occupational mobility, in which western education and fluent linguistic skills play a paramount role, has become more widespread nowadays among young women in the West who are entering professional employment in increasing numbers.

Second-Language Use by Mothers

In addition to women who went out to work, many full-time mothers and housewives also spoke a western language. In the case of Portuguese, women from elite families used it in the home to converse with family members and with peers. Another category of speakers were urban residents of Panjim and Margao and villages adjacent to these towns. Male family members from such Lusophone households were employed within the Estado da India, either in Goa or overseas. Until 1961, when English became the lingua franca, non-working female English-speakers in Goa were predominantly from households with a current or recent history of migration to the British Empire.

Mothers, particularly those with a strong commitment to the international migration of their children and upward mobility, have additional responsibilities, particularly with respect to the education of children. The combination of the traditional reproductive and nurturing roles with new roles and responsibilities I refer to as 'progressive motherhood' (Mascarenhas-Keyes, 1990a).

One of the multitude of ideal attributes and skills that wives require in order to effectively pursue 'progressive motherhood' had been and continues to be relative fluency in a western language. Mothers who have a good command of Portuguese or English create a more favourable linguistic learning environment which fosters educational competence. Thus they can complement the pedagogic efforts of teachers in facilitating western-language acquisition. This endeavour was particularly significant for the promotion of English in Goa during the colonial regime, when Portuguese was the dominant language. Within that linguistic context, it was easier for mothers to encourage Portuguese fluency in their children. It was, however, a bigger challenge for mothers to encourage English fluency, particularly in homes where English was not spoken by other adult members and where a woman's own English-speaking husband was working outside Goa. The approach of progressive Goan mothers has parallels with women in Southern France who tend to abandon the vernacular (Provençal) and are very concerned that their children learn correct French, which is a condition and symbol of improved status (Schieben-Lange, 1977:105).

Progressive mothers are expected to monitor their children's progress at school and 'take up their lessons'. This process involves the mother asking questions from the school book and checking the child's answers against the text. Rote learning is a common pedagogical method, and this facilitates the involvement of mothers with a passive comprehension of Portuguese or English in promoting educational attainment in children.

'Progressive motherhood' necessitates being able to understand the significance of school reports and teachers' comments written in a western language. If a child is under-achieving in certain subjects, particularly language, mothers arrange private 'coaching' classes to supplement school attendance.

The role of a 'progressive mother' cannot easily be played by other women; paternal and maternal grandmothers are usually not of much help here, because of their own relative lack of education and especially of western linguistic skills (Mascarenhas-Keyes, 1991). The absence of both means that grandmothers are at best only able to play a custodial role.

From the above discussion it can be noted that while men deployed the second language principally through employment, women used both the occupational and domestic domains to promote the use of Portuguese/English. Thus the activities of women as teachers and mothers have produced younger generations of females and males literate in Portuguese and/or English. As a result, with each generation of migrants, greater literacy has developed. This is even more apparent in places where settled communities of CGs have been established – in cities and towns all over the world – and in particular where Portuguese or English is the official language.

The Colonial Legacy and the Impact of Women's Second-Language Use on Konkani

In order to understand the impact of women's use of Portuguese and English on the use of the vernacular, it is first necessary to appreciate the historical context in which the Portuguese suppressed Konkani. Apart from the first century and a half of colonialism when Konkani was not only tolerated[9] but both the civil and ecclesiastical authorities favoured its study by missionaries with the principal aim of propagating the faith (Rivara, 1858:168), it was thereafter subjected to much repression at the expense of the promotion of Portuguese.[10] A number of measures were adopted, some of which I have mentioned earlier in this paper. In addition, other specific measures were that students and ecclesiastics residing in the seminaries of Goa were forbidden by the regulations of 1847 to converse with one another in Konkani (*ibid*:215). When the first state schools were set up in the early nineteenth century, children were forbidden to use Konkani in schools (*ibid*:216). The repression prevented the development of the language and its literature, and furthermore diluted both its oral and written authenticity. The Konkani spoken by CGs had been progressively corrupted under Portuguese rule. It contained a number of Romanised words to express Konkani vocables (ibid:158), and its syntax came to reflect that of Portuguese (Sardessai, 1978; Miranda, 1978:88). A number of dialects existed and were associated with particular geographical areas of Goa (Pereira, 1973:27–46; Miranda, 1978:81).

Colonial policy also changed the script in which it was written by CGs. Although Konkani was originally written in Indian scripts such as Devanagari, it came to be written in Roman script under the influence of the Portuguese civil and ecclesiastical authorities. Consequently CGs who learned to read and write Konkani simultaneously learned the Roman script. This was the only script that the vast majority of literate CGs mastered, as there were hardly any facilities to learn Indian scripts in the old Conquests, and indeed few had the motivation to do it.[11]

The colonial linguistic legacy resulted in the undermining of and alienation from Konkani which CGs, particularly the upwardly mobile, internalised and subsequently perpetuated. Those who spoke only Konkani were regarded as not civilised (Rivara, 1858:201) and of low status. 'Civilised' CGs generally kept Konkani to communicate with their servants. This association accentuated the general contempt with which Konkani had come to be viewed under the Portuguese (ibid:220): 'it was fashionable to despise the language: the natives themselves applauded this' (ibid:215). Indeed, many CGs particularly the elite, regarded Portuguese, not Konkani, as their own language (ibid:219).

Against the background of the colonial legacy, the subsequent lack of promotion of Konkani was significantly related to changing norms and values in the ICGC. In the context of international migration and the tremendous opportunities it created for upward mobility, there developed an orientation to achieved rather than ascribed status. An important feature of the ICGC was that unlike other migrant South

Asian communities it comprised a cross-section of castes. The variety of Konkani spoken provided an important clue to the caste origin of the speaker (Miranda, 1978:86). Whereas the syntactical and semantic differentiation in various Konkani dialects served as diacritical markers of ascribed origins, a standard western language disguised them. Since western-language teaching was provided in mixed-caste, not single-caste, community schools, differences in linguistic usage were minimised. Vernacular speaking became incompatible with upward mobility. The desire to jettison ascribed status in favour of achieved status provided an additional motivation for lower caste ICGs to encourage western linguistic fluency in their children.

Within this context, women as teachers and mothers did little to promote the use of Konkani, and hence the trend towards language death (Denison, 1977), particularly in the ICGC, was set in motion. Women in the ICGC, whether in Goa or outside, generally played a minimal role in promoting Konkani use. Their energies were directed towards facilitating foreign-language acquisition. International adult migrants who were habitual Konkani speakers were usually in manual work that did not require a good command of English or Portuguese, but because they aspired to help their children to enter non-manual work, they tended to minimise the use of Konkani in the home.

Indeed, those younger Goans who acquired a knowledge of Konkani lived in homes where it was spoken by the grandparents because they were not sufficiently fluent in English or Portuguese. Hence children who had close and frequent contact with Konkani-speaking grandparents, whether in Goa or outside, were more likely to acquire Konkani.

Over time, the death of the senior Konkani-speaking generation reduced the incentive to learn Konkani, and led to a decline in the transmission of knowledge of Konkani within the family. There was limited opportunity for Konkani to persist as a 'servant's language' outside Goa as it did in the mistress-servant relationship in Goa. Although many Goans employed servants, these were usually non-Goan.

There has been minimal opportunity for women or men to promote the use of Konkani as teachers. Since the majority of schools that CGs attended outside Goa were church schools, Konkani was not a part of the curriculum. In parallel situations that have confronted South Asian, Chinese, Mediterranean and Arab immigrants in the West, supplementary schools and classes to ensure vernacular training have been set up by the community (Saifullah-Khan, 1977; 1983; Grillo, 1989; Warner and Scrole, 1945). In contrast to this, only very minimal provision to learn Konkani has been made by the ICGC. For instance, Konkani classes were set up in Bombay to enable poor working-class Goans to become literate (Report of the Comissão, 1936:8).

The lack of provision was even more apparent in the community schools set up, for instance, in British East Africa. In all these Goan community schools English was a medium of instruction. While there was, for instance, some community controversy in Nairobi, when the first school was established, as to whether it should be Portuguese or English medium (Nelson, 1971:240), there was no question of its being Konkani medium. Nor was the teaching of Konkani part of the curriculum. Its use by children during play periods and extra-curricular activities was not encouraged. Hence the community schools did not provide an opportunity for learning the mother tongue. This contrasted strongly with the different community schools set up by other South Asian communities, where their specific vernaculars were taught. Indeed, the various Asian communities saw illiteracy in their languages as a threat to religion. Konkani, however, was only minimally associated with Catholicism until Vatican II in 1964 promoted the vernaculars. Therefore it did not have the same role in the religious sphere as the vernaculars did in other Asian communities.

Occasionally some elders in the ICGC suggest that Konkani classes should be established, for instance, under the auspices of community voluntary organisations. But they are lone voices, and support from peers or juniors is lacking. Attempts to recruit tutors and students and obtain language books have floundered in the initial stages.

Studies of the Goan community in Kampala, Nairobi and London testify to the fact that most speak English fluently (Nelson, 1971; Kuper, 1973; Mascarenhas-Keyes, 1979:25). The rise of a western language in the ICGC can be borne out by statistics. For instance, the 1957 census of Tanzania found the 31 per cent of Goans regarded English as their mother tongue (Census 1957), and this figure has since risen a great deal.

The low status of Konkani in the ICGC and its association with ascribed caste identity have led to its replacement by Portuguese or English in most community activities (Kuper, 1973:63). The majority of ICGC associations, whether in Goa or outside, conduct meetings and hold social events in Portuguese or English. An exception was associations set up by the Goan tailors, who used Konkani, but with the decline of this low-status occupation among younger generations of Goans such associations have either ceased to exist or have contracted considerably.

The lack of Konkani language use has not, however, precluded a nostalgic attachment to the language in the ICGC. For instance, great sentiment is evoked, particularly among the older generation, when Konkani songs are sung at social gatherings or special Konkani dramas are produced. Such sentiment has also been articulated politically in the support for campaigns to ensure that Konkani, not Marathi, was recognised as the regional language to forestall providing a basis for merger with the neighbouring state of Maharashtra.

Conclusion

In this paper I have examined the role CG women have played in the marginalisation of the mother tongue Konkani and the shift to the use of Portuguese/English. I have argued that the strategy adopted by women has to be understood within a wider political and socio-economic context, which has two main components. Firstly, there was the historical legacy of Portuguese colonialism, which promoted western languages, particularly Portuguese, and suppressed Konkani. Secondly, women were responding to an evolving, dynamic cultural ethos spawned by the CG diaspora, in which the acquisition of non-manual jobs was valued, and achieved status supplanted or at least complemented ascribed (caste) status. Both formally as teachers in schools and informally as progressive mothers, women facilitated and continue to facilitate the transition to monolingualism in Portuguese or English, via the process of bilingualism in which Portuguese/English and Konkani are used, with the latter being gradually marginalised. Thus women played a crucial role in the displacement of Konkani in various domains and its replacement by a western language in the international Catholic Goan community.

Notes

The research on which this paper is based was supported by a UK Social Science Research Council studentship in 1978–81. I am grateful to Professor David Parkin, Dr Ketaki Kushari Dyson, Dr Susan Wright and Shaun Keyes for helpful comments on earlier drafts of this paper.

1. There are a small number of Catholics of tribal origin, called Kunbis and Gauddas, who, some believe, were the original inhabitants of Goa. The term Catholic used in this paper does not include the tribals. Similarly, there are a large number of immigrant Hindus (about 30 per cent of the total population of Goa according to the 1981 census) who are not indigenous to Goa. They are not included when reference is made to Hindus in this paper.

2. Since Goa was a Portuguese enclave within India for 450 years, the term 'international migration' is used here to refer to migration from Goa to elsewhere in India as well as overseas. Although the change in political status in 1961 makes migration from Goa to Maharashtra and neighbouring areas interregional migration, the term 'international migration' is still employed because such migration is a continuation of a tradition that began when the current regional boundaries were national boundaries.

3. Unfortunately such research did not uncover a great deal of reliable statistical information on female education, employment, migration etc. This is partly characteristic of the general invisibility of women in primary and secondary historical and contemporary sources.

4. This contrasts with the Indian renaissance of languages and literatures which received an impetus during the British colonial period (see Dyson, 1978).

5. This is in contrast to elsewhere in India, where converts to Christianity were mainly drawn from the lower castes and untouchables (Diehl, 1965; Weibe and Jogh-Peter, 1972; Forrester, 1980).

6. The castes are, in hierarchical order, Brahmin, Chardo, Gaudde, Sudra, Mahar, Chamar.

7. The colonial attempt to Lusitanise, i.e. make Portuguese, was most intense in the first 200 years of Portuguese rule. During this period only the Old Conquests were under Portuguese rule. By 1670 85 per cent of the population of this area had been converted to Catholicism (Meersman 1972:66).

8. While both Catholics and Hindus migrated, the latter migrated in smaller numbers, and confined their movements to regions within India, usually the regions neighbouring Goa.

9. For a period of time, in an attempt to aid missionary work for which knowledge of the native language was considered useful, the Concilo Provincial, the first of which was held in Goa in 1567, strongly supported the study of Indian languages. In 1606 a Directive was issued to the effect that no priest should be appointed as vicar in charge of a parish unless he was conversant with the local language, and that a priest who was ignorant of the local language should lose that position unless he learned it within six months (Rivara, 1858).

10. For instance, the following decree was promulgated in 1684: 'I assign three years as the period within which the Portuguese language ought to be studied and spoken. Moreover, this language should be used by the people in these parts in dealings and other contact which they may wish to enter into, those using the vernacular being severely punished for not obeying the mandate' (Rivara, 1858:183). The decree further stated its hope that 'in the course of time the Portuguese idiom will be common to one and all, to the exclusion of the mother tongue' (Harrison, 1975:342).

11. This contrasted with the Hindu Goans, who from the last quarter of the nineteenth century, had access to both community and state schools, where Marathi and Gujarati were taught using Indian scripts (Varde, 1977:23).

References

Almeida, J.C., 1965, *Some Demographic Aspects of Goa, Daman & Diu*, Goa: Government Printing Press.

Boxer, C.R., 1969, *The Portuguese Seaborne Empire, 1415–1825*, London: Hutchinson.

'Colonias Portuguese en paises estrangeiros' 1912, *Boletim de Sociedade Geographia de Lisboa*, 89–159; 167–207; 599–609.

'Comissão Administrativa do Fundo Dos Emigrantes 1934–1938', *Relatorio*

Anno dos Trabalhos Realizados Pela Comissão, Bombay.

Conrad, A.W. and Fishman J.A., 1975, 'English as a World Language: The Evidence' in J.A. Fishman, R.L. Cooper and A.W. Conrad, (eds), *The Spread of English*, Rowley Mass.: Newbury House.

Cooper, R.L. and Seckbach, F., 1975, 'Economic Incentives for the Learning of a Language of Wider Communication: A Case Study' in J.A. Fishman, R.L. Cooper and A.W. Conrad (eds), *The Spread of English,* Rowley, Mass.: Newbury House.

D'Costa, A., 1977, 'Caste Stratification among the Roman Catholics of Goa', *Man in India*, vol.57, no.4, pp 283–92.

Denison, N., 1977, 'Language Death or Language Suicide' in W. Dresslker and A. Wodak-Leodolter (eds), *Language Death*, Hague: Mouton.

De Souza, T.R., 1979, *Medieval Goa: a Socio-economic History*, New Delhi: Concept.

Diehl, C.G., 1965, *Church and Shrine: Intermingling Patterns of Culture and Life of Some Christian Groups in South India*, Uppsala: Acta Universitatis.

D'Souza, B.G., 1975, *Goan Society in Transition*, Bombay: Bombay University Press.

Dyson, K. Kushari, 1978, *A Various Universe: A Study of the Journals and Memoirs of British men and women in the Indian Subcontinent 1765–1856*, Delhi: Oxford University Press.

Fieldhouse, D.K., 1966, *The Colonial Empires: A Comparative Survey from the 18th Century*, London: Weidenfeld & Nicholson.

Fishman, J.A., 1975, 'The Spread of English as a new Perspective for a Study of Language Maintenance and Language Shift' in Fishman *et al*, as above.

Forrester, D., 1980, *Caste and Christianity: Attitudes and Policies on Caste of Anglo-Saxon Protestant Missions in India*, London: Curzon Press.

Gomes, O.J.F., 1987, *Village Goa: A Study of Goan Social Structure and Change*, New Delhi: Chand & Co. Ltd.

Grillo, R., 1989, *Dominant Language: Language & Hierarchy in Britain and France*, Cambridge: Cambridge University Press.

Harrison, J.B., 1975, 'The Portuguese' in A.L. Basham (ed.), *A Cultural History of India*, Oxford: Clarendon Press.

Haward, R. Khan, 1980, 'An Urban Minority: The Goan Christian Community in Karachi' in K.A. Ballhatchet and J.B. Harrison (eds), *The City in S. Asia: Pre-Modern and Modern*, London: Curzon Press.

Kuper, J., 1973, 'The Goan Community in Kampala', unpublished Ph.D. thesis, University of London.

_____ , 1975, 'The Goan Community in Kampala' in Twaddle, M. (ed.) *Expulsion of a Minority: Essays on Ugandan Asians*, London: Athlone Press.

Mascarenhas-Keyes, S., 1979, *Goans in London: Portrait of a Catholic Asian Community*, London: Goan Association (UK).

_____ , 1987, 'Death Notices and Dispersal: International Migration among Catholic Goans' in J. Eades (ed.), *Migrants, Workers and the Social Order*, London: Tavistock.

_____ , 1987a, *Migration and the International Catholic Goan Community*, unpublished Ph.D. thesis, University of London.

———, 1987b, 'The Native Anthropologist: Constraints and Strategies in Research' in A. Jackson (ed.), *Anthropology at Home*, London: Tavistock.

———, 1988a, 'Modernisation and the Status of aged Catholic International Returners in Goa'. Paper presented at the Association of Social Anthropologists' Conference on the Social Construction of Youth, Maturation and Ageing, London.

———, 1988b, 'Sorpotael and Feni: The Role of Food in Catholic Goan Ethnic Identity'. Paper presented at Institute of Social Anthropology, Oxford University Seminar series on Food and Ethnic Identity.

———, 1990a, 'Migration, "Progressive Motherhood" and Female Autonomy: Catholic Women in Goa' in L. Dube and R. Palriwala (eds), *Structures and Strategies: Women, Work and Family in Asia*, New Delhi: Sage Publ.

———, 1990b, 'International Migration: Its Development, Reproduction and Economic Impact on Goa up to 1961' in T.R. De Souza (ed.), *Goa through the Ages: An Economic History*, New Delhi: Concept.

———, (forthcoming), 'International and Internal Migration: The Changing Identity of Catholic and Hindu Women in Goa' in J. Bujis (ed.), *Women crossing boundaries: Dilemmas of Changing Identities*, Oxford: Berg.

Meersman, A., 1972, 'The Latin Missions under the Jurisdiction of Padroado' in H.C. Perumalil and E.R. Hambye (eds), *Christianity in India: A History in Ecumenical Perspective*, Alleppey, S. India: Prakasam Publ.

Menezes Bragança, L. de, 1923, 'A Educacão e Ensino na India Portuguesa' in *A India Portuguesa*, vol.11, pp. 18–70, Nova Goa: Imprensa Nacional.

Miranda, R.V., 1978, 'Caste, Religion and Dialect Differentiation in Konkani Area', *International Journal of the Sociology of Language*, vol.16, pp. 77–91, Hague: Mouton.

Moraes, G.M., 1972, 'The Catholic Church under the Portuguese Patronage' in H.C. Perumalil and E.R. Hambye (eds), *Christianity in India: A History in Ecumenical Perspective*, Alleppey, S. India: Prakasam Publ.

———, 1972, 'The Latin Church' in H.C. Perumalil and E.R. Hambye (eds.), *Christianity in India: A History in Ecumenical Perspective*, Alleppey, S. India: Prakasam Publ.

Nelson, D., 1971, 'Caste and Club: A Study of Goan Politics in Nairobi', unpublished Ph.D. thesis, University of Nairobi.

Parkin, D., 1977, 'Emergent and Stabilised Multilingualism: Polyethnic Peer groups in Urban Kenya' in H. Giles (ed.), *Language, Ethnicity and Intergroup Relations*, London: Academic Press.

Pereira, J., 1973, *Literary Konkani: A Brief History*, Dharwar: Konkani Sahitya Prakashan.

Priolkar, A.K., 1961, *The Goa Inquisition*, Bombay (n.p.).

Ribeiro, D.A., 1965, 'The Problem of the Emotional Integration of Goans' in A. B. Shah (ed.), *Goa: The Problems of Transition*, Bombay: Manaktala & Sons.

Rivara, J.H. Cunha, 1858, *A History of the Konkani Language*, Goa. English translation 1958 in A.K. Priolkar, *The Printing Press in India*, Bombay.

Rodricks, G., 1974, 'The History and Survey of Education in Goa', unpublished Ph.D. thesis, University of Bombay.

Saifullah-Khan, V., 1977, *Bilingualism and Linguistic Minorities in Britain: Developments, Perspectives*, London: Runnymede Trust.

———, 1983, 'Mother Tongue Schools and Classes; Implications from the English Context' in L. Dabeire, M. Flasaquier and J. Lyons (eds), *Status of Migrants' Mother Tongues*, Strasbourg: European Science Foundation.

Sardessai, M.L., 1978, 'Portuguese Influence on the Konkani Language' in *International Seminar of Indo-Portuguese History*, Goa: Xavier Centre for Historical Research.

Schieben-Lange, B., 1977, 'The Language Situation in Southern France' in J.W. Dressler and A. Wodak-Leodolter (eds), *Language Death*, Hague: Mouton.

Spender, D., 1980, *Man Made Language*, London: Routledge & Kegan Paul.

Thorne, B. and Henley, N.M., 1975, *Language and Sex: Difference and Dominance*, Rowley, Mass: Newbury House.

Tanzania: Report on the Census of Non-African Population, 1957.

Varde, P.S., 1977, *A History of Education in Goa from 1510 to the Present Day*, Goa: Vidya Pratishthan.

Warner, W.L. and Scrole, L., 1945, *The Social Systems of American Ethnic Groups*, New Haven: Yale University Press.

Weibe, P. and Jogh-Peter, S., 1972, 'The Catholic Church and Caste in Rural Tamil Nadu', *Eastern Anthropologist*, 1, 24, no.1, 88–96.

10

A Note on My Experiences as a Student, a Teacher and an Interpreter of English in China

Liu Hong

I started learning English at secondary school, like most students in China. At the age of eighteen, when I was about to begin applying to university, the importance of studying English was strongly emphasised by our school. In China, upon graduation from university we are assigned a job by the government, and do not have the chance to change professions easily once we are in a work unit. So there we were, my classmates and myself, at the age of eighteen, deciding our lifetime's profession with great effort, not without some 'well-meant' advice from our parents and teachers.

Being a teacher is generally considered an ideal job for a proper woman, as it is assumed to be a quiet and stable occupation, not too competitive, suited therefore to the 'genteel' nature of women. My parents, like most others, strongly recommended that I make that choice. On the other hand, our teachers encouraged us to study English, as they foresaw the need for the language. Because I had done some reading in the language and had become immensely interested in it, I initially chose to study English. But the university I applied to rejected my application, and I was eventually assigned to the English Department of a college for training teachers – which was not really my choice. I did have some interest in teaching English, partly because English teachers seemed more lively and modern than other teachers.

As a student of English at college, I discovered that the attitude of male and female students during lessons differed, for girls were much more active in the classroom, more willing to raise and answer questions. The female students were generally more active in class – they were less shy when it came to making up 'situations' in our conversation classes. Women students were also better at organising extra-curricular activities. In my class most of the 'cadres' (*ganbu*, the people elected to all sorts of responsible office) were women: I was in charge

167

of recreational activities. I was *wenyi weiyuan*, or cultural and artistic commissioner: my first job was to organise a game of hide-and-seek in order to get my fellow students to know each other. This job was actually less frivolous than it sounds: when I proposed the game, I had to face criticism from some of my classmates, who argued that the game was potentially violent.

In the first year we had Chinese teachers of English who trained us in the simplest aspects of language, like pronunciation and oral practice. As we moved on to senior grades, we started getting teachers from abroad, from English-speaking countries such as Britain, the USA, Australia and Canada. They brought with them, along with language skills, influences from their cultures. There was a complete change in teaching technique. We were encouraged to make more use of things we had just learnt and to speak more in class. Changes also came in the teaching materials these western teachers were using: they tended to be more practical and recent, and such courses as 'modern western newspaper and magazine reading' began.

In contrast to our new teachers, who were not only teaching a language skill but introducing the taste and content of their cultures, the textbooks used by our own Chinese teachers were older ones that clung more closely to Chinese culture, and especially to revolutionary thought. We learned revolutionary terms such as 'barefoot doctor' and 'youth league'. I still remember the first English sentence I learned from my English textbook in elementary school. It was 'Long live Chairman Mao'.

The 'principle' for foreign-language teaching prescribed by the government was and still is *Yang wei zhong yong*: to use western thought for Chinese ends. In line with this principle, when our university education ends, we are assigned to a job in a work unit. Those at our teachers' college who refused to be teachers could apply to do further studies in English or other subjects. Many people who applied to do postgraduate work chose subjects other than English, such as 'foreign' history or international relations, subjects which require a good foreign-language background.

I was assigned a job as an English teacher in a science unit and I felt quite privileged at this. I recall it was funny to tell people what your job was. If you said you were a teacher, they would show pity, because they knew the job was badly paid and hard work, but if you said you were an English teacher, they would show respect. For knowledge of English is very much in demand in contemporary China: people would even end up asking, 'Would you kindly teach me (or my son, or my daughter) English?' You also had the advantage of being able to work part-time as a translator or interpreter in a business, which gave you the added pleasure of making teachers of other subjects 'eat vinegar' (feel envy) when comparing their humble salaries to yours.

When I became an English teacher, I taught classes of twenty people, with approximately the same number of women and men. I again observed the different attitudes to learning English among my female and male students. This was most strongly reflected in my 'conversation class', in which girls stood up more frequently and often had more creative and imaginative conversations. I was also adapting teaching methods and materials used by my western teachers. I made sure that the textbooks I used – I could freely select and purchase books with money provided by my work unit – were no longer full of revolutionary jargon. We used instead somewhat more 'modern' English textbooks such as *New Concept English* and *Reader's Digest*, books that in my view conveyed aspects of another culture. The other English teachers at the unit were all Chinese, mostly people 'borrowed' from the English Departments of nearby universities. They also taught at other institutes or did other part-time jobs such as translating and interpreting, making the most of their linguistic skills.

Teaching in the institute was very enjoyable, but it was a closed community, so I was glad when my work unit leader agreed to 'lend me out' as an interpreter for a TV co-production company. Being an interpreter was a very privileged job. Besides the immediate financial advantages, it was also a job which gave me many opportunities to work with foreigners. This was valuable, as some of my former classmates had been assigned jobs which had nothing to do with their studies. On the other hand, it was difficult, sometimes frustrating, to be really conscientious. We were caught between the powerful influences of two cultures, and were not immune to political and social pressure. I once helped to interpret in a co-production between the Chinese Central TV and a western film company. The crew was a very international group with people from eight cultures including Mongolia. We were five interpreters, four women and a man. The budget was tight, and the work was done under considerable stress. I was interested to note that whenever disputes occurred, the women interpreters tended to calm them down and bear the brunt of people's anger. The only male interpreter, who refused to be used as a scapegoat, was eventually dismissed.

When 'sacrifices' were needed, the interpreter was the one to make them. In that sense, I felt that I was somehow trapped by this 'contradiction' between the official policy of refusing western cultural invasion and the natural, unavoidable consequences of absorbing some cultural influences so long as I spoke the language. We believed that as interpreters we had to be very careful to keep a balance between 'professional' conscientiousness and 'political' righteousness.

11
Forging a Bilingual Identity: A Writer's Testimony

Ketaki Kushari Dyson

Being a bilingual writer is probably the most complex form of bilingualism. Besides writing originally in Bengali and English, and translating between these two languages, I have additional skills in some other languages, ancient and modern, from some of which I have also done translations. I shall first explain how I came to develop this identity and then outline its implications in my life.

The roots of this development lie in my Indian education. All people who go through secondary and higher education in India develop some second-language skills. People with some knowledge of three or four languages are not uncommon. In such a scenario some people are bound to develop skills as bilingual communicators, if not as fully developed literary writers then at least as speakers, teachers, or journalists. Because of the multilingual nature of the subcontinent, bilingual skills have always been required in Indian life at business, administrative, political and intellectual levels. For a long time Sanskrit was the pan-Indian language of communication amongst scholars. Persian became the court language of the Mughal Empire, while Urdu emerged as a lingua franca of camps and market-places. Bilingualism was therefore a necessary and even traditional skill for Indian scholars, administrators, politicians, merchants, businessmen and military men long before the British arrived on the scene and introduced English.

Someone like myself could be called the product of the dual heritage of the British Empire and the Indian Renaissance. Born in British India seven years before independence, into a middle-class Bengali family, I didn't have, in the matter of bilingualism itself, any choice. Whether I should have a second language or not, and what that should be: these were not negotiable. History and the social class to which I belonged had set the terms. I would have to get educated; there could be no opting out of education because I was female; I would have to acquire a second language; it would have to be English. What had begun as a requirement of the Empire was replaced after independence by the continuing importance of English as a link language within India and its accelerating importance in the international arena.

If using a second language effectively is in some sense a female role, then this female role was imposed on the Indian elite irrespective of gender. None of us born into a particular social class could escape it. My generation was at least the third generation of the family pursuing it. To what degree we would perfect our use of English would, of course, depend on us as individuals. Here, perhaps, gender could play a role, as indeed it did in my case.

The other side of the dual heritage is that of the intellectual and cultural re-awakening that took place in India in the nineteenth century and continued into the twentieth. It began in Bengal and in its early stages is called by historians the Bengal Renaissance. As a Bengali, I have a strong sense of continuity with this movement. The Bengali intelligentsia welcomed English and the new ideas and influences it brought with it, without throwing all their own traditions overboard. They created a space in which they could experiment with new things and still be themselves, which could not be taken away from them and where the Renaissance could take shape without interference from the imperial rulers. Bengali played a pioneering role in this activity, translations from it helping in the cultural re-awakening of the other linguistic areas.

From my early childhood onwards I was brought up in the atmosphere of a cultural hothouse and an intensely language-conscious family eager to make the most of the twin heritage of the Empire and the Renaissance. My paternal grandfather was a schoolteacher who could recite whole scenes of Shakespeare, earning for himself the nickname of 'Shakespeare Kushari'. My father studied economics at the University of Dacca (now in Bangladesh and written 'Dhaka'), and went into the civil service, but his main interests were literary. He was a devoted reader of contemporary poetry in Bengali and English. He taught himself French and German and read a wide range of literature in these two languages. He published articles in English on Jean-Paul Sartre and Albert Camus. He mixed with those who shared his passion for literature, and knew many contemporary Bengali writers.

My mother's side of the family produced a notable Bengali scholar, Dineshchandra Sen. My mother went to school in Benares and then to college in Calcutta. Because of her residence in Benares she acquired Hindi in addition to her Bengali and English. My early education was in her charge. I don't remember a time when I couldn't read Bengali. My mother put the idea of writing poems into my head when I was very young. We were then living in the country, and life had a very leisurely pace. To develop my writing skills, my mother would ask me to write a poem on a specified subject such as 'Morning' or 'Evening' or 'Spring-time', then disappear into the kitchen. I would write these poems with a chalk on a wood-framed slate writing-board. Soon I showed such skill in versification that my mother felt compelled to copy my good poems into a ruled copybook. This copybook, containing samples of poems written by me from the age of five onwards, has survived. All this poetry was written in Bengali, the only language we spoke at home. While there was no question that I would have to learn English as a second language, it was taken for granted that I would develop my Bengali fully and do my creative writing in it. I was born a year before the death of our greatest modern writer, Rabindranath Tagore, whose figure towered in our consciousness. We read his poetry and prose and sang his songs, including his patriotic songs. My own name and that of my sister immediately after me were taken from Tagore's poetry, the names of two of his favourite flowers. The bonding with Bengali was therefore very strong. The language expressed our cultural identity as well as, in the early years of my childhood, our political aspirations. It also introduced me, through translations, to foreign books. For instance, a Bengali version of *Uncle Tom's Cabin*, suitable for children, was given to me by an aunt on my fifth birthday, and opened new horizons for me.

It was my mother who introduced me to English at home before I went to school. I remember a ragged-looking primer with lists of words like *bat, cat, hat, mat* and *rat*. But soon I moved on to poetry, fairy tales and *Robinson Crusoe*. It must have become clear to my parents at a fairly early stage that I had an aptitude for languages. Things began to happen very fast. They bought me the standard mediaeval Bengali verse-translations of the *Ramayana* and the *Mahabharata*, two fat volumes which I read from beginning to end at the age of seven, sitting up in bed through hot sticky summer afternoons instead of indulging in siestas. A Sanskrit primer too was bought for me when I was seven. When I was nine my father started giving me French lessons. At ten I read classic Bengali novels and started Sanskrit at school. I remember borrowing Somerset Maugham's *The Razor's Edge* from the school library when I was eleven. Our English teacher at school was a very inspiring woman; she made us enact the stories of Greek and Roman mythology as *tableaux vivants*. My father borrowed records for me from the Alliance Française de Calcutta, and took me to French lessons given by Jesuit fathers and to French plays which were put on from time to time. I read Racine, Molière, Baudelaire and other authors with him. To make me read French and to introduce me to Homer at the same time, he made me read the *Iliad* and the *Odyssey* in French prose. He also gave me

German lessons. I read some of the lyrics of Goethe and Heine and Goethe's novel *Die Wahlverwandtschaften* with him.

We were four siblings, and all of us acquired English. My brother showed a special interest in languages, and dabbled with Italian while still at school. Perhaps because he was a boy, it was first physics at university and then civil service for him. But, indomitable, he surfaced again as a linguist in his career as a civil servant. Serving in the state of Jammu and Kashmir, he has acquired a good knowledge of Urdu and Kashmiri, and has written a manual for the learning of Kashmiri which is used to teach the language to other civil servants. However, amongst all the siblings I have been the only one who has wanted to be a writer and pursue linguistic skills in a literary context.

Through my father's friend Buddhadeva Bose, who was the editor of a highly-regarded poetry magazine, I gained an early entry into the contemporary literary world. My parents used to show him my youthful poetic effusions, and he reckoned that they were promising. My first publication was at the age of seven in a hand-produced children's magazine edited by Bose's two daughters. Then at the age of nine I saw myself in print in the school magazine and went with my father to hear Auden at the British Council. I couldn't have made much sense of Auden's poetry at that age, but the idea of seeing a famous English poet with my own eyes gave an importance to the occasion. Later I also heard Stephen Spender in Calcutta.

Looking back, I can see clearly how my identity was shaped by my education in Calcutta. I was made by that city. My debt to it is difficult to convey to outsiders. Calcutta is a much-maligned city, conjuring images of slums and poverty to the western imagination. But Calcutta was the seat of the Bengal Renaissance, and is still the cultural capital of India. It is, intellectually and artistically, a very lively, open and generous place. Calcutta University permitted women to take degrees in 1883, just five years after London granted that permission and decades before either Oxford or Cambridge did the same. One important determinant in my development was the fact that my higher education had a broad base. For instance, I did three languages up to university level. English was my honours subject; a paper of Bengali was compulsory; and Sanskrit was one of the two other subsidiary subjects. I did my degree course at Presidency College, noted for its teaching of English literature and descended from the celebrated Hindu College of the early nineteenth century. For our Sanskrit classes we went across the street to Sanskrit College, another old and famous institution. At these two places we had a strong sense of continuity with the traditions of the Bengal Renaissance.

The advantage of Sanskrit was that it gave me firm roots in India's classical cultural tradition and enriched my Bengali style. The literary vocabulary of Bengali is strongly linked to Sanskrit. Sanskrit is of special help if one wants to write in Bengali in an intellectual and analytical mode. For the writing of scholarly prose in Bengali, the back-up of Sanskrit is indispensable. I had this valuable empowerment in my student days at Calcutta, a tool which has enabled me to continue on my own in Britain as a Bengali writer. The other advantage of Sanskrit is that once its grammar is mastered, the grammars of other Indo-European languages are easy to learn. It is like a key that opens many doors. It helped me to read French and German; it helped me with Anglo-Saxon; and later I have taught myself to read Spanish as well.

My student days in Calcutta were heady with literary activities. In a sense I was already, by the age of eighteen or nineteen, a bilingual writer. Having done a degree at Calcutta, I came to Oxford on a West Bengal Government scholarship to do a BA in English once again. This was common practice in those days in Commonwealth countries. The Oxford degree course in English was supposed to be the ultimate training for one aspiring to teach the subject at university level. I was sent to be trained for that job, and at the age of twenty arrived in Britain for the first time in my life.

After the multicultural, hothouse atmosphere of Calcutta, the Oxford English School in the beginning of the sixties seemed tame and provincial. My tutors treated my knowledge of Sanskrit with evident respect, but my fellow students in English were not interested in Continental figures like Baudelaire or Thomas Mann, as my friends in Calcutta were. My cultural identity was usually unclear to most people, who seemed to have no idea of India's complexity and diversity. They tended to assume that I had always spoken English at home and that Bengali was a dialect rather than a language. Dialects hadn't acquired class in those days. While I knew a great deal about Britain's history, geography, religion and literature, my fellow-students knew almost nothing about India. Such general ignorance amongst educated people about a part of the world which had been within the British Empire only a few years before astounded me. In my search for peers I began to associate with foreign graduate students and with scientists, with whom I felt more at ease. This was to have its consequences in my personal life. There were no opportunities for literary involvement as I had had in Calcutta. I continued to write poems in Bengali, and began to publish them in a well-known literary magazine in Calcutta.

When I returned to Calcutta I found that I was regarded as one of the promising new poets. People were quoting me in the coffee house where we used to discuss poetry in our own student days. I began to teach at a new university, and wrote my first proper academic 'paper' in English. At the request of editors, I began writing prose in various Bengali journals and newspapers. They thought I had potential as a prose writer as well.

At the end of a year one of my Oxford contemporaries came to Calcutta to marry me and brought me back to Britain. On the eve of my departure a group of my 'fans' came to see me and told my husband that he was taking away one of their promising writers. He promised them that he would always encourage me to write in Bengali, and I made a solemn promise never to give up writing in that language.

This return to Britain was the turning-point of my life. An academic career in English combined with some writing in my spare time was how I had envisaged my life. But the insuperable difficulties I faced in giving shape to an academic career in this country turned me towards full-time writing. At first I lived in Brighton, as my husband was doing a doctorate at Sussex. Unable to get any job near home, I travelled to London three times a week to teach sixth-form English. During my train journeys I read new books which I then reviewed for Calcutta. I had a column of my own for reviewing foreign books. I also wrote an autobiographical sketch based on my student days at Oxford and a holiday in France I had had. And I wrote poetry. I was now being called a writer of the sixties generation, and my life as an expatriate Bengali writer had begun in earnest.

But I hadn't given up the idea of an academic career. After a brief spell in Canada we returned to Oxford so that I could do postgraduate work. I worked very hard for some years, working for a doctorate and rearing two small infants at the same time. I thought that an academic career would be possible once I did a doctorate. But this proved not to be the case. After many unsuccessful applications for jobs and fellowships, and after being told by the Equal Opportunities Commission that I was being discriminated against but would not be able to prove it in court, I went to West Bengal for a year at the invitation of a provincial university. I renewed my literary contacts, and an editor urged me to write a novel set in Britain. A year after my return to England I decided to do just that and to devote myself to my writing in a full-time capacity. This decision was more or less simultaneous with the coming out of the book based on my doctoral thesis. By then I had become disillusioned with the British academic scene. I began to find a life of writing both exciting and comforting, and couldn't face any more unsuccessful applications.

Even if I had never come to Britain, I would have been, to some extent, a bilingual writer. Having written from childhood, I would clearly have continued to do some writing in Bengali, and editors would have made me write for their magazines. And teaching English at university, I would inevitably have written some papers and books in English too. It is not uncommon for academics in India to develop this kind of bilingual expertise. But obviously living in Britain has made me a different person, given me a range of experiences I wouldn't otherwise have had, polished my English in a different way, exposed me to British English and to the nuances of western life and culture. Books, music and films, opera and ballet, television documentaries and discussion programmes to which I wouldn't have had access if I hadn't lived here have educated and enriched me. Living in Britain has given me the confidence to write poetry in English, something which I might not have attempted if I hadn't lived here. So far I have written poetry, articles, reviews and scholarly work in both languages, and have done translations into both languages. But fiction I have written only in Bengali. I have felt no urge to write a novel in English. At the request of an amateur theatrical group based in Calcutta, I have also just completed (summer 1990) my first play – in Bengali, of course.

*

The consequences of being a bilingual writer who writes in Bengali and English but lives in Britain have been far-reaching for me. In essence it has meant that though I live in Britain and have been a British citizen for half my life, my career has consolidated itself in India. I have been writing in magazines published from Calcutta for three decades, I was given recognition as a writer there when I was still a young woman, and naturally all my Bengali books are published from there. I am well-known in West Bengal and Bangladesh, and I don't mean known just to the sophisticated. Many ordinary people have read me or noticed my name because I have written for the weekly *Desh* on and off since 1961. *Desh* has an extensive circulation in both West Bengal and Bangladesh, and is also read by expatriate Bengali communities all over the world. I have had the moving experience of having my poetry quoted to me by a customs and immigration officer at Calcutta airport, which, I am told, could never happen at Heathrow to any poet, no matter how famous. Poets have their fans in Bengal in a way they don't in Britain. I also achieved wide publicity by having my first novel serialised in *Desh*, receiving fan mail from Bengalis in Europe and North America. For the past ten years I have contributed regularly to the quarterly *Jijnasa*, gaining a new group of readers in both Bengals.

To maintain my expatriate writing career I have to visit West Bengal at regular intervals, maintain contact with my publishers and other sponsors, press for my royalties, give interviews and so on. To keep in touch with the language, I have to buy books, talk to people and let the spoken language swirl round me. A sponsorship for the passage cannot be found every time, and passages are expensive. Also, most of my royalties are paid in Indian money and have to be spent there. This means that I have to get there first before I can spend the money I have earned, and the passage costs more than what I can earn in India from *my* kind of writing in a normal year. Most serious writers there have other jobs which are their main sources of income. But my writing does provide me with spending money when I am in India, which is very handy. Unfortunately, because of the British treatment of Indians entering Britain, India has now introduced a visa-system for British passport-holders entering India. For me this is a new inconvenience.

A consequence of being well known in Bengal has meant that it has been easier for me to publish most of my English-language books from India also. Two books of poetry have been published from Calcutta and two academic books from Delhi. In India there are still no middlemen between authors and publishers, everything being done through informal personal contacts. As a result, I have never acquired the experience of dealing with an agent. Here even agents seem to have their agents, a situation that scares me. I have never registered with an agent. The case-history of the publication of *A Various Universe*, the book based on my doctoral work, may be of interest here. I sent it first to OUP here. Their reader was very enthusiastic and recommended some changes. I made the changes according to his suggestions and submitted the MS again. This time OUP sent the MS out to a new reader, who proposed some radical changes in the arrangement of material. The book would have to be totally restructured. I took the MS back and gave it to Vikas at Delhi. OUP Delhi's general manager at the time, whom I knew slightly from my undergraduate days at Oxford, came to know of this, retrieved the MS from Vikas and decided, over a weekend, that he would publish it. In the end OUP Oxford took 500 copies of the first imprint for sale in Britain, but because my contract was with OUP Delhi my royalty on all copies sold was on the Indian price only.

My first real British publication was a pamphlet of poems published through a poetry workshop at Oxford in which I used to be active, but which is now defunct. A number of us had pamphlets published; there was some financial assistance from Southern Arts; there were no royalties; and we had to sell our own books at readings. The poems in this pamphlet were included in my next collection of English poems published from Calcutta.

While I opted for the convenience of publication in India, I lost out on distribution and publicity in Britain. It is very difficult to persuade British journals to review Indian publications and British bookshops to stock them. The review of an Indian-language book in a British periodical seems unthinkable, although western books are reviewed in India all the time. But even English-language books published in India are given a similar treatment. My collection of poems *Spaces I Inhabit*, published from Calcutta, was liked by some poets I know here. One of them – let us call her X – persuaded the *TLS* that it should be reviewed, then sent in her article, reviewing me along with some American women poets. The article was published with the paragraph on me cut out. I was Indian and therefore could not be reviewed with Americans. X then reviewed me with a group of Indian poets who write in English. This time the paragraph on me was cut out because thirty copies of the book were going to be distributed in Britain by Y, to whom X was then married. The *TLS* reckoned that in such circumstances X could not review my book. Shortly thereafter X and Y broke up their marriage, and I had neither a review nor a distributor.

But these are merely symptoms of the deep-seated and radical problem which I face as a bilingual writer in England. I have said England deliberately, because there are some bilingual writers among the Scottish and the Welsh. The problem can be summed up in one sentence: the English do not really believe in bilingual writers. Yes, they believe in translators. Translation is seen as a valid use of second-language skills. The English do it themselves. But for historical reasons the English seldom become bilingual writers: they have no need to. What they do not practise themselves they neither appreciate nor respect. Not only do they not understand the fine skills that go into the making of a bilingual writer, but they are also suspicious of the *quality* of the work produced by such a writer.

Writers of Indian origin who win the approval of the London establishment tend to be those who write in English only and cannot write in any other language, though they may speak other languages to some extent. Anita Desai, half-Bengali, half-German by birth, writes in English only. Her recent novel, *Baumgartner's Bombay*, partially set in Calcutta, shows that she has some access to German. But her access to Bengali remains unclear, and this does affect the novel adversely. Salman Rushdie interlards his English with Urdu words and phrases as a naughty teenager interweaves his speech with swearwords, but he cannot write a book in Urdu. The English applaud his style whether they understand these bits or not, but never analyse the intellectual implications of his inability to write in an Indian language. He may be a cosmopolitan, but he is a monolingual writer. His use of Urdu adds colour to his texts, but does not lead us to an Indian intellectual world. Had he been an artist in Urdu, I doubt if he would have used that language to pepper his English in the facetious way he now does, and had he been in touch with an Urdu-speaking reading public, he might not have made the *faux pas* he has made in *The Satanic Verses*.

One of my Calcutta publishers quoted a statement of T. S. Eliot on the back of one of my books: 'I don't think that one can be a bilingual poet, or know of any case in which a man wrote great or even fine poems equally well in two languages.' My publisher was trying to make the point that T. S. Eliot had got it wrong, myself being the proof. Others have humorously pointed out that Eliot used the male gender in his pontification. Perhaps *no man* wrote fine poems in two languages; but perhaps a woman could. Eliot himself wrote one or two poems in French. Perhaps he wasn't satisfied with them.

For my life in England the fact that I am a bilingual writer is a problem; the fact that one of these languages is South Asian makes it worse. My bilingualism, instead of bringing me extra honour, as in India, is an embarrassment here. Most people around me automatically assume that everything I write must be in English, and express surprise when they hear otherwise. One Oxford don, himself a scholar in other languages but suspicious of bilingualism in writing, thought that I was *very brave* trying to write poetry in English. The fact that I have written several books in Bengali does not really add anything to my status here. The only value of my Bengali books in this country is as physical objects, when I go into classrooms to work for multicultural educationists. They come in useful to demonstrate to children that there are other languages and scripts in the world. Here I must acknowledge that a number of dedicated people are trying to bring a multicultural perspective into British schools, and I have done some work for them, as a writer and an ESL teacher. But so far the tertiary sector of British education, which ought to be multicultural almost by definition, has not responded adequately to the challenge of multiculturalism. And that is the level where I would be more useful. We often hear that the schoolteachers themselves are products of a monocultural education. If British universities and teacher-training institutes had hired people like me in the sixties or seventies, we might have seen a difference in the perspective of schoolteachers by now. But British society, instead of allowing bicultural people like myself to make a genuine contribution to it, has on the whole alienated, marginalised and trivialised us.

I don't know what the situation is now, but only a few years ago the Arts Council wouldn't entertain applications for writers' bursaries from anybody intending to write a book in a language other than English.

This was the cause of some resentment among writers in the ethnic minorities. But the Arts Council wouldn't help me even when I was writing a book in English. My Bengali work couldn't be assessed by the bursary committee members, therefore couldn't be taken into consideration by them. So in this country my bilingualism casts a shadow on my stature as a writer and on my English writing, making it suspect, in spite of my Oxford degrees. Not only is my Bengali writing invisible in England, so is my English writing. The lack of distribution and of reviews in Britain deprives it of status and authenticity. If it is good English writing, then why haven't we heard about it? If we haven't heard about it, then how can it be good? This is the circular logic of the gatekeepers. Among the general reading public there could well be some who might be interested in my books if they were available, but the gatekeepers decide who is going to be visible. When one of my Bengali books won an award in Calcutta, the event, as far as I am aware, was not noticed anywhere in the British media. When one considers the enormous attention some authors of Indian origin (who write in English) do get in the British media, this extreme of invisibility in my case deserves to be noted. One would have thought that a British citizen getting an award abroad for a book written in a language other than English had at least some news value as a curious item, but it is not so.

In a society dominated by the media, by the values of the commercial and advertising worlds, invisibility is a considerable handicap. It means isolation from one's peer-group. It means that one's name doesn't get known to the people who control writers' bursaries. Thus it means even less access to the already scarce writing funds that are available. It is difficult for me to develop myself in a British context, and I have to depend on Indian friends and contacts for both peer-interaction and future sponsorship.

Another problem is the gap that exists in Britain between creative and scholarly writers. I am both; so the hiatus affects me. Not being employed by a university department, not having notepaper with the name of an institution at its head, I am at a disadvantage when trying to get any kind of assistance for research. For instance, when I was working on my last English academic book, on Rabindranath Tagore and the Argentine writer Victoria Ocampo, at a time when I badly needed some financial support, I was refused funding by five institutions to which I applied: the British Academy, the British Council, the Leverhulme Trust, St Antony's College (Oxford) and the Arts Council. The only help I received was from India and Argentina.

Recently I have faced a disturbing reaction to the book that came out of this project. One British male writer who has translated from Bengali has, in correspondence with me, commented that while my scholarship is impressive, I have written a book for insiders in the language of outsiders, that it is far too scholarly for a book on Tagore written in English. According to him, any book on Tagore written in English, unless aimed exclusively at the Indian market, should be in the nature of a general introduction. My book is published from Delhi and is oriented towards a general literary and academic market, both in India and elsewhere. It grew out of the task of editing the Tagore-Ocampo letters, which are in English, and the story has a connection with an eminent Englishman (Leonard Elmhirst) who went to Argentina with Tagore and also became a friend of Ocampo. So a large amount of archival material in English needed to be presented, and it seemed appropriate to write the entire book in English in order to reach a wider audience. In view of the importance of English in India as a language of academic discourse, and the number of books and journals in English published annually from India on a variety of subjects, the opinion expressed by my correspondent seems strange to me. Is this an example of gatekeeping, asking me to keep off a marked territory and go back to writing in Bengali? I know that the book has had excellent reviews in Argentina and that many in England and Continental Europe have also read and enjoyed it. Why should I be debarred from reaching this audience?

The point I made earlier about translation being more acceptable here than writing in two languages is borne out by the fact that I received a modest bursary from Southern Arts for a translation project. I have been translating a selection of Tagore's poetry and songs into English. The project was initiated by Visvabharati University, Santiniketan, India, but the bursary enabled me to begin work on it in England. This was my first access to British public funds available to writers. I had to work in Santiniketan for three months, and this time even the British Council gave me a travel grant to get there. I have also found a British publisher for the projected book, by-passing London and agents, by contacting the printer of my poetry pamphlet, who in the years since then has become a poetry publisher based in Newcastle-upon-Tyne.

To understand the British suspicion of Asian languages we have to go back in history. When the British were establishing themselves in India under the aegis of the East India Company in the latter half of the eighteenth century, they were marked by a relative lack of arrogance. Intellectually they were shaped primarily by the Enlightenment, which meant that they were curious about India's social, political and religious institutions. They enjoyed spiced dishes, hookah-smoking, nautches, Urdu ghazals and Indian mistresses. A surge of British Orientalist researches relating to India took place in the closing decades of the eighteenth century and the early years of the nineteenth. Its landmarks were the foundation of the Asiatic Society of Bengal in Calcutta, the regular publications of which, the *Asiatick Researches*, were widely read in Europe and ushered in a new era of scholarship, the first English translations of classic Sanskrit texts, and the foundation of the College of Fort William in Calcutta for the training of British civil servants who would be acculturated to India and fluent in Indian languages.

But as the British gained political confidence in India, these positive attitudes were gradually replaced by attitudes which were negative towards India. Waves of Christian fundamentalism in the shape of the Evangelical revival and of secular radicalism in the form of Utilitarianism gathered strength in Britain and hit India. To men moulded by such movements at home, the Company's Indian territories seemed a stage ready for action. The Evangelicals wanted India to be opened up for missionary enterprise; the Utilitarians wanted to see India westernised by means of effective legislation and strong centralised administration; other radicals wanted India changed by means of English education. One of the strongest anglicisers was T.B. Macaulay, whose 1835 memorandum on education routed the Orientalists and provided the basis for a new official policy on language and education. Macaulay's document is notorious in Indian history. It swept aside the modern Indian languages as rude dialects and all oriental literature as intrinsically inferior to western literature, maintaining, in an incredible mixture of ignorance and arrogance, that 'a single shelf of a good European library was worth the whole native literature of India and Arabia', that 'all the historical information which has been collected from all the books written in the Sanskrit language is less valuable than what may be found in the most paltry abridgements used at preparatory schools in England'. Macaulay proposed that a class of anglicised Indians should be trained to become interpreters between the British rulers and the Indian masses, 'a class of persons, Indian in blood and colour, but English in taste, in opinions, in morals, and in intellect'. In this new climate of ideas language-learning became a one-way affair. The Indian elite learned English to the best of their abilities, but the British did not learn Indian languages to any depth. It was the British understanding of the modern Indian languages that suffered most from this change. The foundations for the study of ancient India had already been laid, and in 1837 James Prinsep deciphered the rock edicts of the emperor Ashoka, the key to the rediscovery of Buddhist India. A few British scholars would continue to study Sanskrit and Pali, without a cultivation of which modern disciplines like comparative philology or comparative religion would not have devel-

oped, but the modern languages of India, in which exciting developments were beginning to take place, which were becoming the space in
which the Indian Renaissance was taking shape, were neglected. The
British had no further involvement with this space, in spite of their earlier involvement in the introduction of printing technology, which had
been, in any case, mainly spurred by missionary motives to facilitate the
translation and printing of the Bible in the languages of India.

Generally speaking, this legacy of the Empire is still the prevailing
situation in the cultural interchanges between the English-speaking
world and the world of the modern South Asian languages. If translations from the latter have to be done, it is usually the Asians themselves
who have to do it. It is they who have to be the mediators and bridge-
builders. Yes, there are some small signs of change right now, but on the
whole the English-speaking literati are much more at ease with those
authors of South Asian origin who produce literary works in the English
language. These texts require no mediation – at least so the English-
speaking readers think – and many of them have been quickly and con-
veniently appropriated into the new academic category of 'Commonwealth literature', bypassing the bulk of modern literature in the subcontinent, which continues to be written in the South Asian languages
and is invisible in the English-speaking world. A new leviathan called
'Third World literature' is also beginning to appear in discussions, and
certain authors of Indian origin who write only in English are being co-
opted by the West as representatives of the Indian segment of this mam-
moth category. This tendency to co-opt authors who write in English
(and publish from the metropolises of the West) to represent Indian
writing is essentially a form of cultural neo-colonialism, a continuation
of Macaulay's old reliance on 'a class of persons, Indian in blood and
colour, but English in taste, in opinions, in morals, and in intellect'. For
writers of Indian origin the decision to write in English and publish
from the West is therefore, whether we like it or not, to some extent a
political act.

It seems to me that to succeed as an Indian writer in London one
needs to pursue a career dedicated exclusively to writing in English, in
which it is difficult to escape from perpetuating neo-colonial images of
India. This is why I have felt no urge to write a novel in English. In
poetry the 'I' speaks very directly, and scholarship aspires, or should
aspire, to be objective. So in these cases I don't mind writing in English.
But writing fiction for the global market in the world's number one
'world language' is a different affair. Here success can bring great
financial rewards, so the temptations to sell oneself must also be great. I
have written two novels in Bengali, both set in England and deeply con-

cerned with women's lives. Both are highly regarded by critics whose judgement I respect. The first one is in the form of letters and diary entries. The second one combines fiction with research work, and won an award. I could be completely myself in these novels without interference. I didn't have to pander to the tastes of neo-colonial gatekeepers, follow prevalent western fashions, or fulfil any expectations about what 'black British writing' should be about. I was doing what an expatriate British novelist would do wherever she was in the world, writing in her first language about the life she saw around her. Knowing that it was the fate of a bilingual writer to be caught, to some extent, in the politics that results from the power-relationship between the people who speak the two tongues, I was determined to maintain as much independence as I could. Writing in Bengali preserves my freedom, dignity and integrity. It is my private space in a society that is in some ways hostile to me.

As I see it, history played a big initial role in the development of my bilingual skills. Subsequently both race and gender have played their roles in the story of how I decided to use those skills as a writer. In the discrimination I have faced in Britain, race and gender have been compounded. My very assets have been turned into my disadvantages. The more skills I have had, the more I have been discriminated against. But the more discrimination I have faced, the more determined I have been to show that I am not dependent on the approval of British society for my survival as an artist and an intellectual. I can always write in Bengali; I can always publish from India. The way I gave up the pursuit of an academic career because of the difficulties I faced and concentrated on writing, allowing myself to be supported by my husband, was a female decision to cut my losses and make the most of my situation, and a diplomatic decision taken by an artist with her long-term interests in mind. A man in my shoes might have returned to India or gone to North America or Australia, with or without his English wife. People say to me that I could have found a niche in a university in the USA. But if I had had an academic career in the USA, the pressure to keep publishing in English would have been overwhelming. It was my jettisoning of money-earning that enabled me to spend three whole years writing two long novels in Bengali. But everybody needs money; I need it too. I sometimes spend morbid weekends looking at 'Situations Vacant' in the *Oxford Times* newspaper, wondering how I could earn some money.

Here in Britain there are some male academics from my own community who have established themselves. Is it possible that they could have helped me, maybe not to get a job, but to get research funds when I was battling to get some, to meet other scholars or be introduced to publishers or editors? Could they have asked me to give a paper or a poetry reading, just as I have been invited to contribute to this workshop on women and bilingualism? In short, could they have helped me to get known, to overcome some of the obstacles I face? Perhaps gender is a strong factor in my relationship to these ambitious male expatriates. Is there a fear that I might take away a slice of their territory? Supportive networks in Britain do seem to be gender-based. Interestingly, the only English poet-friends left from my poetry workshop days are female. I had one male workshop friend, but he retreated within himself. Whereas I had many male friends in my undergraduate days at Oxford, one of whom became my husband, I haven't really acquired new male friends in my subsequent British life. Most of my male literary/intellectual friends are now from India. They help me, are proud of me and enjoy socialising with me. It must be noted that the Calcutta editors I work for are men, and that from time to time I do experience those tensions which beset the relationships between writers and their editors. There are also disquieting signs that such tensions are likely to increase in the future. Men who were glad to be my 'patrons' when I was a younger woman (and therefore in a kind of 'filial', deferential relationship to them) seem less benign as I become older, more 'established', more their 'equal'. Doesn't this show us the patriarchal face of such patronage?

The lack of social interaction with a peer-group can be a deprivation for a writer. In that way too I feel deprived of adequate nourishment in Britain. And I have not talked about other problems I face, of racism in the streets, or as a mother of mixed children, though such problems affect me and are therefore relevant in my life as a writer. In my experience when race meets race, race is the more dominant factor, but gender also plays a role, less dominant but by no means insignificant. These issues are like fierce currents. They may not always be visible to the eye that surveys the surface, but the body under water feels it. It is in the midst of such currents that I have had to survive. But it is not all bleak. There is nature in the four seasons. There is food for the body and for the mind. There are books, BBC 2, Radio 3, Channel 4, even the advantages of a word-processor. My husband and children are very supportive, and I do have a few good friends here. It is true that only half my full identity as a writer is visible to them, but friendship, intimacy and sympathy can usually imagine the other side of the moon. And my long-distance friends, themselves bilingual, who can at least read all I write, even if not catching all the western nuances, are, as I said, supportive. So I go on, trying to make my ambidexterity a strength, so that in each of the two languages in which I write the other culture acts as another horizon or an enriching counterpoint, giving the work additional complexity and a deeper perspective. I hope my condition has given me more knowledge of human nature, more compassion and a finer sense of humour than I might otherwise have had, made me a little wiser and more tolerant than I otherwise would have been.

12

Engendering Language Difference

Elizabeth Tonkin

The women and men considered in this book speak clearly different languages. But what is a language? And how different must language varieties be for us to talk of bilingualism? It is often hard to talk *about* language *in* language, and language takes up a great part of our lives. It is report and action, medium and message. We do different things with language and it also does different things with us. Using it may identify our social or regional origins, our age, our sex.

Linguists and literary critics may ask different questions about language, and so may philosophers, historians or information technologists. Given the daunting mass of research, one has to clarify a perspective, to see which may be the key aspects of language for answering one's own question. Of course, one cannot then rest in comfortable ignorance of what may be crucial knowledge about other aspects, but one may also find that the question is a new one, and has not been systematically addressed. That seems to be the case with our questions about women and bilingualism in this volume.

Much sociolinguistic and psycholinguistic research has centred on questions of identity and inequality, but it has been gender-blind. If, for instance, one scans the titles of books and articles on education chronologically, it is easy to see the rise and spread of references to women. Such references are only beginning to appear in sociolinguistic research. Yet here is a crucial part of social life. A recent monograph on bilingualism (Romaine, 1989) really ignores gender issues, and the complexities of asymmetry which they entail. In bilingual families – a long-standing study area – how different are the inputs of mothers and fathers, and are there any differences in the learning patterns of sons and daughters? Romaine reports Ochs' findings that 'if the child's ties to one parent are stronger, then that language will develop faster and stronger' (Romaine, 1989:192), but she fails to mention gender implications here. To direct the questions already being asked elsewhere on gender to the study of bilingualism and education, for instance, would surely be very illuminating. There have been many studies aimed to
186

show how school practice in bilingual or multilingual situations affects the success of 'the child'. For one short but thoughtful study of bilingual and bicultural gender-learning, see Steedman (1986). There are also gender-focused studies on schools – which generally find some discriminatory effects on girls. Surely these latter researches should be informing the work on bilingual learning, and the usefulness of the ungendered 'child' as unit of analysis should be queried as it has been in other educational research?

Other studies have taken existing research on class or ethnic distribution in a given area and asked how this correlates with language varieties used by such 'groups'. An advance on this approach is the analysis of networks, their differing qualities, and their relation to language variety. This approach also directs attention to sex-differences in networks. An objection to network as the unit of analysis is that it misses the individual's repertoire and thus the range of language varieties commanded, their deployment and any restrictions on their use. Milroy's study of working-class Belfast speakers (1987) nevertheless shows how some groups of women were much less terrritorial than the men, in a small urban area characterised by dense networks (overlapping in occupation, kinship and locale) because they crossed the city for work, and that this affected their speech patterns. 'Female native speaker' has become gendered in this way – as in others.

Questions of gender are questions of social relations. They are questions of making difference, of power, authority and 'alternative voices'. The themes of gender studies include socialisation, subjects and subjectivity, hegemony and subversion, and 'mutedness', another language-loaded term. Our questioning of language and of bilingualism must also be focused in this way. And it can be, because the boundaries of languages are social categories, not essential natural classes. People use language and language 'evidence' to make differences in the same ways that they use the other symbolic means on which anthropologists have written so much. One excellent study which does make these points is Hewitt's (1986) study of black and white friendships in South London.

Hewitt shows how ethnic density affects both the familiarity and the significance of Creole use by teenagers, as it does their friendships, and that these differences vary also with sex and with age. Like Milroy, he emphasises that stigmatised language varieties survive when to use them is simultaneously to make a claim of positive identification. '"Ethnic signs" are . . . pre-positioned by the very act of selection itself. They declare simultaneously "I am strong" and "I am weak"' (1986:204). Milroy reports sanctions against modifying a shared accent in a world of poverty and discrimination where solidarity is an overriding virtue.

Hewitt also shows how Creole and Cockney are not best seen as separate closed varieties, but that – as so often happens elsewhere – items of Creole lexis, syntax and phonology are manipulable entries, or cues of context; in this sense Creole can be a signal, whose speakers make and claim certain identifications and assertions about power and culture.

As elsewhere, girls are less identified with the stigmatised variety, and it is said that black mothers are more keen than fathers to control Creole use by their sons. Creole use is part of street energy and aggression: it thus asserts young male culture, though girls can sometimes appropriate its male power in limited arenas. Creole is also an 'ethnic sign' along with dress and music choice. Sometimes a strategy, it is also part of black culture (often musically envied by young whites) in which as always the participants are gendered, and not always as females wish.

Because literates tend to learn about languages as objects, with written rules and structures represented on the page, it is less easy to see language as social activity. But language is always a part of human culture, and its use is alike a lived practice, coercive, and a means of choice. For this reason I suggest that it is more profitable in issues of gender to work with 'language varieties' rather than starting from the assumed category of 'a language'. A language variety can be said to exist because it is identified as different from another variety, and the choice of one as against another signals social meanings to listeners or readers.

In terms of linguistic form, Scandinavian languages can be called closely related dialects. In terms of use, they signal national identities. The history of Scandinavia includes the building up of distinct nation-states and language engineering to promote written languages for each. Their citizenry's use of 'dialects' within each country likewise has distinctive connotations. To speak Swedish in Finland means something different from speaking it in Sweden, and, given Finnish as the national language, it implies bilingualism, too. But one could also be bilingual in Norwegian and Swedish or Danish in Norway. Here is a case where different languages are in fact distinguished by small linguistic differences, and where purely linguistic definitions of 'language' and 'dialect' (which may be hard to make) do not help one to recognise socio-linguistic usages. Here, these distinguish language and dialect as part of a historically complex politico-social enterprise.

From the perspective of social use, we can also focus on acts and choices: on shifts between different languages, between a standard and non-standard dialect or a mixture of all these, according to the social situation. There are many shades of social meaning which people make by their choice of sound, word or grammar, and it is common for them to code-switch, that is to move from one variety to another, even in the course of a sentence. In England, regional varieties contrast in class terms with the non-regional Received Standard Pronunication (RSP), as well as with 'ethnic' varieties, themselves diversified in status. Where working-class women become secretaries and learn a 'good telephone voice' this may prove a resource which they employ on behalf of their families and which their partners have had no practice in achieving. Social access and social valuation are at stake here. The degrees of difference between such language varieties are not regarded as slight, though they are slight in formal terms, as anyone familar with language usage in England can work out for themselves.

As practice, operating such distinctions – women's command of two language varieties in this case – seems to be useful, and thus enabling. But its significance in gender identification can be complex and contradictory. Different varieties may be appropriate for different places such as office and workshop, thus mingling – and reinforcing – class and gender specifications of occupation. Middle-class values and approximations to RSP are taken as evidence of one another, so men in the two places may evaluate each other's masculinity differently; 'polite' correctness is rejected if it is felt to detract from the (male) workers' camaraderie. The reluctance of English males to study foreign languages is striking, compared with the numbers of girls, and it starts in school. It suggests constructions of masculinity which cross class, and have as corollary the view that bilingualism is 'feminine'. Such femininity is disparaged, because it is constructed as malleable to the point of two-facedness. But of course male imaginations are limited by such constraints, and females are enabled to do interesting work – though it is easily put down and, as a woman's job, underpaid.

Languages – and language varieties – are not equal. Among the criteria of 'a language' is its existence in written form. Varieties not so authorisable are disparaged as 'dialects'. They are not taught in school, and the literate forms tend to be chosen as the national spoken standard on radio and television. With the development of broadcasting, BBC English – a style consciously developed under the direction of Lord Reith – made one form of RSP the standard 'accent' as well as grammatically and lexically standard. In the last few years efforts have been made on Radio 4 (the middle classes' news and features channel) to employ announcers with non-standard accents: the first announcer with a Scottish accent has spoken on radio of the hostile letters she received from listeners. Female news readers on Radio 4 are recent too: it was argued that female voices were not authoritative; male ones were. Hewitt describes 'toasting' as an oral art (practised by young blacks non-commercially, as well as by DJs) in which girls were put down on similar grounds.

There are many places where different language varieties co-exist, but school education demands the mastery of one in particular, which is the language of reading and writing. Examples of diglossia, as this pattern is called, include classical Arabic, which may be very different from the Arabic spoken throughout a country. In so far as literacy is a tool of power, ability in the written standard is obviously crucial. Many educationists have pointed out that those who speak the standard variety at home are advantaged; thus children from the Italian South whose home dialect is non-standard have a harder start. In sub-Saharan Africa the children of educated, successful urban parents will not only get better schooling than rural children, but will also be much more likely to hear local-standard English or French at home. Since in most African countries these are national languages as well as international ones, this is a very important resource.

Diglossia thus spells inequality and the reproduction of inequality. Considering the world-wide inequality of educational access for females, we can see how their access to national, authoritative and international language varieties is made doubly difficult. If one wants to understand women's and men's language opportunities, one needs to grasp how strategies and resources mesh. Some varieties are forced on speakers: they are born into them. Their opportunity to learn other varieties may be limited: it may also be made gender-inappropriate. This can be done by refusing certain types of education to girls. Latin was an interesting case in Europe, a variety which was also inaccessible to most of the male poor. It is also possible for women to use prestige spoken and even written forms without necessarily gaining public power, when these skills become accomplishments (c.f. Abu-Haidar, 1989) – possibly rather useful ones in the marriage market, but also important as class or status markers.

Pierre Alexandre tells the story of the administrator in Africa who 'had learned the local language in bed' and gave 'great joy' to his subjects by inadvertently using 'feminine mannerisms': these would not be a female dialect as such; rather, as he pointed out, there can be in Africa as elsewhere points of pronunciation as well as of topic and vocabulary which distinguish male from female, and old from young (Alexandre, 1967:140). It would be easy to say that in Britain such divisions, both linguistic and social, have broken down, but I believe there are still many barriers of appropriateness which perhaps assert the power of youth over the advantages of gender.

These examples also show that the problem can be not of ability to control two language varieties in which access to books, schools and teaching is necessary, but of the social rank of one variety over another.

Sometimes use identifies gender, or gendered use in turn defines particular linguistic choices as evidence of gender. Gender difference, like other differences, works through symbolic value. Objectively, the basis of differentiation may be small. Rights over resources that are naturalised as gender-specific may well be practically organised so as to limit access, but again, male gender hegemony works through the acceptance and reproduction of gender difference: females wear this, say thus and are therefore female – and may in changing circumstances be further distinguished by men as desirably upper-class or accessibly lower-class females. Voice, of course, is a universal sex discriminator, but the realisations of voice are gendered. In England, female voices, not male ones, are soft (+) or shrill (-), and Italian can be characterised as a feminine language.

Seen comparatively, peoples use different linguistic means for the same ends. In tone languages, tone contributes to lexical meaning. English uses word order where others have case-endings. Particular themes in one place may be presented through particular registers or styles, but in another may be bound to particular languages – languages of religion or diplomacy, for instance. In Britain, production of certain features of phonology and syntax is still important for political success, though the boundary lines have changed, and a regional accent can be a political asset. In many countries political success demands fluency in a national language quite different from any indigenous language of the country. The tensions between the political need to identify with a local-language constituency and also to operate in a national, and different, language arena are everywhere. The native speakers of an international language variety, such as English, have evident advantages over those who may even speak the same language at home and nationally, but whose type of English is still not internationally current.

Women's opportunities and limitations in these conditions can vary, as I have been arguing. Struggles for recognition by 'nationalities' and ethnic minorities are growing all the time, but women's issues seem strikingly absent in them, and this includes language, which is so often made a key area of identification struggles – struggles in which all the issues of unequal educational, economic, media and political access are at stake. We don't know, therefore, how to categorise properly or theorise the conditions in which females and males have an identical interest in minority-language varieties and in which where they do not.

We do not know either how far women may profitably mediate between language barriers. The choice of females to interpret may be a sign that men believe them to be politically irrelevant except as smoothers-away of aggression. However, the female trader or merchant, multilingual and indomitable, coolly crossing the borders, or keeping material life going by her market ventures, is a feature of Africa, and is found elsewhere, too. In such cases, their language abilities are part of the skilful and intelligent practices of women. Women have managed to learn, and not by the light of female nature, as is suggested by popular sexist representations. The 'sleeping dictionary' evoked by Alexandre is, of course, an example of race and sex inequality, though even this cliché testifies that women are perceived to speak different languages better than men. I argue that such achievements may be held against them, but they are achievements of resource nonetheless. Yet the implications of diglossia seem particularly serious for women. Since varieties of language are unequally valued, it is particularly important to see that women fare equally in their opportunities to speak and write with authority.

References

Abu-Haidar, F., 1989, 'Are Iraqi Women more Prestige Conscious than Men? Sex Differentiation in Baghdadi Arabic', *Language in Society*, vol. 18, pp. 471–81.

Alexandre, P., 1967, *Langues et Langages en Afrique Noire*, Paris: Payot.

Hewitt, R., 1986, *White Talk Black Talk*, Cambridge: Cambridge University Press.

Milroy, L., 1987, *Language and Social Networks*, 2nd edn, Oxford: Basil Blackwell.

Romaine, S., 1989, *Bilingualism*, Oxford: Basil Blackwell.

Steedman, C., 1986, '"Listen how the Caged Bird Sings": Amarjit's Song' in C. Steedman, C. Urwin and V. Walkerdine (eds), *Language, Gender and Childhood*, pp. 137–63, London: Routledge.

Name Index

Subject Index